Trip to Idaho
1938

MANU DE LA SOTA

Trip to Idaho 1938

Edition:
MAITENA IRAGORRI

Book cover:

Anton Irala, Jose Villanueva Amezketa, (?), Manu de la Sota and John Archabal.

With the collaboration of JOSEBA SARRIONANDIA. Translated from Spanish by TERESA BOUCHER

Thanks to Pedro de la Sota, Patty A. Miller, Megan Overgaard, Larraitz Ariznabarreta, Koldo San Sebastián, and Steve Mendibe.

This book was published with generous financial support from the Basque Government.

EUSKO JAURLARITZA GOBIERNO VASCO

Alrica Goldstein, Center for Basque Studies Press http://basquebooks.com

Design and photo composition: Pamiela
31014 Pamplona-Iruña (Navarra)

ISBN-13: 978-1-967179-08-4

Library of Congress Cataloging-in-Publication Data
Names: Sota, Manuel de la author | Boucher, Teresa Claire, 1962- translator
Title: Trip to Idaho 1938 / Manu de la Sota ; translated from the Spanish by Teresa Boucher. Other titles: Viaje a Idaho 1938. English
Description: Pamplona-Iruña, Navarra : Pamiela, [2026] | Series: Diaspora and migration studies ; 20 | Includes index. | Summary: "In a tragic moment of Basque history marked by defeat in a civil war and his own exile in 1938, Manu de la Sota wrote this previously unpublished diary of his journey to the states of Utah, Nevada, Idaho and Oregon. His objective was to gather in solidarity the scattered Basque community, accompanied by Antonio de Irala, for those territories of the American West but instead discovered hundreds of Basques distant in space, and perhaps also in time, of that country. His interesting reflections, humorous at times, about the character of the people and about the ideas around which we live, are shared in this diary of the trip with original discourses to the Basques of the Far West issued by the radio or published in the newspaper of Boise"-- Provided by publisher.
Identifiers: LCCN 2026007479 (print) | LCCN 2026007480 (ebook) | ISBN 9781967179084 paperback | ISBN 9781967179121 epub
Subjects: LCSH: Sota, Manuel de la--Travel--Idaho--Boise | Basques--Idaho--Boise--Social life and customs--20th century | Basques--Idaho--Boise--History--20th century | Boise (Idaho)--Description and travel | Basques--United States--History--20th century | LCGFT: Travel writing | Diaries
Classification: LCC F754.B65 S6813 2026 (print) | LCC F754.B65 (ebook)
LC record available at https://lccn.loc.gov/2026007479
LC ebook record available at https://lccn.loc.gov/2026007480

Printed in the United States of America

Who Was Manu Sota?

By way of a foreword

The son of Ramon de la Sota Llano and Catalina Aburto Uribe, Manuel, Manu, was born in Getxo, in 1897. He earned a law degree from the University of Cambridge, where he also taught for several years. Upon returning to Bizkaia, he joined the Basque Nationalist Party (EAJ-PNV), and after the party split in 1921 between *Aberri* and the Basque Nationalist Communion, he joined Aberri, the socially more progressive and openly pro-independence branch of EAJ-PNV. Within Aberri, he took charge of the organization's propaganda work along with Eli Gallastegi and Jose M. Uzelai.

Manu de la Sota developed a multifaceted cultural activity. He began writing very early, publishing literary texts in *La Gaceta Literaria*, *Euzkadi*, *Hermes*, *Jagi-Jagi*, *Excelsior*, *Euzkerea*, and other publications. He founded the Bilbao cine-club, he was the editor of the mountaineering magazine *Pyrenaica*, and president of the Athletic Club de Bilbao soccer team. His theatrical work deserves special mention, as he was one of the architects ("The Basque Cocteau," as he was called) of the Basque theater renaissance, made possible by the relative freedom enjoyed after the fall of Alfonso XIII's dictatorship. Some of his productions were very successful: *Itxaro-ixaŕa* (Star of Hope, 1931), *Oztin* (*Blue*, 1932), *Negaŕez igaro zan atsua* (The Old Woman Who Walked Past in Tears, a version of W. B. Yeats's *Cathleen ni Hoolihan*) (Bilbao, 1933), *Uŕetxindoŕa* (*The Nightingale*, 1934) and *Buruzagijak* (*The Leaders*, an adaptation of Patrick Pearse's *The Singer* into a Basque context), and many others. Joseba Altuna "Amilgain" collaborated on the Basque version of almost all the works, and the poet Esteban Urkiaga "Lauaxeta" translated *Iru gudari* (*Three Soldiers*, 1933). Manu de la Sota collaborated with the best Basque visual artists and musicians of the time, as a part of aesthetic avant-garde linked to a popular movement for the independence. All that, unfortunately, was cut short by the uprising of the Spanish Army against the Spanish Republic.

After the outbreak of the war in 1936, Sota began collaborating immediately with the Basque Government. When his father Ramon de la Sota died in 1936, Manu inherited part of his father's wealthy estate, but after Bilbao was occupied, the rebel government confiscated the family's assets in Bizkaia and imposed a heavy fine on most of their members. Sota was forced into exile and continued to collaborate actively with the Basque Government in exile. He was one of the main promoters of the Basque national soccer team, Euzkadi, which represented the Basque Government on a highly successful world tour. He was also director and promoter of the musical group *Eresoinka*, which likewise undertook a world tour of great artistic merit and international critical acclaim. During this time, he composed and wrote the libretto for the musical piece *Akerlanda*.

After a few months on the European continent, Sota arrived in the Americas in 1938 to establish a delegation of the Basque Government in the United States alongside Anton Irala. In August 1938, Jose Luis de la Lombana traveled as a delegate of EAJ-PNV to the United States to participate in the Second International Congress of Youth for Peace. Upon returning to the Basque Country in November of that year, he left behind a report detailing the political and diplomatic position of the United States concerning the War of 1936. Lombana noted that American society was not entirely indifferent to the conflict. The general public had followed the war through the press and had formed a fairly clear opinion about the Basque reality and the nature of the Francoist regime.

Just a month later, in December 1938, Sota and Irala traveled to Idaho to explore the possibility of establishing a subdelegation of the Basque Government in Boise. And this book deals precisely with this episode of his life.

Despite the initial misgivings of Irala and Sota, the exploratory trip of December 1938 and January 1939 was a success. In 1940, Jon Bilbao was sent to Boise, to establish the subdelegation of the Basque Government in the US. Bilbao was a young man of twenty five, driven by a vivid thirst for adventure. Between 1932 and 1936, he had lived in Madrid, where he earned a degree in medieval history, studying Latin and Arabic. Influenced by some of the leading intellectuals of the time, he developed a deep interest in Basque history. At the outbreak of the Spanish Civil War in 1936, he joined the Basque army. After the fall of

Bilbao in 1937, he fled into exile. He continued his studies at Harvard and Columbia, completing his degree in 1939. That same year, contacted by Manu Sota and Anton Irala, he was appointed sub-delegate of the Basque Government in Idaho.

Soon after his arrival in Idaho, Jon Bilbao met Jose Villanueva Amezketa, "the most *abertzale* (Basque nationalist) man in the area." After a few weeks, Jon Bilbao established his residence in Emmett, a town located about thirty miles northwest of Boise, staying at a hotel owned by the Villanueva family. Along with Damian Telleria and Gregorio Landaluze, Villanueva was one of the main supporters of the Basque representation in that part of the country. Bilbao also made contact with several local politicians who were interested in attracting the votes of Idaho's sizeable and influential Basque population. At the annual shepherds' ball of 1939, a collection was held to purchase blankets for imprisoned women in the Basque Country.

Jon Bilbao's first months in Boise were marked by frenetic activity. He began studying Bizkaian Basque to better connect with the Basque immigrants, who overwhelmingly came from the Gernika area. As he recounted in a letter to Manuel Sota on January 3, 1940:

> The first thing I did was to gauge the mood of some Basques. Most were indifferent—you know how naturally reserved shepherds are. Some prominent Basques, like Tomas Ysursa, predicted I would fail. In Zenon Izagirre, I sensed a reluctance—perhaps even a wish—for Ramon [Sota Mac Mahon] not to come [to Idaho to engage with and support Basque sentiment among local immigrants]. Seeing that I had no support from the more prominent Basques, I turned to the Americans.

In this regard, he struck up a friendship with Camille R. Powell, a Spanish professor at Boise Junior College, and thanks to her and the Bidaurrazaga family, Ramon Sota's visit was organized for Christmas 1939. The visit received coverage in the local press, and the initial mistrust of the local Basque community was overcome. Ramon Sota was invited to speak at the annual shepherds' ball.

Following these early efforts, Jon Bilbao requested funding from the New York delegation in January 1940 to open the Boise sub-delegation. After consulting with the Basque Government headquarters in Paris, Manu Sota informed Jon Bilbao on February 24 that he would be assigned a salary of one thousand dollars as the initial annual budget to take the necessary steps to solidify the Idaho subdelegation. The project gained urgency when it was learned that the Spanish government of General Franco planned to appoint Julio Anduiza as consul of their delegation in Boise. Thus, on March 11, 1940, the office of the subdelegation of the Basque Government in Boise was opened, housed in a small office in the city center.

In a report sent to New York, Jon Bilbao described his three main projects. The first was the publication of an informational magazine. The second was to expand the subdelegation's reach to the states of Idaho and Nevada. Bilbao designed a system of local committees, modeled on the organizational structure of the Basque Nationalist Party. This led to the creation of agencies such as the one in Emmett, headed by Villanueva. As his third and final goal, Bilbao proposed mobilizing the youth and creating a Basque cultural center in Boise. Accordingly, he worked with Basques in Emmett to establish a Basque dance group. In addition to these efforts, he taught classes on the history of the Basque Country at the subdelegation.

But these were not his only activities. Jon Bilbao also helped find work as shepherds for Basques who had deserted ships arriving on the East Coast, locating their relatives or corresponding with families of these refugees in the West. During those days, following Manuel Sota's recommendation, he used his military rank from the Basque Army. As a result, much of his correspondence appears under the name "Commander Jon Bilbao." He even intervened in a sensitive legal case, defending a Basque shepherd who had written bad checks.

But none of these projects came to fruition. The German occupation of Western Europe led to the disappearance of *lehendakari* [Basque President] Jose A. Agirre, and after the occupation of Paris on June 14, 1940, the German—and later the Francoists—seized the central offices of the Basque Government in exile. This caused the immediate breakdown of communications and the suspension of financial transfers to all Basque government delegations. As a result, despite the industrious efforts of Jon Bilbao and those around the subdelegation, it was forced to close its doors at the end of June 1940 due to lack of funds.

Jon Bilbao then wrote:

> Four months of struggle. Result: failure. The Delegation I dreamed of so much has closed. Today I sold the last remnants of my office and turned in the keys. By three in the afternoon it was all over, and I left the Eastman Building, formerly the Overland Hotel of Boise. I went home and changed clothes. I kept on my pants and shirt. I stopped by the library where, after reading a few magazines, I picked up two books and read them in the park. After dinner I went to the pool with Bertrand Russell's *The Problems of Philosophy*. As I read, new ideas came to my mind. To completely nullify all that my spirit has received in all the years of my life and then begin building a philosophical structure of my own. That night I wrote a page and a half on the matter.

Nevertheless, Bilbao's efforts in Boise were not in vain. In 1949, the town's Basque Center was founded, and it remains open to this day at 601 Grove Street. Today, this block in Idaho's capital city includes the Basque Center, the Leku Ona restaurant, the Gernika Tavern, and the fronton court, making it known as "The Basque Block."

Despite all the obstacles, Manu Sota, as delegate of the Basque Government in New York, continued to work in close contact with the Basque National Council in London, led by Manuel Irujo. The Basque National Council served as the de facto Basque Government during the absence of Jose A. Agirre, who was missing in occupied Europe from May 1940 to October 1941. During these years, Sota worked with Anton Irala to organize the Basque intelligence services and a propaganda campaign in support of the Allied war effort in South America. After *lehendakari* Agirre arrived in New York in 1941, the New York delegation became the official headquarters of the Basque Government in exile until 1946, from which all Basque activities in occupied Europe and South America were coordinated.

At the end of World War II, Sota returned to his home, *Etchepherdia*, in Biarritz in the Northern Basque Country. He was one of the organizers of the 1948 Basque Studies Congress in Biarritz and was named Secretary General of the Basque PEN Club. He was also appointed a member of

Euskaltzaindia, the Basque Language Academy, which was reconstituted after the war. In the years following the conflict, he wrote *Yanki hirsutus* (Wild Yankee), a collection of casual conversations about the inhabitants of the US, published in 1949.

During a meeting in May 1949 at *Intxausti-Baita*, the home of Manuel Intxausti in the town of Uztaritze, Joxe M. Lasarte, Telesforo Monzon, Intxausti himself, and Manuel Sota conceived the idea of promoting *Euskara Eguna*, or the Day of the Basque Language, to be celebrated both in the Northern Basque Country and in Basque centers throughout the world. At a second meeting, they were joined by Piarres Lafitte, a Basque writer and scholar, and Louis Dassance, mayor of Uztaritze and president of *Euskaltzaleen Biltzarra*, a Basque cultural organization. At that meeting, it was decided to launch the initiative, and Intxausti proposed that it be held on December 3, the day of the death of Saint Francis Xabier, patron saint of the Basque language. Since then, *Euskara Eguna* has been celebrated annually in various parts of the Basque diaspora.

As a member of *Euskaltzaindia*, the Academy of the Basque Language, Sota played a significant role in the compilation of the Retana Dictionary of Authorities, published in multiple volumes starting in 1977.

He amassed an important library, which he donated to the Basque Museum in Baiona. After the death of the dictator Franco, he remained in Biarritz until 1979, when he returned to Getxo in Bizkaia, and died on December 16 at the age of 82.

In many ways, this diary of a journey to Idaho serves not only as a chronicle of events, but as a mirror of Manu Sota himself—his lucid and purposeful style, his unwavering optimism, and his tireless commitment to action. It reveals a man deeply devoted to the Basque cultural and political cause, whose pen moved with the same passion as his steps, always in defense of democracy and human dignity. Against the tides of Fascism, Nazism, and Spanish National Catholicism, Sota stood firm. His life and work are a monument to those who resisted tyranny in one of humanity's darkest hours.

Xabier Irujo

Trip to Idaho 1938

Mama.

1 Diciembre

Hoy a la tarde, a las 3.20, hemos dejado New York en un bus greyhound [galgo] rumbo a Boise, capital del estado de Idaho.

Este viaje puede realizarse por tres medios de locomoción diferentes: por avión ~~tradan~~ tardándose 17 horas; por tren en dos días y por autobus en cuatro, ~~p~~ no habiendo entorpecimientos por la nieve.

Nosotros escogemos el autobus, pues ademas de ser más barato, nos permitirá ver mejor el paisaje. Para llegar a Boise, Idaho, tenemos que atravesar los estados de Pennsylvania, Ohio, Indiana, Illinois, Missouri, Kansas, Colorado y Utah.

El autobus es grande, comodo y con buena calefacción. A traves de la ventana se desliza el paisaje nevado. No hay nada que ayude mejor a pensar y a fantasear con la imaginación.

Cuando se viaja, el pensamiento tiene propensión a exajerar las cosas, y a darlas proporciones heroicas. Por eso, tal vez, yo voy pensando que nos hemos lanzado a una gran aventura; la de descubrir una colonia vasca establecida desde hace años en una región remota de los Estados Unidos.

Para los que tenemos cariño a las cosas de Euzkadi, el descubrir en el extranjero a un hombre que lleva un apellido euzkeldun, ó un escrito que hace referencia a nuestra patria, o simplemente la palabra vasco, consideramos que es un hallazgo casi trascendental. Entonces nos invade la emoción del coleccionista, en presencia del raro ejemplar que enriquecerá su colección.

Y es indudable, que si la persecución franquista contra todo lo vasco continúa por más tiempo, el euzkeldun va

December 1

This afternoon, at 3:20 we left New York on a Greyhound bus to Boise, the capital of the state of Idaho.

This trip can be made by three different modes of transportation: by plane taking 17 hours, by train in two days and by bus in four, if not hampered by snow.

We have chosen to go by bus because, besides being cheaper, it will allow us to see the landscape better. To get to Boise, Idaho, we have to cross the states of Pennsylvania, Ohio, Indiana, Illinois, Missouri, Kansas, Colorado, and Utah.

The bus is large, comfortable and well heated. The snowy landscape glides past the window. There is nothing like it for the imagination to help you think and fantasize.

When traveling, thought has a propensity to exaggerate things and to give them heroic proportions. Perhaps that is why I am thinking that we have embarked on a great adventure, that of discovering a Basque colony that has been established for years in a remote region of the United States.

For those of us who are fond of things from Euzkadi, the Basque Country, discovering a man with a Basque surname abroad, or a document that refers to our homeland, or simply the word Basque, we consider it an almost transcendental find. Then a collector's emotion invades us, in the presence of the rare specimen that will enrich his collection.

And there is no doubt that, if Franco's persecution of everything Basque continues for much longer, the Basque-speaking person will become a rare specimen.

It is interesting to think that among the states of Idaho, Oregon, and Nevada there is a Basque community, more than twenty thousand in number, still fully preserving all its racial characteristics.

The characters that populate this small Noah's ark in which I travel are of no great interest. They are people, men and women, repeated models of the endless series created by God, the way Ford makes cars in these parts.

In the seat immediately behind the driver, there is a pretty blonde lady, with an unlikely feather in her tiny hat.

The driver is a tall and photogenic young man wearing an impeccable uniform, a garment that, as is well known, has great power of attraction for the female sex.

Above the driver is a small plaque that reads:

Your operator
V. Heiser
Safe. Reliable. Courteous

The lady with the feather contemplates him with the attention that is the precursor to love. She seems to ask herself: "How safe will this man be? How reliable is he? To what extent will he be able to be courteous to others?" Apparently the young lady wishes to acquire direct information on these issues, because she soon strikes up a lively conversation with the subject in question, which becomes more intimate and affectionate as the evening wears on.

Next to the driver, there is also a sign warning travelers not to offer him alcoholic beverages. I am of the opinion that it should also be forbidden for ladies to offer him conversation, because, on more than one occasion, we have been at risk of crushing into cars that look like dwarfs compared to our bus.

In Easton, where we had dinner at 8 p.m., I saw the driver and the lady sitting at the same table. And then I don't know what became of them, because we changed buses and drivers as well.

We continue traveling throughout the night. We pass an endless number of little houses on the side of the road. Their lights are on and I can see what is going on inside: peaceful scenes of home, a father reading the newspaper, children playing... I can't help but remember with melancholy our broken homesteads, our shattered homes, and our wandering life as exiles. I experience a longing for home, for homeland, for family, which hurts me like a thorn in my side.

All the towns we pass through are decorated for the Christmas holidays.

Garlands, flags and Christmas trees are everywhere: in the streets, outside the stores, and inside the houses, next to the windows, so that they can be seen from the outside. Illuminated with colored lights: red, blue, yellow… In the middle of the main squares, there are bigger Christmas trees that, amidst the solitude of the night, seem to spread the spirit of Christmas with their lights, the whole essence of Christianity: peace, love, understanding, respect for others.

And once again, my memory harks back to my small homeland devastated by the hatred of evildoers, by the barbarism of foreigners, and by the brutal intransigence of a minority that uses brute force to impose an ideology—materiology, I should say—that no Basque can accept.

Greyhound Lines
Something about the
SUPER-COACH
Designed exclusively for Greyhound, this famous SuperCoach offers the most luxurious ride on the highways . . . combines travel comfort with scenic enjoyment.
A LOT MORE TRAVEL . . .
FOR A LOT LESS MONEY!
GREYHOUND

December 2

We continue navigating the American highways inside the motorized monster. It glides smoothly along the flat surface of the lanes, and every two hours it stops in front of a small hotel or restaurant where we disembark to stretch our legs. The landscape we pass through as the miles monotonously go by is desolate, immense, and deserted. Rarely do we see a person, and only every once in a while a lone ranch, with its huge pile of dried wood and its herd of cattle.

The small towns we pass through are newly built, and all of them have the endearing grace of improvised things that the passing of the years makes definitive. It is true that from time to time we pass a huge city with its apartment buildings that rise up to look like skyscrapers, but in general, during the five days of the trip, we have seen nothing but a great desert, and, from one hour to the next, a new and cozy little village.

One realizes immediately that the United States is a land of promise, full of opportunities for enterprising and tenacious spirits who want to make money in direct contact with the land, far from big cities, which here in America are even more overcrowded than in the Old World.

And soon one can see why Basques who have come to the United States have triumphed. The villager from Amoroto, Ereño, or Arrieta, transplanted to the states of Idaho, Oregon, or Nevada, finds himself a bit as if his mountains had suddenly flattened out and his homestead had been upgraded with radio, heating, a Frigidaire, and an electric stove. In these Americas, he can largely develop his personality without prohibitions or restrictions, because the men who surround him—and not very closely, by the way—are free and respectful like him, far from all those medieval conventions imposed by a ridiculous European pride that suffocate his spirit and abort his initiatives. The Basque—European democrat par excellence—marks his freedom, the true one, the one that ends where his neighbor's begins, and it is well known that this is the nourishment that best suits a Basque, to grow and develop spiritually.

That is why it is not strange that, suddenly, a Basque national minority has sprung up like a bed of mushrooms on one side of the United States. And getting a little pretentious, we could say that the newest and richest democracy in the world wears on its chest, as if it were an ancient jewel, a piece of the oldest democracy.

Intellectually immersed in these more or less transcendental disquisitions, I had not noticed the appearance among the bus passengers of a rather picturesque character. He is a Black man, but so black and shiny that he looks like patent leather. He has the diabolical expression of a character from a horror novel, a long, sharp moustache à la Mephistopheles, and curly hair laboriously combed with some greasy brilliantine. In the middle of the patent leather of his face, and under a menacing frown, his eyes stare with captivating fixity.

His attire is worthy of close scrutiny: bow tie collar, red tie with beadwork worthy of Churriguera, morning coat trimmed with braid, light speckled vest, striped pants, and yellow shoes. When he takes off his cream-colored gloves, he wears a ring with a hundred reflections that, after fogging it with his breath, he rubs giddily on his sleeve. His hands play continuously with a bamboo cane, handling it with the dexterity of a circus dandy. An important part of his attire is a bowler hat of the dynasty of those worn by Charlie Chaplin, which he periodically puts up on the luggage rack and takes down from the luggage rack to place over his tousled curls. Sometimes upright, other times leaning back in his seat, he looks like one of those kings of the Black tribes of central Africa that explorers show us in photographs surrounded by their 777 wives, a cabalistic number that must be restored as soon as it occurs to him to order the head of one of them to be cut off.

He is a terrifying man, capable of bringing a whole nursery school to tears. And yet, as soon as the bus makes a stop and its occupants get off to go to the restaurant to get something to drink, swinging his bamboo cane, he humbly slips into a dark room over whose door is a shameful sign that reads: "Reserved for Colored People." Once again I was convinced that appearances can be deceiving.

On the other hand, this woman who just got on the bus with a little boy in her arms—or rather, under her arm—is unbearable, her hair disheveled and dirty. We soon learned she is going to San Francisco; she comes from Chicago; she is sick and tired of traveling by bus and even more sick and tired of her little boy, whom she would gladly throw out the window. You can tell she's a product of that ill-mannered and scandalous Latin race.

She questions everyone, berates the driver, moves her packages, and walks around with the little boy as if he were just another package, utters exclamations of disgust, at all times displaying her rudeness with ostensible delight.

In short, this feminine product of the Latin race amidst the congeniality of American travelers sounds like an out-of-tune trumpet blast that breaks the harmony of a choir of muted violins.

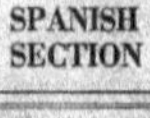
SPANISH SECTION

BOISE CAPITAL NEWS

BOISE, IDAHO, SATURDAY, DECEMBER 3, 1938

SPANISH SECTION

Para El Dia Vasco En Boise

A Traves de Mis Ideas

Por Damian Telleria

Musica de Baile

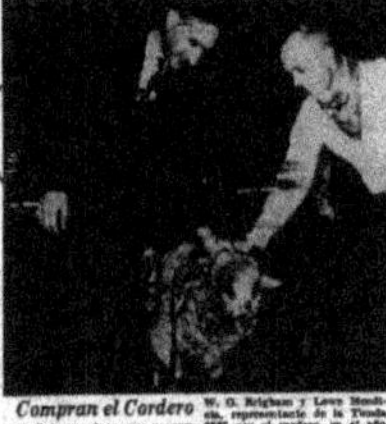

Compran el Cordero

La Donación de la Colonia de Idaho Llega a Las Victimas de la Guerra

Gran Baile de Pastores En Boise 22 de Diciembre

Alvarez del Vayo Regresó de su Visita a Madrid

Los Alemanes Activos en la Ciudad De Tánger

Periódicos de Barcelona Alaban A Estados Unidos

Boise Capital News, December 3, 1938.

December 3

We continue traveling. I look out the window: still only plains. Occasionally, a grain silo. Clear skies with sunshine. Outside, too cold; inside the bus, too much heat.

The quirky Black man is no longer here. He must have gotten off in some remote town, and now, perhaps, he is surrounded by his kids, who will kiss his cheek as if it were a patent leather boot.

The scandalous Latina has also disappeared. We rejoice, although we feel sorry for the little boy, who has been carried off, mixed in with her suitcases and packages.

But two new travelers have appeared who attract attention. Two different travelers and a single person, for by all appearances they are a married couple, all the more united because they are Black. They are young and, by those of their race, would surely be considered handsome. They dress well, and it soon becomes clear that they are well off.

One can immediately guess that they feel acutely stigmatized by their Blackness and, even more so, for being highly educated people. When they move, they look at us whites with a reverent smile, as if to say: "You must forgive us for being Black. Nothing we can do about it. God's whims."

When the bus stops and we whites enter the café, they don't dare approach the counter where refreshments are served. They know the custom here of not allowing Blacks to sit and eat with whites. So, while we have something to drink, they walk around absentmindedly as if to imply that they are neither hungry nor thirsty.

In WaKeeney—a tiny town in the desert—we get off at a diner and all of us white people sit at the counter for a snack. As I eat my sandwich, I see the young Black man approach and cautiously sit down next to me. Apparently his hunger has overcome his shyness. The waitresses who serve us—blondes, light-colored uniforms, white caps—pay no attention to him, as if he didn't exist. Finally, the Black man makes up his mind, calls one of them and asks her for something. The waitress takes some foodstuffs and a little milk, puts them in a paper bag, which she hands to the Black man very curtly.

But I hear the Black man say to her:

"—No, not to go; I want to have lunch here."

She quickly answers him:

"—We are not allowed to serve Colored people at the counter. If you want, you can take the paper bag with you, and eat outside or on the bus."

The young man stands up holding back his indignation, looks at me in embarrassment and leaves.

When I get back on the bus after dark, I look at the Black couple dozing in close embrace, as if trying to drown out the curse that weighs on them with their mutual love. Feeling despised by those around them, they seem to want to isolate themselves, sheltering in the affection they have for each other. Perhaps, for the same reason that they are despised, they are proud to be Black. I feel an enormous sympathy for them, and I would like to show them this affection in some way. But the world will never react against these great injustices; we worship Christ, who was of the Jewish race, and yet most Christians feel an invincible repugnance for the Jews.

These American people are good, deeply human. They experience childlike reactions as soon as they learn of any humiliation suffered by any national minority. Nevertheless, in their own midst, they treat the Indians as inferior beings, and they avoid contact with the Blacks as if they were pariahs. It is clear that no general rules can be applied to people, for soon there are exceptions so great and so eloquent that they nullify the validity of the general rule.

At this very moment, all American people have been outraged by the persecution unleashed by the German Nazis against the Jews. They are scandalized because in Germany they do not allow Jews to go to certain places, to occupy certain positions, etc. They see the log in the Nazi's eye, but they do not notice the splinter in their own eye. Because here in America, Blacks are not allowed to enter restaurants and in some states, even in streetcars there are separate places reserved for them.

These anti-Christian measures are flagrant exceptions in a nation like the United States, where the general rule is true democracy. But what can you do? Humanity is too complex for me to explain the reason for its contradictions with pen and paper.

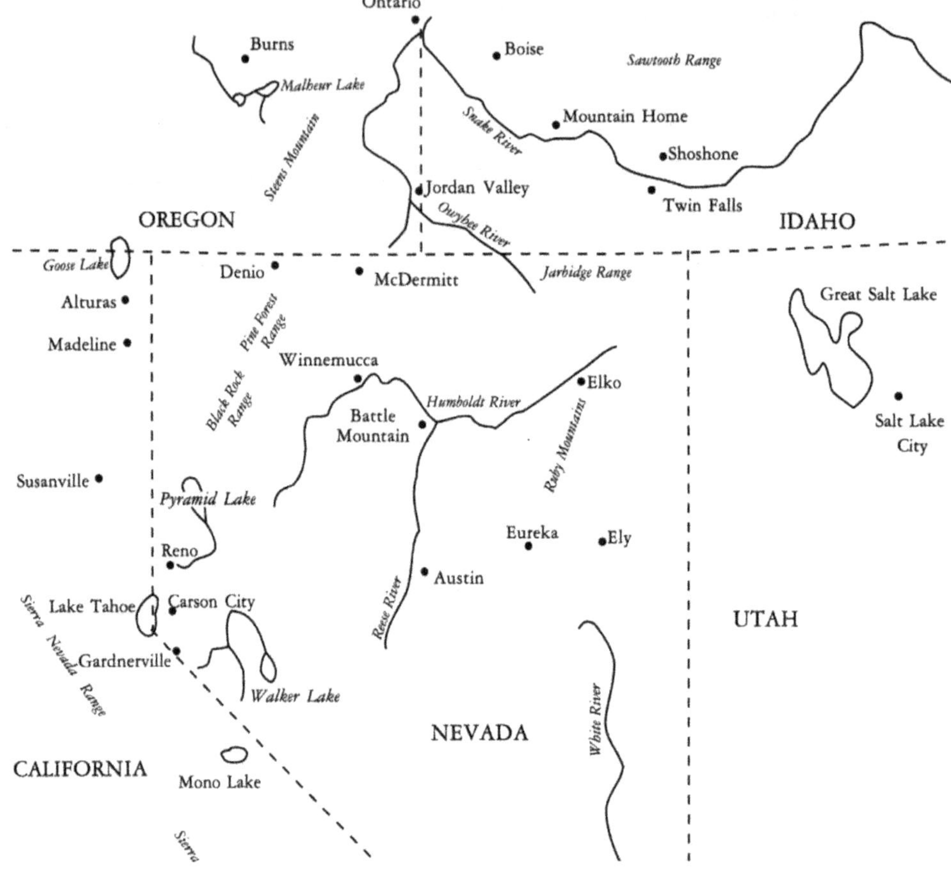

Amerikanuak! Basques in the High Desert, The High Desert Museum, and the Idaho Humanities Fundation, 1995.

December 4

One feels happy traveling on this bus surrounded by Americans. They are easy-going, friendly, straightforward and, above all, extraordinarily nice. Accustomed to traveling in England, where being a foreigner is something akin to rudeness, here I feel like I am in my own country.

In Europe every nation believes itself to be the best, and every national is plagued by a superiority complex that induces him to feel an Olympian contempt for foreigners. I remember a friend of mine traveling in Portugal, irritated by the condescension with which the natives treated him, approached the clerk at the bank where he went to change money and said, "Although I have the misfortune not to be Portuguese, would you be so kind as to change this money for me?" In the United States, on the other hand, and perhaps because its population is made up of all the races of the world, the foreigner is considered to be one of many, to the point that not even in hotels do they ask for identification papers, as happens in Europe. The United States is a democracy for everyone, nationals and foreigners alike.

After coming from Europe, it is a pleasure to travel among Americans. They are neither excessively formal like the English, nor dirty and ill-mannered like the Spanish. (For me, the best definition of hell is a working-class excursion train full of Madrileños or Catalans.) The American has an easy-going courtesy, which, aside from being very comfortable, has the right balance: he does what he wants without bothering his neighbor, and in not bothering his neighbor I include acts such as taking off his boots in the train or cutting his nails with a knife and then offering us a piece of omelette carved on the tip of that same knife with a polite "Would you like some?"

I talk to my neighbor, who, like most Americans, wears glasses, is clean-shaven, has a nasal voice, and is a model of friendliness.

—Now we're in the state of Utah – he tells me. The name comes from the Utes, an Indian tribe that our ancestors, as a consequence of trying to civilize them, managed to wipe out.

—Don't you agree that no one can be civilized by means of force? Unless civilization consists of granting eternal life to the civilized, which could also happen. When you hear that a European state has decided to civilize an African tribe, for example, ask for the job of undertaker: I guarantee you will become a millionaire. What do you want to bet that in Abyssinia that job is held by a relative of Mussolini?

—I'm interested in this state of Utah – I tell him – because there are already some Basques here, although not as many as 20 years ago.

—This state has an area of about 85,000 square miles with a little over five hundred thousand inhabitants; about six inhabitants per square mile. As you can see, it is not heavily populated. It has some mountain ranges, but most of the state is made up of a plateau six thousand feet above sea level. Here in America every state has a symbolic flower: Utah's is the sego lily, because, it seems, the first Mormons who came to Utah fed on the roots of this lily.

—What about the weather?

—It is dry and healthy. Hot in summer and quite cold in winter, but with a sky so clear that for three hundred days of the year it is unblemished by a cloud. In the extreme northwest corner of the state, bordering Nevada, is what we call the Great American Desert.

—Through that desert the Basques would surely have reached Utah with their herds – I tell him.

—Are you going to Salt Lake City? – he asks.

—No – I replied. We're going to spend the night in Ogden, and tomorrow morning we'll go on to Boise.

—You'll like Ogden; it is a very nice town, with about 40,000 inhabitants. Like most Utah towns it was founded by the Mormons.

—Are you a Mormon by any chance?

—Oh, no! I'm not a politician.

I look at him strangely, for I know that the Mormons are a religious sect and not a political party. But he continues:

—In the United States, my friend, religion is politics and politics is religion. Some believe in Roosevelt, others in Hoover, and others in God. And the worst thing is that there are many Americans who take orders from Stalin, Hitler, or the Pope… I assure you that the United States will not lift the arms embargo on Spain until the Vatican wants it lifted... Religion? No, politics... Disgusting... This does nothing but corrupt our little human perfections... And besides, it doesn't make any money.

It's already nighttime when we arrive in Ogden. Sam Maruri, whose real name is Saturnino, is waiting for us and takes us to the Royal Hotel, which he owns. It is at 2522 Wall Avenue. He's tall, bow-legged, light-eyed, and walks with a sturdy step like all Basques. He is from Amoroto, married to a sister of Mateo Osa, the boxer.

Sam is the prototype of the hospitable and noble Basque. He goes out of his way to make our short stay with him as pleasant as possible.

As it is 11 o'clock—here they have dinner at 6—Sam's wife prepares us a chorizo omelette and some pork chops that we eat together in the kitchen, while we fill up our glasses with red wine—at least I do. In the meantime we talk.

Sam's wife says:

—You won't find much Basqueness here; it's not like Idaho or California.

Sam nods:

—That's right. A bunch of Basque families, nothing more. In the olden days...

Between Sam and his wife they tally the number of Basque families in Ogden. Here is the list I wrote down:

John Etcheverry and family	from	Baygorry
John Balan and family		Baygorry
J. P. Etchart and wife		Tardets
Pedro Hualde and family		Valcarlos
Micaela Aguirre and family		Bergara
Julia Laucirica		Ibarrangelu
Margarita Bengoechea		Ispaster
Domingo Ydo		Ereño
Ramon Varela		Arteaga
Tomas Uribe		Arteaga
Jesus Varela		Arteaga
Peter Ospital		Aldudes
Simon Nachiondo		Ispaster

Nicolas Totoricaguena	Garai
Juan Aberasturi	Arteaga
Juan Bilbao	----

—This Bilbao, I don't know where he's from – Sam tells us –, but he's a fine man. For a long time he lived in Jordan Valley, Oregon, where he was a cattleman of much renown. Besides sheep he had two thousand acres of the best land on Clerk Ranch. Twenty-five men he employed, all of them Basques. And now here he is…

—Bankrupt or something? – I inquire.

—I don't think so… Now here he is.

And beyond this "Now here he is" I can't get any more out of Sam.

—And don't you remember Higinio Sendagorta, Sam? – asks his wife.

—I don't have to remember… From Gautegiz Arteaga that guy is, and now about sixty years old he'll be. His mother Maria Goitisolo he had. Off to Cuba Higinio went first, where he got a job as a chocolatier, and it was through the influence of an American soldier that he came to the United States, because he assured him that his father would give him a job in Cleveland, Ohio… With this objective to the United States he came, but the address that his friend gave him he lost, and there you have Sendagorta, a *gixajo*,[1] wandering around Cleveland not knowing where to go.

—What a fool – his wife interrupted. If he had remembered the name of the American soldier, with that at least he could have found out his father's address.

—Did he even know the soldier's name?

—Since he was blond, he called him Peter *Gorri*.[2] And Peter *Gorri* here, Peter *Gorri* there, and Peter *Gorri* everywhere… Finally, after a week, poor Higinio went west. In Nevada he went to work on a ranch in Rebel Creek, then he went to Winnemuca and later on to Willow Creek for about five years. From there, he went back to Rebel Creek again, where he worked on Buffalo Ranch for three years, and he came within an inch of marrying an Indian woman whose name was *Bonita Voz*[3] and

1. *Gixajo*: a poor gay.
2. Peter *Gorri*: Peter Redhead.

who learned to sing in *Euskera*, in Basque… She was so in love with him! But one fine day to Oregon he went, to Mount Steen, and there he worked as a sheepherder for seven years without coming down from the mountain. Then he bought flocks, made a lot of money, and was one of the top sheep owners in Ogden until the Depression came... He's told me that story so many times!

—Higinio – adds Sam's wife – married Marta Corta in Winnemucca.

—And where is he now? – I ask.

—That guy gets itchy feet. In Reno he must be now.

—At least a month ago he was there. Julia Laucirica saw him...

I am deeply moved by these inconsequential stories, a mixture of adventure and loafing. How many of these Basques there are in every corner of the world, little unknown heroes of our race!

As I am very curious to learn more about the lives of Basques, I ask:

—And who is this Julia Laucirica?

—Her father, Jose, was from Ea. In 1899 he arrived in New York City with a big bunch of young Basques, avoiding the draft. Here in Ogden he worked as a cook until 1906, when he opened this hotel, which he later transferred to me. Now he is in California.

—The one I don't know what has become of – Sam's wife intervenes – is that man from Navarre, Juan Lugea, who had sheep…

Since it is already 12 o'clock, we all go to bed. My room is large and simple, with a big double bed. It reminds me of the bedrooms in our homesteads, clean and traditional. Through the window panes I see that it is snowing. I hear bells ringing constantly in the station across the street.

3. *Bonita Voz*: Beautiful Voice.

Basque Delegates In Boise

Basques driven from their homeland by the conquest of Fascist armies are scattered throughout the world, particularly France.

That was the statement today of Manuel de la Sota, official Basque delegate to the United States, in Boise today with a party of his countrymen.

With Antonio de Yzala, de la Sota was in the office of the Boise Capital News, the only newspaper in the world which publishes articles in the Basque language.

De la Sota described the growing Basque colony near Paris where native songs and dances entertain refugees while the great powers of the world quarrel over Spain, the northern part of which was once the home of thousands of Basques.

In addition to the Paris colony, Basques are scattered throughout the French Basque country, the northern slope of the Pyrenees.

In order to weld all the Basques into a united front for their homeland, the Basque delegation was in Boise today making arrangements for the showing of a motion picture taken in the Basque country and featuring the holy city of Guernika, native city of many Boise Basques.

De la Sota said Basques in Europe and America looked to The Capital News as their foremost medium of expression. Publication of articles in the Basque langauge is prohibited now in Spain. They hoped showing of the motion picture here (time and place as yet are undecided (will help the growing spirit of unity and solidarity among the Basques which may eventually result in restoration of their homeland.

Boise Capital News, December 6, 1938.

December 5

Before leaving the hotel, Margarita Bengoechea comes to visit us. She's from Ispaster, the widow of Juan Bengoechea *(Bixar)*, of whom there is much talk in these parts, as he was a millionaire and then lost almost all the money he had.

Bengoechea came to the United States at the end of the last century, working as a morroi in several cattle ranches, especially in one known as Rancho Español, in Palo Alto, California. With the money he made, he bought a flock of sheep that became the foundation of his fortune. Tenacious, enterprising, this man who never learned to read or write expanded his business eventually becoming vice-president of the Bank of Mountain Home, and then he had to undertake the most difficult enterprise of his life: inventing a signature.

He acquired many properties, and in 1910 built the Mountain Home Hotel in Mountain Home, surrounded by parks and gardens, which was, they tell me, one of the finest hostels in southern Idaho at the time.

But Joe Bengoechea hit a rough patch, and when he died, he left his wife a modest sum. His widow, Margarita, now lives in Ogden, and his two sons are attending college in Washington. One of them, Joe, is one of the best football players at the university.

After saying goodbye to Sam Maruri, his wife, and Margarita, we boarded the bus for Boise. We travel among rocky mountains, through a gray and deserted landscape as always. At noon we eat in a lonely canteen, and soon we enter the state of Idaho, whose representative flower is the syringa.

In any case, Idaho—where there are more than twenty thousand Basques—is located in the western part of the Rockies and is bordered to the north by British Columbia and Montana, to the east by Montana and Wyoming, to the south by Utah and Nevada, and to the west by Oregon and Washington. It has a population of about 446,000 inhabitants, and is sparsely populated: 5.3 inhabitants per square mile.

4. *Morroi*: a ranch hand.

Its topography is mountainous, with large plateaus. Its lands, when fertilized by irrigation, are extraordinarily productive, but there is a very large tract of land where water does not yet reach and which remains uncultivated, with its extraordinary reserves untapped. Hence the state of Idaho offers a wide field of experimentation, full of possibilities for the enterprising man who is not afraid to live alone with nature. The climate is dry and very healthy.

The altitude varies from 726 feet on a certain part of the Snake River to 12,655 on Mount Borah. Surrounding the flat, desert scenery in which Basque herders operate exclusively—not a single American is to be found there—rise the mountains called Bear, Blackfoot, and those of the Snake River. Basques ascend these mountains with their herds in the spring, where they remain until autumn. Many times a peak has been pointed out to me which they call *Gabonmendi*, Christmas mountain, because a group of Basque shepherds once spent Christmas Eve there.

In the mountains there are bears that the shepherds can kill easily and that are not dangerous as long as their young are not attacked. There are also rattlesnakes in great abundance, but the greatest enemy of the shepherds is the coyote—a species of predator almost as large as a wolf—which wreaks great havoc on the herds, and which they catch with traps, because the state gives a cash prize for each coyote skin that is turned in. At night they make howling cries that keep the novice shepherds awake. In addition, there are large elk that it is prohibited to kill; several species of deer, coati, cougar (a lion or an American panther), ocelot, and wild cat, which is very similar to a small tiger.

Idaho's major cities are: Boise (population 25,000), which is the state capital, Pocatello (17,000), Idaho Falls (10,000), Twin Falls (9,000), Coeur d'Alene (9,000), Lewiston (10,000), Nampa (9,000), and other smaller ones, such as Caldwell, Emmett, Moscow, Payette, etc., scattered through all of which many Basques live.

We stop in Mountain Home and three travelers get on. It's foggy; the bus is going slowly and we can't see a thing. One of the passengers is sitting in the seat in front of us. He is a man of about forty five, neatly dressed, clean, and clean-shaven. He wears his hat cocked to one side and chews gum, which gives him a blasé air. Short and strong, when he hears us speak Spanish, he looks at us with a mixture of curiosity and distrust. I think to myself, "This guy is Basque."

It is strange; Basques are eminently hospitable people, and nevertheless, it is difficult to get to know them, to get them to open up to you right away, to extend their friendship spontaneously as soon as you meet them. They are like those mastiffs at our homesteads, that, when they see a stranger approaching, look at him with suspicion, pacing close by, like a wild beast in a zoo. José Ortega y Gasset once said in one of his essays that we Basques were crustaceans, with an innate tendency to withdraw into our spiritual shell.

This suspicious position adopted by Basques in the presence of a stranger is perhaps due to the fact that, in their native land, they are accustomed to being mistreated spiritually by Spaniards, especially when they do not express themselves well in Spanish. Spaniards, with their facile dialectics, their superficial and adaptable character, and, above all, their conviction that they belong to the privileged race of Spain, treat Basques with superiority, like the colonizer treats the colonized. Hence, Basques grow up dominated by a sense of distrust towards strangers, which envelops them like an armor. But, undoubtedly, as soon as Basques shed this shell, they are the best people in the world, and the most faithful companions. One does not get to know Basques until the third or fourth day of dealing with them; as great psychologists, they soon discover the moral qualities of their new acquaintance, and then accept or reject him. I have been able to observe this phenomenon in all the Basques I have met here in America.

Poor Basques! If Spaniards had not deceived them so many times, today José Ortega y Gasset would not have to say that we withdraw into ourselves like turtles when we notice the presence of a stranger. However, as noble as dogs, after growling inwardly, we jump affectionately to the owner of the hand that petted us.

We are still in a dense fog, as if it were cotton batting. My two companions speak in Basque; I notice that the new traveler, who is sitting with his back to us, pays more attention and watches us as if he had eyes in the back of his head.

I enjoy reading the Basque page of the Boise newspaper, *Boise Capital News*, which is published every Saturday. The issue I have in my hands is the first one published (October 1, 1938), a true monument to Castilian literature. The ads, above all, have no equal in the history of Spanish advertising. See this one which must refer to some knitted jackets sold at Logan's store, Sportsmen Co. of Boise. It goes like this:

"Loganknit
All *sarterios* (wardrobes) should include one or two
Don't *chimerse* (deny yourself) a Loganknit!
You can replayce three ordinary clothes".

The following advertises the Walker Drug Company, a pharmacy, with the following enigmatic words:

"En su trabajo para el necesita de todos"
"Dari, el gente de este community
un professional ethical prescripción
servecio segundo ha nada.
Register Pharmacistas con
años de experiencia,
hombre este departamento,
cosas siempre son frescos y
completos, y los precios siempre bien".[5]

Another calls out to the passerby:

"Veas las ventanas y venir adentro del
estor y escojes su magnífico abrigo de
estas featured precios. ¡Cuando tienes tiempo!".[6]

A fur coat is described as follows:

"¡Mui cirimilau con hermoso fur!
¡Adentro tiene cotton y aguanta mucho tiempo!".[7]

Here is an advertisement for chinaware:

"Novelty Pottery sets de 6 piesas.
Regular $ 1.98 tiene un pato de asucar,
uno de cream, sal pimiento, uno pato de tea
y para pan honey.........$ 1.29".[8]

5."In your work for it needs of all to give the people of this community a professional ethical prescription servece—second to nothing. Register Pharmacists, with years of experience, man this department, things are always fresh and complete, and the prices always well."
6."Sees the windows and come inside the estore and you chooses your magnificent coat from these featured prices. When you have time!"
7. "Verry cirimilau with beautiful fur! Inside it has cotton and holds out a long time!"
8. "Novelty Pottery sets of 6 peases. Regular $1.98 it has one plat of zugar, one of cream, solt pepper, one tea plat and for bread honey....................... $ 1.29"

Undoubtedly this advertisement page is written by a Basque who speaks Basque and English, and barely knows Spanish, which is what happens to most Basques living in the western states of America. His phrasing is the same as that used by those fellows—half-wits, half-idiots—who imitate Spanish charlatans and who are found in all the taverns of our villages. It is unquestionable—and this was already noted by Cervantes—that Basques are the foremost butchers of the Castilian language living in the Peninsula. And the fault is not theirs, but that of the Spanish rulers, who insist on putting Castilian into their heads—notice I did not say teaching them—by hook or by crook, instead of adopting a gradual teaching method based on bilingualism. As long as the current school curriculum continues in our villages, the Basque-speaking child will never learn the Spanish language, and when he grows up, he will mistreat it when he needs to use it. The Spanish page of the Boise Capital News is an eloquent example of this phenomenon.

Nevertheless, the advertisements in this newspaper in Basque—which also exist—are of no better literary quality. See this one referring to J. C. Penney department store, one of the best in Boise:

"Onche Ettoreche daus Penney otoñako
Jaque Barrisek".[9]

And below:

"Calleako nai jasteako claseak daus.
Pielesko colluekin nai collu badik evelcheko clasiek daus".[10]

It is interesting to note that, in order to attract Basques, Boise department stores make use of the names of the compatriots they employ. For example:

"Ben at Falk's *sutureno*[11]
and Teresa Arriola is at your service
to show or sell any item".

Another:

9. Advertisement in dialectal and oral Basque: "Now just arrived the new Penney Jackets".
10. "There are both, for street and dress models. With fur collar and without".
11. *Sutureno*: stitcher.

Boise Capital News, October 1, 1938, page 8.

"These Golden Rule staff members
want their friends to visit them at Golden Rule *Estore*:
Victoria Letamendi
Toni Garechana
Josephine Garechana
Millie Anchustegui
Marie Ocamica
Domingo Abarrate
Joe Letemendi
Antonio Lopez".

*"Asko estimancot etorri eitie, ezta deriora erosi eitie,
posik legundu ein got estoren erasein lecuten".*[12]

The Boise Friendly Store, meanwhile, advertises as follows:

*"Tenemos cinco Basque personas de trabajo, encima de nuestra
corporación, para ayudarais con gusto y servicio pronto:*[13]

Joe Anacabe -Departamento de los hombres.[14]
Phyllis Anchustegui -La primera abitación.[15]
Marie Bastida -El balcón de faciones.[16]
Regina Madarieta -Cosas de acosa.[17]
Marie Anchustegui -En el desk o oficina".[18]

Undoubtedly, if you go to any store in Boise, you will be able to find—despite the disconcerting indications of these ads—a young Basque man or woman, a model of politeness and friendliness, who will speak to you fluently in English or Basque. And the same happens in restaurants and banks, not to mention bars (whether they are called *Pools*, *Pastimes,* or *Cigar Stores*), the owners of which are mostly Basques.

12. In a very dialectal and spoken Spanish, with a strong influence of Basque: "Really appreciate you coming, no need to buy anything, I'll be happy to help you anywhere in the store".
13. We have five Basque working people, on our corporation, to you help with pleasure and service soon:
14. *Departamento de hombres*: Men's department.
15. *La primera abitación*: The first room.
16. *El balcón de faciones*: The blacony of fashuns.
17. *Cosas de acosa*: House stuff.
18. *En el desk o oficina*: At the desk or office.

This shows how perfectly Basques have acclimated to this environment, and how esteemed they are by Americans. On this point I would like to cite the fact that Spaniards, when they come to the West to look for a job, hide the fact that they are Spaniards, and say either that they are Basques, or that they are Basque-Gallegos, Basque-Asturians, etc. I have heard this repeatedly from people here.

But let's get back to our advertisements. On other occasions, the names of the best-known ladies of the Basque community are mentioned in them. Here is an example:

> "Basque people know the quality of Lennox *Torrid Zone Furnaces.*
> Their friends own one! Mrs. de Bastida,
> Mrs. de Aldecoa, Mrs. de Asumendi, Mrs. de Abarrate.
> They will tell you how advantageous it is;
> for our stoves and housework they are very useful".

My reading was interrupted by the voice of the stranger who finally decided to question us.

—Are you Spaniards? – he asks, turning around.

—Basques – the three of us answered at the same time.

We soon got into a lively conversation in Basque. His name is Rufino Uriarte, and he is from Errigoiti.

—I'm a bartender in Mountain Home – he says. I used to work at the nightclubs in Boise until they closed. Now there's not much money.

From the conversation we soon discover that he is a good Basque and that in the current war he is a determined opponent of Franco.

—I haven't heard anything from my family – he says, They were caught in the bombing in Gernika, and since then they haven't written to me... That damned Franco!

We move on to talk about the Basques in Boise.

—Although there aren't many, you'll find some snitches among those who carry more weight.

Uriarte calls the rebels snitches. The biggest snitch, according to him, is Jack Anduiza, the hotelier, who, as a result of the bombing of Gernika, declared in a dispute that it was a pity that more Basques of that kind had not died.

This worries us, because we will be staying precisely at Jack Anduiza's hotel.

—But don't pay any attention to him – he added. He's the most stubborn man in the world. He says things without thinking, and he'd rather die than back down.

And so he goes on to tell us a string of gossip about the people of Boise.

Since my arrival in America, I have noticed in most Basques an inordinate inclination to gossip. Each one tells things about the others, and not exactly very kindly things, and there is no way to form an accurate idea about a given Basque, because everyone expresses a different opinion about him. And as soon as it concerns the present war, the difficulty increases, because everybody is branded a fascist.

Women are distinguished by their sweetly acerbic criticisms. They arrive at the hotel, sit on the edge of the armchair, put their purse on their knees and their hands on their purse, and begin their "Some people say…", "What they are saying about you, although I don't believe it…", "Some people are already saying…", etc., followed by an endless series of gossip.

But, then again, I suppose this is a defect of all races, exacerbated by the subconscious pain of feeling far from the homeland.

Uriarte now tells the famous story of Tirripitirri of Natxitua, when he was in Idaho as a sheepherder. It seems that Tirripitirri spent 10 years without leaving the mountain, tending his flock and reading one issue of the newspaper from Bilbao, *Noticiero Bilbaíno*, which he learned by heart, without knowing a word of Spanish.

Now someone says to him, "Tirripitirri, tell us what the *Noticiero* says from line 32, column 4, page 2." Immediately the guy from Natxitua parrots the lesson, reciting the whole text of the newspaper, as written from top to bottom, with advertisements, obituaries, etc.

We finally arrive in Boise. We take a taxi to the Anduiza Hotel. Suddenly, we hear the driver who utters a loud *Arraiyua*![19] because he is forced to brake. We ask him in Basque if he is Basque.

—From Ispaster – he answers.

His name is Jose Garate, and he runs a taxicab business with his brother. He is short, stocky, and strong, and like most Basques he made

19. *Arraiyua!*: Damn!

some money during Prohibition with alcoholic beverages. Decidedly, smuggling is a vocation of all Basques.

We enter the Anduiza Hotel, which, more than a hotel, is a *sui generis* boarding house that is dedicated exclusively to lodging Basque sheepherders, like all the Basque hotels in Boise. The main part of the Anduiza Hotel is a beautiful *fronton*, which, as if it were a courtyard, is surrounded by a wooden balcony that all the rooms of the house overlook. On the first floor, at the same level as the court and all along the court is the kitchen and a long dining room with two very long tables. Then there is a small living room, the office, and a large living room with gaming tables, pool tables, and a huge stove.

Jack Anduiza is a herculean Basque who walks like an orangutan. He is old, clean-shaven, and has a tuft of white hair on his head. A native of Natxitua, he was one of the first Basques to arrive in the Western States of the United States. Gruff and very stubborn, but noble at heart. He does not believe in what is written or in words. Everything is "imaginashun," he says. Jack Anduiza believes in nothing but himself. He speaks English well, but almost always expresses himself in Basque. He mumbles a rather picturesque Castilian; for example, he calls heating, *"calificasión."*

Jack was one of the first Basques to arrive in the western states of America. He started out as a sheepherder, then owned sheep, which he later sold to become an innkeeper. The house in which he lives is his own, and he owns some land in Idaho. He is a man of money, as evidenced by the fact that his oldest sons, Julio and Pete, attended the Deusto Business School of Bilbao, and his son Johnny is now at the University of Portland (Oregon).

Jack is the lifetime secretary and handy-man of a Basque Mutual Aid Society, which by the way is in a fight with another one run by the Ysursa, Iriondo and Abarrate *(Arboleda)*. The Basques of Idaho do not like him because of his domineering and intransigent character. His wife Juana, from Gizaburuaga, has no other merit than that of being an excellent cook. She understands nothing, is very short-sighted, lacks prudence, and talks nothing but nonsense. Before marrying Jack, she was a maid in Barcelona, where malicious tongues say that she led a life that was a little too amorous.

As soon as we arrive, Juana takes us all around shouting: "Here we have very little politics; it's not like in Spain", referring to the lack of proper etiquette we find in her house.

We also meet Matilde, the only daughter of the family. She is a pretty, polite, and smart girl, who does all the housework: she tidies our rooms, serves us dinner, etc. All this with a naturalness, a distinction and a lack of pretension, which makes her very likeable. She is a Basque young lady educated in the democratic principles of the United States.

When we arrive, the eldest son Pete is also at home. He is married to one of Isidro Madarieta's daughters, and is a clerk in one of the Boise banks. He is an earnest, good, and friendly man. During our stay in Boise, he has formed a close friendship with us, helping us in all our endeavors.

Anduiza's family is a typical Idaho Basque family: by their upbringing, their way of life and their means of expression, in Basque and English.

A curious detail: Jack and his family belong to the Democratic Party, despite the fact that their convictions—Jack's—are completely anti-democratic, and that the vast majority of Basques vote for the Republican ticket.

As soon as we arrive, we sit down at the table, which is clean and neat like in a house in Euzkadi. The dinner is excellent and with the proverbial Basque abundance: a succulent and comforting broth, a white and very tasty cauliflower; halibut (fish) in the manner of fried hake (a gastronomic delight); beef tongue in tomato sauce, tender and expertly seasoned; lamb chops (a Boise specialty) with fried potatoes. (The Idaho potato is reputed to be the best in the United States.) For dessert, peach pie (*escabeche de alberrechicos*, as our villagers say) homemade by Juana's expert hands. All this, with the excellent company of a select red wine from California. And to top it all off, *akeita, txola, eta txokorra*.[20]

To any Basque who is lucky enough to go to Boise, I highly recommend eating at Anduiza's one day. I guarantee you a gastronomic delight that you will never forget.

While we are having dinner, we have our first visitors: Justo Echebarria

20. *Akeita, txola eta txokorra*: coffee, brandy and a cigar.

and his wife. Justo is a strong and healthy man and wears a light-colored ad hoc hat. He is from Ea and came to America when he was seventeen years old (he is now fifty three), before the draft, like all Basques here. He owns a beautiful ranch on Dry Creek, near Boise, and owns flocks of sheep. He has plenty of money.

His wife Raimunda Aldamiz appears wrapped in a thick black fur coat and a fashionable hat. She is a perfect Ibarrangeluan lady, somewhat pretentious and deliberate, but deep down, a naive person. From the conversation, we soon deduce that Raimunda, above all, breathes fascism. But they are nice enough and harmless.

Another notable visitor is Tom Uranga, *Urtubiya*. He is a fine specimen of an American Basque. He left Ea in the year 1893, and first worked as a sheepherder in Winnemucca, Nevada. From there he went to Paradise Valley, Nevada, where he was employed on the Bacon cattle ranch, and then was in Hagerman, Idaho. He now lives in Boise, and has sheep. His wife's name is Maria Sabala, and they have five children. Anton has a very beautiful home on Bannock Street, Boise. He has had many ups and downs in his economic career, and at the present time, as the sheep business is in a downturn, he is not doing very well at all.

He is the perfect Basque adventurous type, easy-going, friendly and obliging, with the invaluable experience of one who has had to struggle to live far from his homeland. He is very popular in Boise—he knew it when there were hardly any houses—and is a great friend of the Indians in the vicinity. I suspect he has a child or two among them.

We are also greeted by Don Antonio Azcuenaga y Basterrica, one of the most renowned Basques in Idaho. This 71-year-old native of Bilbao is one of the pioneers of Basque immigration, and one of those who contributed the most to bringing his compatriots to these lands. He arrived at the age of nineteen in New York, where he heard about the opportunities that the western states had to offer, and decided to come to this country.

—My trip by railroad, without knowing English – he tells us – was a real odyssey, and I remember that I got off at Saint Louis thinking I had to change trains, and I had to spend the night sleeping in a freight car. In Winnemucca, where I finally arrived, I met Jose Navarro and together we decided to go to Jordan Valley, Oregon, to try our luck. We made the trip on foot, and as the roads were very lonely, we wandered lost for five days in the desert. When we thought we were dying of hunger and exhaustion, on the sixth day we came upon one of the inns where the stagecoaches stop. In Jordan Valley we had a five and dime store, and with the money we made we bought sheep. We had some luck, and by the year '30 I had a few hundred thousand pesos in the bank. But also, the year of the Depression, when the banks closed, they really took a good bite out of me. But, anyway, there is no need to complain; for our daily *lapikoko*[21] and to give *instrusion*[22] to our children we have enough…

Azcuenaga lives in a very nice house with his wife Consuelo Uberuaga and their children Adrian, Fernando and Ines. He is a man who is seldom out and about.

Chatting after dinner, while some drink cognac and others rye whiskey, Justo Uranga, Antonio Azcuenaga and Jack Anduiza tell tales of the most famous Basque guys around, or rather, Justo does not tell any stories; he empties glasses by the gulp and laughs with satisfaction. Azcuenaga talks about a certain Pete Gastelu, who at first worked with him, and later with an Irishman named John McDonald, who kept sheep near Bingham Canyon:

—Pete and MacDonald grew to love each other like brothers and understood each other in an English that no one else understood except them. While working in the *parisión*[23] MacDonald had to give Pete orders for the next day, and Pete said to him: "John, tomorrow morning, seven o'clock sharp, *bijar goixian etorriko nok…*".[24] To which the Irishman replied grimly: "All right, Pete, *mi sabi-de-boro*".

This *"mi-sabi-de-boro"* produces great hilarity, although frankly I do not understand it. Justo Echebarria, especially, chuckles enthusiastically and does nothing but repeat:

—So mi sabi-de-boro…

And then, big laughs.

21. *Lapikoko*: stew.
22. *Instrusion*: education.
23. *Parisión*: birthing.
24. *Bijar goixian etorriko nok*: I'll come tomorrow morning.

After that, they talk about Antonio Popolo's *chirenadas,*[25] and it is *Urtubiya* who recounts an anecdote:

"One afternoon, Antonio Popolo went hunting in the mountains of Pocatello, and before leaving, his wife put a couple of little sausages in his pocket for a snack. Suddenly, a *mendiko auntze*[26] comes into view. It was getting dark and he was in a big hurry; he put his hand in his pocket and, instead of putting a cartridge in his shotgun, he put in one of the little sausages. And, curious, curious, without so much as a squeak, Popolo went towards the auntze while saying to himself: *"Oraintxe bai, neu ondo nau azertauten bot au antelope au…"*[27] And bang! Popolo fired, eta *uts ein dau Popolok beren eskopetiegaz.*[28] Sad, sad Popolo went to the sheep camp, and went to bed without supper that night. When he woke up the next morning, it turned out that the mendiko auntze was once again next to the sheepherder's wagon. And Popolo picked up the shotgun while saying to himself, *"Ongüen bai ilgot, urrien dau ta… ".*[29] But as soon as he began to shoot, the mountain goat looked at Popolo, raised its *buztena* (tail) and ran away. Then Popolo said to himself very convincingly, *"Igarri entsost onek mendiko auntzek txorizuen usañagaitik neure eskopetie!".*[30]

These anedotes make our guests laugh as if they were the wittiest jokes. Juana and Raimunda also join in with great laughter over the Pete Gastelu and Popolo incidents. Apparently they are funny, and I'm the only one who doesn't understand them. Could it be that my imagination doesn't match these people's? That could be. Anyway, I am going to tell two other stories recounted by Anduiza, which, for better or for worse, belong to the folklore of the Idaho Basques.

25. *Chirenadas*: nonsenses, silly things.
26. *Mendiko auntze*: a mountain goat.
27. *Oraintxe bai, neu ondo nau azertauten bot au antelope, au…*: Yes, right now I'm sure I'll hit this antelope…
28. *Eta uts ein dau Popolok beren eskopetiegaz*: And Popolo has missed the shot with his shotgun.
29. *Ongüen bai ilgot, urrien dau ta…*: This time I'm going to kill it, because it's close…
30. *Igarri entsost onek mendiko auntzek txorizuen usañagaitik neure eskopetie*: This mountain goat discovered me by the smell of chorizo from my shotgun!

The coyote's mockery

Back there, on the ranch in Jordan Valley, there was a bunch of Basques who hunted *azeriak* with *adakiak*.[31] One of them was Pedro Artiondo, a very experienced man. One day they went to the mountain. It was snowing, there was *lañua*,[32] and it was already night when they approached the location where they had placed traps. Artiondo told Canuto Olletxe that there were coyote tracks in that area, and added: *"Ementxe bai badau kakaldi da azerí"*[33] Then, Olletxe, because of the darkness there, or because he did not notice, or perhaps to make a joke, *"ta aldi ezarri urdai, bereziaz miñiban abarkanarrura en el adaki"*.[34]

After nightfall, the hunters returned to see if any prey had fallen into the traps. And, astonished, they saw that there was nothing at all, and then there was an argument! They all blamed Canuto, and Artiondo said to him: *"Heuk dekok ogena guzti onena…"*.[35] Then, Canuto confessed that he had put *abarka*[36] instead of *urdai*[37] in the trap. But the azeri mocked the two when they left, because the azeri had *kaka tranpien ganien, burlez azeri orrek, eta aztertu bere lurra.*[38]

On the Crosby ranch

On the Crosby ranch in Oregon one spring they were shearing Txanton Pipirri's sheep. The sheepherder, whose name was Micke Allu, was angry with a Mexican shearer because his shearing was so bad that the sheep were bleeding.

Then the Mexican shearer answered him: "Son of a bitch, you think you're going to teach me how to shear sheep, you bastard." Allu did not understand what the Mexican was saying, but assuming it was something bad he said: *"Ipiztarreko semie naz gero, eta kontua euki zer ezan duzun nigatik"*.[39]

31. *adakiak*: traps.
32. *lañua*: fog.
33. Here there really is shit and coyote.
34. instead of putting bacon he put straw sandal leather in the trap.
35. You are to blame for all this.
36. *Abarka*: straw sandal leather.
37. *Urdai*: bacon.
38. Popped on the trap; the coyote mocking them, had stirred up the dirt.
39. I'm from Ispaster, so be careful what you say about me.

"Son of a bitch", the Mexican replied, "you, Basquito, speak Christian to me, I don't understand what you are saying".

Allu, who was getting angrier and angrier because a few hours later quite a few sheep had died from the blood they had lost because they had been so badly shorn, shouted to the Mexican: *"Nire ardiak il en diez zeugatik eta jateko emongotzut ardien okelia, zeuri oparituko dotsuaz gaur gabian bere garaunak".*[40]

The Mexican, believing that Allu was going to shoot him, started running from the ranch, but Allu managed to show him the brains of the sheep that had died because of the bad shearing, and then the Mexican understood that the Basque was not going to retaliate because of the argument they had had.

From then on, the two became close friends, and Allu told the Mexican: *"Emendik aurrera garaunak jango dozuz emen ardi-kanpuan, uzabak Txanton Pipirrik esan dost neuri ta".*[41]

"All right, Basquito," replied the Mexican. We will both eat the brains of Mohammed.

But Txanton Pipirri gave the Mexican shearer the bill from the Great Captain:

For 800 dead sheep	120
For eating sheep brains	5
For Basque lessons	60
Remaining balance	15
	200

And since he had to pay $200 for shearing one thousand sheep, the Mexican went home without a red cent.

The $60 Txanton gave to Micke as the good Basque language teacher he was, and then the latter said to his boss: *"Ostabe ekarri, urrengen be treskiladorak datorren udaberrian, Txanton… ".*[42]

40. My sheep have died because of you, so I'm going to give you sheep meat today and tonight I'm going to give you their brains.
41. From now on you will eat sheep brains here at the camp, because that's what the boss, Txanton Pipirri, told me.
42. Bring more sheep shearers next spring, too, Txanton…

We head to bed to rest. My room is full of pillows, rugs, colorful seat cushions, all sweetly tacky. My bed is huge, a double bed, covered with a satin bedspread of very garish Arabian drawings. But all very clean, and saturated with the bad taste of the Basque emigrant.

I fell asleep thinking about these men of our race, who have left our small homeland for every corner of the world, triumphing and giving a good name to Euzkadi because they are true knights of adventure and have the pioneer spirit.

Zenon Izaguirre, John Archabal, Tony Basabe, Juan Coscorrosa and Anastasio Odiaga.
Juanita Uberuaga Hormaechea Collection. BMCC.

December 6

This week when I went down to breakfast, I found some sheepherders who were already having their cornflakes with milk in big bowls, reminiscent of the breakfasts in Venta de Baños and Casetas. Almost all of them are from Biscay. Serious and concentrated, they eat, listen to the news on the radio, play cards, and sleep inordinately. Since they are on vacation, they get up late and do nothing but eat and sleep. They are taciturn men, who speak very little and in Basque, and spit in the spittoons, after making unbelievable noises with their throats. This, at least, is my first impression.

Breakfast was interrupted by the entrance of Jacinto Anchustegi, a Lekeitian of about sixty years of age, blue-eyed, bespectacled, with a graying mustache and a clear voice. He has a ranch in Spring Valley, near Boise, and is engaged in selling eggs, milk, etc., and by all accounts is well off. He is a jolly man, and at the banquets when Anchustegi is in attendance, there's never a lack of song. His two daughters, Marie and Phyllis, are sales clerks in the department store at Boise's Friendly Store, and Millie at the Golden Rule.

In the state of Idaho we have met other Anchustegis: Gregorio, from Berriatua, is married to Fermina Iturri and they live in Homedale; George and Joe, in Boise, and Pedro in Mountain Home. The latter must be Jacinto's brother.

We leave the hotel and, for the first time, we come in contact with the capital of the state of Idaho. It is a clean, new city, with nicely laid out streets and some beautiful buildings. It has 25,000 inhabitants. It is located in the Boise Valley which is divided into two parts by a river also called Boise. The southern part is amazingly fertile, so there are countless ranches. To the north rises a chain of snow-capped mountains that surrounds the capital under a continuous blue sky, presenting a beautiful picture.

One of Boise's main sources of wealth is sheep ranching, which is almost exclusively in the hands of the Basques.

This morning we visited the most important Basques in Boise, and we started with Don John Archabal.

His real surname is Achabal, but when he became an American citizen he added the "r" and, when pronouncing it, accentuating the first "a", the result is Arechabal, which sounds the same as Archibald, and is easier for Americans to pronounce.

Among the Basques naturalized in the United States I have noticed that all those who have long last names, shorten them: Zabalandicoechea, for example, is Zabal, and Idoyaga, Ido, which in English is pronounced EYE-doe. The most curious transformation is that of a Domingo Marcuerquiaga, from Orovada (Nevada), who is now McErquiaga, giving him an Irish or Scottish appearance.

Archabal is from Ispaster, and he came to the United States at the age of twenty, with two dollars in his pocket and seventeen in his gerriko,[43] so that people would believe that he had only two, and that way he would not be robbed. The ship he was on was shipwrecked, and after being on the verge of drowning, he finally arrived in California.

Since for Basques all of the United States is California, and since he did not know how to read or write, nor did he know English, he showed the first policeman he met the paper on which he had the address where he was headed. The policeman could not make Achabal understand that on that paper was not written the address of a house in San Francisco, but that of a house in Boise in the state of Idaho. Finally, the policeman took him to a French sailors' lodging, where he found a Basque who explained the misunderstanding.

Today Archabal is not only one of the largest landowners and flock owners in Idaho, but in all the Northwest states. He owns eighty thousand sheep and two beautiful 2,000-acre breeding farms. In addition, he rents five thousand acres for grazing his sheep. His business requires the constant attention of fifty to ninety employees and, during the lambing season, double that number, all of whom are Basque.

He is married to Benedicta Aldecoa and has three daughters: Casilda, married to Zenon Izaguirre; Matilde, married to Julio Anduiza; and Jane,

43. *Gerriko*: waist pouch.

who has just finished her studies at the university. His son's names are John, married to an American, and Fidel, who is a university student. All of them speak only Basque and English, and the firstborn, above all, has inherited all the Basqueness of his father.

A few years ago Archabal's fortune was valued at $1,000,000. Today his financial situation is not as good, but he enjoys great standing. His name travels all over Idaho, Nevada, and part of Oregon, which is where his herds graze.

Archabal makes a very good first impression on me. Unfortunately, in this first visit I hardly talk to him, because, since I hardly speak Basque, he avoids me and prefers to talk to Irala, who speaks it. But he is a perfect Basque, intelligent, straightforward, and affable.

Although he does not know how to read or write, he has an accounting system that he invented, so no one deceives him. He is very popular among all the Basques, because, although he does not smoke or drink, he is always in the bars frequented by Basques, whom he treats with his natural cheerfulness. He is very fond of jokes, and of organizing *pelota* challenges.

His wife Benedicta is a perfect Basque, who speaks only Basque, and takes care of their home as if she had no money.

We are presented with pastries and liquors, and soon we feel as if we were in our homeland. Here we meet Zenon Izaguirre, Archabal's son-in-law, who runs his business. He is very nice and has considerable influence among the Basques, since he is always traveling around the state for business. He has siblings and relatives in New York who are very patriotic, but he is indifferent, and is interested in nothing but his business. He speaks in Basque all the time and is very Basque in his manner.

Then we visited the dean of the Basques in Boise, Don Jose Navarro, who is from Akorda, and came to the United States when he was nineteen years old.

Just as Don Antonio Azcuenaga told me about Navarro when he told me his story, I asked the latter to tell me his own version, and so he did:

—Yes – he tells me – in Wimmenucca I met Azcuenaga, and we decided to try our luck in the state of Oregon.

Full of optimism and youthful enthusiasm, they bought a horse at

McDermitt to carry their supplies and clothing, and set out across the desert. The first day they walked about 12 miles through a sheep camp where they spent the night. The next day they set out again, going toward the Owyhee River which they had to cross before reaching Jordan Valley, but when night came they were still in the desert with their water supply exhausted. They turned the horse loose to graze on the weedy grass, and made a fire, beside which they spent the night.

Again they set out, reaching the Owyhee River, where they were able to quench the thirst that was tormenting them. The environs of the Owyhee were not as had been described to them, and, knowing that there was a steep pass between McDermitt and Jordan Valley, they traveled in that direction. But they lost their way and strayed into the dry, barren wilderness, suffering untold hardships for lack of food and water.

Completely exhausted, they decided that Navarro should take the horse and go in search of water, and if he did not return until late, Azcuenaga should light a fire to guide him back to the camp, since they could not call out to each other because they were too weak.

Guided by the setting sun, Navarro reached Battle Creek, where he got some provisions and returned in search of Azcuenaga, finding him faint. He placed him over the horse and they returned to Battle Creek, where, after spending the night, they continued on toward McDermitt. They rested two days at a stagecoach stop, and finally reached Jordan Valley.

Navarro recounts that, after two months, they returned to the same places and found the clothes they had been forced to leave behind.

Today, Jose Navarro is well off and owns two large ranches. He is married to Pia Azpiri, from Lekeitio; she is the sister of Monsignor Francisco Azpiri, who perished in a shipwreck off the coast of Galicia, and behaved heroically, on his way back from America. A street in Lekeitio bears his name. Jose Navarro lives with his nephew Manuel.

We also met the brothers Joe, Juan and Luis Mendiola, who are sons of the late Jose Mendiola de Ispaster and Juana Aldecoa, who died in a car accident. Jose Junior is married to Maria Goicoechea.

Luis is a great hunter, as evidenced by a very colorful news release I've copied from the *Boise Capital News* of October 1, 1938:

HUNTS A DEER WITH A ERRIFLE

"They say Louis Mendiola has experience hunting deer this year. The day to hunt is open on Wednesday. Last year he says he used a 410 shotgun, but this year he says they're going to use an *errifle* like kids use to kill birds."

The surname Mendiola is quite common here. In Boise I know four others: Carlos, Isidro, Lorenzo and Gervasio, from Bedarona, married to an Ostolaza.

Another odyssey similar to that of Navarro and Azcuenaga was related to me by Don Jose Uberuaga, whom everyone here knows by the nickname of *Arotza*, and who today is a 71-year-old man who lives in a very nice house of his own, with his children and his wife Felipa Juarrochena, from Durango.

Arotza, who was born in Gizaburuaga, found himself in Reno, Nevada, at the age of 19, with no money and no knowledge of English. He and two other Basques decided to go to Idaho, and they crossed the desert on foot with a horse carrying foodstuffs, which ran out on the eighth day. After 13 days they arrived in Boise where they worked building sewers. Then Arotza opened a Basque restaurant, put up a boarding house called Star Rooming House, and built a *fronton* that still exists. But he made his money raising sheep.

The Uberuaga family name is also quite common here. In Boise alone live Demetrio, Felipe, John, Lino, Sabino and a rather pretty lady, Sara, who is in sales at Falk's department store. After these visits we returned to the hotel for lunch. At a long table next to ours, we meet the sheepherders, all of them in shirtsleeves. It takes about 10 minutes for the sheepherders to eat three or four courses. And that's because here in Boise, instead of serving the courses separately, one after the other, they place them all on the table at the same time, and eat them interchangeably. I am surprised by this innovation at the Basque table, as there are few people in the world who like to eat as leisurely and as well. All Basques are *maikides*, that is, friends of the table. That's why I find the idea of gobbling down four or five dishes at a time in ten minutes to be an influence of American haste which, when combined with Basque abundance, results in a slight gastronomic aberration.

Miguel Gabica, Luis Bermeosolo and Joaquin Solozabal come to have

Confer on Basques Manuel de la Sota (left) official Euzkadi (Basque) delegate to the United States, his secretary, Antonio de Irala (center), and Damian Telleria, Basque editor of the Boise Capital News, confer on the condition of refugees from the homeland. They talked things over in the editorial offices of The Capital News, only newspaper in the world publishing articles in the Basque language.

Boise Capital News, December 3, 1938. *Jose Villanueva Collection. BMCC*

coffee with us. Gabica is from Ereño and has a 128-hectare homestead called Sand Creek Ranch in Nampa. His brother Elias died in Nampa. I know another Gabica in Boise, Victor, and a Miss Carmen, who must be their sister. Luis Bermeosolo, of Amoroto, has a hotel in Nampa, with two pool halls, a barber shop and a confectionery shop in the mezzanine. He is married to Venancia Gabica and has a son, Jess, about 30 years old. He has a brother named *Boney* (Bonifacio) who also lives in Nampa and is also married to a Gabica, Jeronima. Joaquin Solozabal is from Cenarruza and is married to Pilar Silloaga.

After lunch we went to pay an official visit to the *Boise Capital News* newspaper, which publishes a page dedicated to the Basques every Saturday. From the offices we soon see that it is a serious and important newspaper. It is published in the afternoon, and is considered in Idaho as the second in importance—the *Statesman* is the oldest—although in my opinion it has better information than the latter. Regarding the war, it maintains a partisan impartiality toward the Government. The Statesman has a pro-Franco bias. The editor—who speaks Spanish well—receives us with great affection, and we make plans to improve the Basque page. He gives us the paper for free.

In the editorial office we meet Damian Telleria, with his frightened eyes and his picturesque speech. He runs the Basque page. He is a magnificent fool, but at the same time a very good person. He's from Ea, and he's been going from one place to another, failing in all his jobs. First, he worked for Standard Oil Co. of Cuba; from there he came to Ogden (Utah), where he put up a modest hotel; then he was employed in a tailor shop; from there he went to Jordan Valley as a shepherd, then to Winnemucca, etc., etc. Recently he was in the Philippines and from there he has come to Boise, because he knows, and it is true, "that here a Basque does not starve to death".

How Damian writes will be apparent from the following editorial, with which he introduced himself to the public as editor of the Basque page, which appeared in the Capital News dated October 8:

> According to the United Press and according to public opinion, I'm here to inform you about this partisan ideal, that the Spanish Civil War will remain in equal proportions, and equal to what was done by "The Allied Powers at Chekoslovakia," well my dear readers, as to the situation of Europe, it is almost the same with the Spanish

Peninsula, and with her Colonies and Islands of the Mediterranean, in proportion will be amipulated by Italy, Germany and England, as intermediary on the partition of her Provinces in Spain, divided in North, South, East, West, each of these of the four Powers; they will each partially administer their own, in their agricultural and mining industries, especially in Bilbao; the mining Corporations in the Cuenca and Castro Urdiales, Dos-Caminos, Baracaldo, and these corporation are controlled under the regime, with all the principal members of Bilbao, and other areas of the Provinces of Bilbao, Santander, which according to external reports they credit to the Government of Franco, 40% of the Utilities of the mentioned Government and the rest for these above mentioned Nations.

Instead of entering the Bask Capital, and Bask Mining Company, and it is quite the opposite, in a Bask Country, what happens in the rest of the Spanish Peninsula, and has following this in my agreement, it should be a mutual Basque capital 70 % and 30 % of the product that is taken abroad for the benefit of the Government, and this indicates that Italy, Germany and England take this mineral in exchange for war armaments, and other essential products such as flour, oils, gasoline, hides, fabrics and other war materiels.

Here is another editorial in which our friend Telleria protests against the criticisms that his writing merits according to the Basques of Idaho. It is called *Colonial Union* (?) and reads as follows.

Some people believe that the articles that are written in the Saturday paper are believed to be absolutely outragious to these comments that are made in local public establishments.

In Boise, and I feel very much in my duty to be, about this minority that is entwined among persons of no mental capacity; imagining to such information of tolerance to these articles, because according to the public opinion of the majority of our readers, they are proud to have such reports on this matter, and what we must accomplish, and be more humble in this matter, of course here in Boise, than the editorial staff of this newspaper in Basque Spanish, in the *Boise Capital News* local Basque readers should be very proud that they have a newspaper of their loving homeland in Euskera, Spanish, written by a Basque, the daily news of this local newspaper, which gives them all their daily information and events of the news of Europe and of the local area in Boise.

But Telleria is also a poet, although I suspect that his poems are mere fusillades, for, although equally bad, they make some sense. See this short piece entitled *Problem*.

En abismo hondo *Todo bien mirado;* *Nada es redondo* *ni cuadrado…*	In deep abyss All things considered; Nothing is round nor square…
Si el mundo *Es igual arriba que abajo,* *Nada es profundo,* *alto, ni bajo…*	If the world Is the same above and below, Nothing is profound, high, nor low…
Son meras conjeturas, *Cuestión de alturas,* *Síntesis, demencia.* *Hipótesis de las artes* *Que en todas partes* *Forman la Gaya Ciencia…*	These are mere conjectures, A question of heights, Synthesis, dementia. Hypothesis of the arts That everywhere Form the gay science…

And since in political matters it is always advisable to light one candle to God and another to the Devil, we left the *Boise Capital News* and went to its journalistic competitor *The Statesman*, where we were very well received and were interviewed for a piece that came out the next day, which did not please some prominent and profascist Basques, because we strongly condemned the atrocities committed by Franco against the Basques.

Next, we visited the most influential hoteliers in the locality, as it is well known that the politics of attracting Basques from these states has to be carried out at counters and around tables.

Moreover, hoteliers, and I don't know by what rule of thumb, enjoy great prestige among the numerous sheepherders who stay in their establishments, and their opinions constitute advice and even rules of conduct.

The first hotel we visited was that of the Ysursa brothers (Benito and Tomas), two very smart businessmen from Durango, who in our country would be known as *trapasalsas*.[44] It is the most popular hotel in Boise among the sheepherders, and during the Christmas holidays there are usually one hundred fifty or more. Tomas is reactionary in his way of thinking, and almost as stubborn as Jack Anduiza. Benito, on the other hand, is cheerful, friendly and a good guitar player and is the one who runs the business, since in addition to the hotel they own some five thousand sheep.

Benito is very volatile in his way of thinking, but he has been very good to us, perhaps because his guests are all very Basque and anti-Franco. He invited us to dinner several times, and what's more, this year, the proceeds of the Basque Mutual Aid Society Ball that he manages have been donated to the Basque refugees in France.

At the Ysursa's house every night, a good number of sheepherders gather to talk, drink and sing, and there are often lively dances that last until the early hours of the morning. The Ysursas have a sister who is very patriotic. She is married to Ruperto Iriondo, a sheep owner who is in good standing and thinks just like his wife. In Boise there was another Iriondo from Markina, whose name was Ramon, and who was married to Segunda Maruri. He died.

Afterwards, we visited Anastasio Jayo, owner of the Royal Hotel, where about twenty sheepherders stay. He also has a dance hall. He is a very good person, very Basque and anti-Franco. His wife, Anunciacion Amias, is very cheerful and an excellent cook. They have a son and two daughters. In Boise there are other Jayos from Nabarniz: Francisco, Juan, Segundo and Tomás. The latter works in the Bruneau Sheep Company of Mountain Home.

Then we go to visit Mateo Arregui, from Berriatua, owner of The Delamar Hotel. When we enter the lounge, there is a group of young ladies sewing and speaking in Basque who disappear as soon as they see us. Mateo is one of the best people I have met in Boise. Very religious—I think he is one of the few Basque men who go to Mass in Boise—he is a Knight of Columbus, but not at all reactionary, and very anti-Franco. His wife's name is Adriana Celaya, and they have a son and two daughters. Arregui fought in Cuba, and after returning to Euzkadi, he embarked

44. *Trapasalsas*: busybodies.

for the United States in 1907. He arrived in Winnemucca, Nevada, with $20, and as he paid fifty cents a day for room and board, his funds were soon depleted. He went to work as a sheepherder with Taylor, in Golconda, earning $15 a month. From there he moved to Mounty City, Nevada, where he worked with the Bacon herds. From there he moved by stagecoach to California, to Rancho de Palo Alto, better known as Rancho Español.

From Rancho Español he went to work with Don Jose Bengoechea, earning $25 per month, and later with Thomas Mellen, of Mountain Home, and W. Johnston, of Boise. He also later worked with Castor Aldecoa, bought a herd, was lucky and made some money, with which he bought the Delamar Hotel.

In the evening we visited Frank Aguirre, from Segura, who, besides being a shoemaker, has a guesthouse and a *fronton*. A good Basque, a bit of a slacker and a stock market player, he is anti-Franco, which is a good sign when you have money. His wife's name is Gabina Goitia, and his daughters, Bonifacia and Florentina, beautiful and elegant, were Anton Irala's favorite partners, when he devoted himself to Terpsicore, daughter of Zeus and Mnemosine, one of the nine muses, "she who delights in dance", in the dance halls of Boise.

In Boise there is another Aguirre, named Candido, who has a barbershop on Main Steet.

I should point out that all the Basques we have visited own their own automobiles.

In addition to the aforementioned hotels, there are others of lesser quality owned by Basques, which, as Anton Uranga assures me, are frequented by some cheerful ladies who comfort the sheepherders when they feel *errimiña*.[45]

Other Basques we met today:

Antonio Ocamica, from Ispaster, married to Anastasia Osa. His daughter Marie is employed at The Golden Rule department store.

Manuel Gabiola, owner of sheep and a ranch on Middle Creek, married to Dolores Azpiri. I also met their son Miguel, age thirty.

45. *Herrimin*: homesick.

Women workers at the Modern Hotel. Angelina Urquiaga, Juanita Uberuaga, Marie Uberuaga and Consuelo Mallea. *Juanita Uberuaga Hormaechea Collection. BMCC.*

Three more Gabiolas live in Boise that I know of: Cristobal, Juan and Julio.

Juan Uranga, from Ea, married to Bonifacia Llona. Their son Ricardo is twenty eight years old.

Ventura Beristain, of Ondarroa, married to Rita Bengoechea. He was the owner of the Hotel Moderno, in Boise.

Bonifacio Garmendia's album with the pictures and names of the Basque sheepherders to whom he helped to establish in the West. *Bonifacio Garmendia Collection. BMCC.*

December 7

This morning Justo Echebarria came to pick us up in his car. He takes us to visit the region around Boise. He shows us ranches all around that belong to Basques.

We stop for a while in Nampa, which is a small town where there are quite a few Basques.

I have noted down the following names: Timoteo Acordagoitia, Jose Arrizabalaga, Joaquin and Pedro Artechebarria, Ignacio Badiola, Juan Cruz, *John*, Bastida, Ignacio Beitia (Cenarruzabeitia), Ciriaco Bicandi, Ms. L. Calzacorta, Doroteo, Jesus and Juan Ereño, Louie Garmendia, Tomas Izauro (who owns the Spanish Hotel), Luis Larrinaga, Ana, Louie and Frank Luque, Antonio Menchaca and Gregorio Urquiaga. I have already spoken of Miguel Gabica. He lives in Nampa with his sons Luis, Jose, John, and Jess.

Here are the names of some Basques from other small towns in the state of Idaho.

In Aberdeen, Dionisio Bollar.

In Belleme, Jose F. Landa, who works with John Broson's herds.

In Bruneau, Eustaquio Ocamica. Twenty years ago Luis Goitia, from Markina, and Juan Lascagne, from Biderrai, lived there. I do not know their present whereabouts.

In Burley, Luis Acaiturri, Leon Bilbao, John Goitiandia, Martino Ydoeta, Paul Zuazua, Dionisio Menchaca, and Joe Varela.

In Carey, Constantino Elorriaga.

In Cascade, Jose Onaindia (hotelier).

In Castleford, Valentin Barinaga, Pedro Oñarte-Echevarria, and Miguel Rementeria.

In Firth, Silverio Olaso.

In Challis, Maximo Ansola.

In Gooding, Joe Acorda, Jose Ignacio Alberdi, Manuel Areitio, Alexander Asueta, Toni Azcuenaga, Pedro Badiola, Tomas Celaya, Luciano

Eguia, Balbino Mallabia, Luciano Uria, Florencio Uriaguereca, and Juan Uribe. Years ago there was a Domingo Azpitarte, from Bolibar, but I don't know what has become of him.

In Grand View, Raimundo Aldamiz, Abraham Azpiri, Nemesio Baraiazarra, and Domingo Solozabal.

In Hagerman, Marcelino Larragan. His daughter Carmen is the only girl from Idaho employed as a stewardess for United Airlines. Her father owns a hotel.

In Hailey, we have the Astorquias – Rosie, Maria, Julio and Joe –, the Batiz – Pete and Tomas –, Antonio Beitia, the Cenarruzas – Jose, Manuel and Pete –, Andres Echevarrieta, David Inchausti, Carmelo Mendiola, Ignacio and Santiago Naberan, Moris Olien and Juan Orueta. Years ago Felix Unamuno, from Lekeitio, and Eusebio Arriaga lived in Hailey, but at present I do not know their whereabouts.

In Hazelton, Felix Eiguren.

At Homedale, Antonio Aranzamendi, Lucas Bicandi, Marcos Ibarriaga, John Landa, Leon and Santos Mancisidor, Telesforo Hormaechea.

In Jerome, Francisco Arizmendi, Cornelio Muñozguren.

In Lowman, Pedro Ayarzagüena.

In Leniston, Antonio Martiartu.

In Mackay, Justo Arrien.

In Marsing, Frank Churruca, Agustin Cilloniz, Michel Quintana, T. Erquiaga, Agustin Sollube and the Muguira family, who have a ranch.

In Middleton, Gregorio Aranguena.

In Mullan, Gabina Goicoechea, Ignacio Mingo, Pascual Totorica, Angel Uriarte and Pedro Armolea (who has a hotel).

In Murphy, the Elordi Sinker Creek Sheep Co. is located.

In Murtough, Raymond Goitiandia.

In Parma, Jose Jayo, Vincent Mendiola, G. Ocamica.

In Pine, Julian Azpitarte.

In Pocatello, Domingo and Francisco Eguileor, Justo Goiri, Timoteo Icazuriaga, Henry and Juan Landa, Jose Uriona, Luis Zabala.

In Rupert, Basilio Artia, Manuel Bengoechea, Saturnino Guerricagoitia, Pio Lekeitio, Luis Munitibar, Alejandro Otazua, Johnny and Manuel Trebiño, Jose Maria Urigüen, Leon Zubieta, Roman Zubieta, Castor Lete.

In Shoshone, Ramon Andrinua, Antonio Arguinzoniz, Salvador Arrien, Eusebio Arrizabalaga, Telesforo Arrizabalaga, Manuel Beitia, Carlos and Ignacio Berriochoa, Felipe and Eusebio Elorrieta, Julian Garatea, Antonio Goitia, Isaac and Mildred Gojenola, Manuel Guerricagoitia, Simon Lopategui, Casimiro Madariaga, Jose Mallea, Francisco Onaindia, Charlie Sara, Domingo Zuluaga, and Julian Pagoaga, from Mutriku.

In Spring Valley, years ago, a very popular Bilbao native, Jose Ondarza, who everyone knew as Jose Alastra, had a ranch, but he is now deceased. He was married to Escolastica Arriandiaga. He owned 20,000 sheep.

In Star, Lazaro Urruzuno, married to Ines Echebarri, who has three children, Joe, Maria, and Aurora.

In Tendoy, Felipe Bilbatua.

In Terrenton, Pedro Artechebarria.

In Twin Falls, Alejandro Alberdi, Pedro Arteche, Candido Batiz, Lorenzo Celaya, Frank Egaña, Mauricio Guerricagoitia, Joe Juaristi, Miguel Juaristi, Martin Iturbe, Lorenzo Celaya, Eusebio Zubizarreta, Frank Legarza, who owns a hotel, and Frank Zabala, married to Florentina Irazabal.

In Wilder, Buenaventura Zabala.

It would be very difficult to attempt an exact census of the Basques in each of the cities where they live, since there are a great number of them who are constantly changing their residence among the states of Idaho, Nevada, Oregon, and California. Those who move to the states of Utah and Montana are few in number.

But the principal difficulty is that it is an arduous task to know the real names of the Basques. Almost all of them are known by their nicknames or by the name of the town where they were born. If you come across a Garay, for example, you don't know if that is his real surname or if he is called that because he was born in Garai. An American gentleman who handles life insurance for almost all the Basques here—I don't remember his name because he is also known by the nickname "Montes"—told me that, in order to be able to work properly, he had to have as an employee a Basque whose only mission is to know the nicknames of all his compatriots. He is known here as "Artia."[46]

46. Paul Arruti, from Arteaga (Biscay).

Furthermore, a Basque doesn't mind being asked his name, age, place of birth, etc. But as soon as you begin to write down these data on a piece of paper, the man becomes scandalized, and begins to foresee who knows what evils that will befall him for not having complied with conscription.

For all these reasons, it is very difficult to carry out an accurate census of Basques abroad.

Justo took us to eat lunch at his brother Juan Echebarria's ranch, which is about fifteen miles from Boise. He is married to Alejandra Cilloniz, sister of Crescencia from Laida, which is very popular among those of us who usually go to that beach in the summer. With them live their daughter and son-in-law, a Basque who is known by the nickname Cuba. Their two sons, Pedro and Julio, are employed in the capital.

Only two weeks ago Juan finished building his new homestead, and around it he has established the ranch with livestock, orchards, etc. It is located in a small solitary valley, surrounded by snow-capped mountains. The house is a small, one-story wooden chalet—the standard type here—very well furnished, and with all the conveniences that characterize American life: Frigidaire, electric stove, indoor heating, potato peeler, potato ricer, etc. As the land here costs very little, given the immense extension that is uninhabited, these constructions are very cheap. In addition, the Government provides many incentives for this purpose.

I can't help but make unfair comparisons between the Basque homestead in America and the one in Euzkadi: the old homestead in our mountains, ramshackle and unhealthy, which has to be reached by muddy paths and which has, to top it all, a despotic and mean owner, full of medieval prerogatives! Considering how stately the Basques live here, it is not suprising that little by little their yearning to return to their homeland is fading away. Their children especially, born and educated in a land of democracy and freedom, where even the humblest villager has a car, how can they have any desire to return to the homeland of their parents, which is constantly threatened by wars, revolutions and continuous internal unrest? A mild curiosity to get to know it, which will probably not be greater than the curiosity they have for visiting the Universal Exposition in San Francisco. This second generation of Basques in the United States is doing enough to keep the Basque language alive, and to evoke the homeland of their parents with true veneration. It should not be forgotten, moreover, that the Basques born here are Americans, and that the United States is a homeland worthy of being loved, because it provides nothing but joy and well-being to its children.

We sat down at the table and were served a succulent meal. In addition to the appetizers on the table, we had soup, stews (chickpeas, cabbage, chorizo, etc.), croquettes, halibut in the style of fried hake, slices of lamb, beef tongue in tomato sauce and roast chicken. Two or three kinds of dessert, cherry jam, coffee, cigar and various and repeated brandies (I want to state that this is the type of food, give or take a dish, that the Basques here have offered us in their homes).

During the meal, Raimunda, Justo's wife, and Alejandra, Juan's wife, while serving us, encourage us to eat more, comment on the dishes in Basque, giving the meal a completely Basque flavor. I can close my eyes and imagine that I am in the house of the priest in Mendexa, or in the house of the doctor in Arteaga during *Sanpolikarpos*, the feast of Saint Polycarp.

Juan Echebarria and his son-in-law are dedicated in particular to poultry farming. They show us the chicken coops, installed with the latest advances. The hens are very cute, with small muzzles on the upper beak that prevent them from hurting each other when they fight.

Since Justo, apparently, has insisted that we meet his entire family, he then takes us to the ranch of his other brother, Elias. Another beautiful ranch. He is married to Maria Irusta and has three children, Angel, Luis and Victoria. They are mainly engaged in selling milk. They milk the cows mechanically, bottle the milk, etc.

This couple's sons, Angel and Luis, have made a great impression on me. Two young, handsome boys: two all-American guys, speaking to each other in proper Basque. Dressed in their blue and white striped overalls, with their gloves and high, white rubber boots, clean, neatly groomed, white teeth... What splendid specimens our race produces in this land of freedom!

Justo then takes us to the home of his nephew Julio Echebarria, Pedro's

Victor Echebarria with his son in law Santiago Achurra and grandson riding a sheep.
Idaho State Historical Society.

son, at whose house we had had lunch. Julio is very gentlemanly, recently married, and is employed at the First National Bank. He lives in Boise, in a very nice house, and it soon becomes clear that he is more Americanized than his father, like all of the generation born in the United States. He treats us to cocktails.

The last Echebarria we visit is Elias. According to Justo, he is the slacker of the family. His brothers have set him up in various businesses and he has failed at all of them. Now they have a boarding house. He is married to Joaquina Badiola, a sassy, plump woman, who is always in a good mood. In the dances organized by the Basque community she is the one who always leads the women's *aurresku* dance.

Her daughter, a bright and cheerful little Basque girl, takes off her black outfit and puts on a green uniform. She tells us to take her to the restaurant where she works as a waitress. So we do, and since there is not enough room in the car, she sits on top of us with the carefree nonchalance of a movie.

Apart from these Echebarrias, I have met three others in Boise: Victor, Esteban, and Aquilino, the latter the owner of the White House Cigar Store.

The different members of the Echebarria family that we have visited provide us with interesting elements to study what we could call the *family colonization* of America by the Basques.

Around 1875 an Echebarria from Ibarrangelu arrives, settling in the state of Idaho. He brings his sons, Juan, Pedro, Justo and Elias, who arrive as adults. They always speak Basque, live in a completely Basque way, and return to their homeland from time to time, as they feel an evident desire to visit it.

Their children, now in their 20s and 30s, are U.S. citizens, living a completely American life, but they still speak Basque and speak it correctly.

Their children, still young, speak exclusively in English, with the exception of some who still speak Basque, but this is tending to disappear.

I do not think it is far-fetched to prophesy that, with this last generation, what we might call the living characteristics of the race will disappear. Then there will be nothing left but a surname and a memory.

In the evening we attend a dinner offered by Zenon Izaguirre. In addition to Zenon, John Archabal and his son, Julio Anduiza,

Mendiola—married to Zenon's sister—Fermin Achabal, John's nephew (he has not yet added the "r" to his last name), and Damian Telleria are seated at the table. The dinner is Pantagruelian and delicious, served by Zenon's wife (Casilda Archabal), Julio Anduiza's wife (Matilde Archabal), and Mendiola's wife.

Incidentally we talked about religion. I soon see that none of these gentlemen are concerned about the Church. They don't go to Mass on Sundays, but they don't attach any importance to this fact. They have no sympathy for priests (*manufacturers*, as Archabal calls them), but they don't worry about speaking ill of them either.

They speak of the only Basque priest that there has been in Boise, Don Bernardo Arregui y Machinandiarena, from Tolosa, who, from what I hear, must not have behaved very well.

Don Bernardo arrived in Boise in 1911, because at that time the bishop of Idaho, Monsignor Glorieux—who apparently was a man whose common sense was not absorbed by his mitre—asked Cadena y Eleta for a Basque priest.

Good old Don Bernardo must have been quite ambitious, and he charged the Basques for burials, baptisms, etc., with the demands of a Motilon friar. In addition, the government of His Majesty the Catholic had the brilliant idea of making him Vice-Consul of Idaho, and if Bernardo charged from the altar with too much prudence, he lost this prudence when it came to consular affairs, outside the jurisdiction of the Church.

Because of all these things, Don Bernardo was not well regarded by the Basques, and if we add to this the fact that the American priests resented him for carrying off the ecclesiastical contributions of the colony, one fine day he decided to leave for California.

As a noteworthy legacy, Don Bernardo left a niece named Petra Iraola, who had a Spanish school in Boise, and who also used to play the organ with Don Narciso Aramburu, who was the organist at Saint John's Cathedral in Boise. By all accounts, Petra now lives in Tamarillo, California.

Damian Telleria, who, when his wife is not present, gives free rein to his concentrated foolishness, recites a poem that, according to him, is titled *Emotional Impressionism*.

The first stanza is somewhat physiological and disconcerting:

"Head, fecund womb of bone
mother of the idea..."
"A mouth of love that smiled".

Then, in his eagerness to talk, Damian begins to deliver confused speeches in a rather picturesque oratory. He gets everything wrong: speaking of Gernika, for example, he sometimes calls it the *holy city* of the Basques and other times *holly wood*, as if it were the Mecca of Basque cinematography. To his speeches he lends a packaging and a pomposity that match very well with the absolute lack of meaning in his sentences.

But, apparently, he touched on a sore spot in his speech: the union of the two Basque mutual aid societies that exist in Boise. This causes quite a lot of suspicion among the diners, who argue animatedly and even make speeches—without standing up—expounding on their point of view. From what I gather from all these discussions and speeches in Basque, it is clear that, if the two mutual aid societies were to unite, they would form a kind of Basque Club, where they would serve squid, bacalao in pil-pil sauce, etc.—words of one of the diners—to the undoubted detriment of the owners of the boarding houses, that is to say, Anduiza, Ysursa, etc.

To calm the mood, Anton Irala sits down as a *bertsolari*[47] and sings some *bertso zarrak*[48] urging reconciliation, which does not have the desired result. Then, I stand up and say a few words in English—in Spanish they would not have understood—making them see that in these times when the Basque people are suffering so cruelly, it is absurd for Basques to become divided into two camps over such a spurious thing as societies and innkeepers.

But it is very much in the psychology of the Basques to give excessive importance to, and even to quarrel over, town gossip. On the other hand, they do not attach any importance to the magnificent fact that they came to America penniless and after a few years have become the drivers of Idaho's prosperity. Perhaps this is a facet of the generosity and humility of the Basque race.

47. *Bertsolari*: improviser poet-singer.
48. *Bertso zarrak*: old verses.

In spite of Telleria's foolishness, I come away from the encounter very satisfied. During the whole dinner we spoke exclusively in Basque, and we have been in a completely Basque atmosphere. And yet, these men who do not know how to speak Spanish always refer to the Basque Country as Spain: "There, in many homesteads in Spain...", "The last time I was in Spain...", referring to Natxitua... Undoubtedly, the Basques have a propensity to generalize using one single name.

For a villager from Mendexa, for example, all of North America is California, and for a Basque from Idaho, anything that involves crossing the Atlantic is going to Spain. But they don't do it out of premeditated love of Spain and all things Spanish. For the Basques here, anyone who comes from the Peninsula and does not know Basque is a *maketo*, but they do not speak of him with contempt—for the Basque there is no such feeling—but as a stranger separated by language, which for the *Euskaldun*[49] is the soul.

It must be emphasized that the preservation of Basque in America is largely due to the Basque mother. She clings so stubbornly to the Basque language that she does not learn English. The wives of the most prominent Basques here, who arrived in America fifteen or twenty years ago, barely know English, having completely forgotten Spanish. Hence, the children born in America have no choice but to learn Basque to understand their mothers. I know many young people of both sexes born here who speak English with everyone, even with their father, but as soon as they address their mother they do so in Basque. This is a very interesting detail, which brings to light the strong personality of Basque women.

It is curious to note that the latter, although transplanted, has not changed in the slightest. Mrs. Archabal, Mrs. Aldecoa, Mrs. Uranga, all of them, are preserved exactly the same as when they were in Euzkadi. None of them have servants: accompanied by their daughters they keep house, cook the food, etc., making the Basque home in America a more Christian institution than our European home.

It is striking to see these ladies, of excellent social standing, whenever their husbands have invited us to a meal, the naturalness and social

49. *Euskaldun*: Basque speaker.

nonchalance with which they prepare the delicacies, the maternal charm with which they serve the meal and, then at dessert, they join in the after-dinner conversation. This is a completely Basque trait.

I have also observed that when a married couple has been invited to the meal, the husband sits at the table, but the wife goes to the kitchen to help the hostess cook and serve the meal.

Boise Capital News, October 8, 1938.

December 8

This morning I amused myself by reading some Spanish ads from *Boise Capital News*, written in the inimitable style of Damian Telleria. No matter how much imagination a writer has, he can't improve on them. One of them reads:

"Nosotros arreglamos sus eratios furiosos de invierno."[50]

This other one advertising *"Huchas para grano"*:[51]

"Butler son similares para hucha grano; son las mejores piezas del mundo, no tiene palanquete, ó barra alguna. Este herrumbre galvanizado resistirá áa hucha de grano, y le dará un servicio usuál para años y bien reparando para Ustedes. Calidad superior, escojan el repartero. Tres precios escojan Ustedes mitodicamente."[52]

Oxford shoes:

"Lindamente ejercidos por profesión para llevar de día casual. Hermoso negro suede lindamente emoremido, con cococrilo de Calcuta. Cortado arriba sobre la garganta al pie."[53]

Advertisement for *"Mantas de lujuria"*:[54]

"Hermoso Pomposo confortable y eso es agreste áspero por la parte de atrás en miniatura."[55]

"Tejidos de lana cerdoso de Nueva Zelandia, materna-manta, en blanco, o en casca-recto en línea."[56]

Fashions:

50. "We fix your raging winter eratios."
51. *Huchas para grano*: bins for grain.
52. "Butler are similar to grain bins; they are the best pieces in the world, it has no lever or bar. This galvanized rust will withstand grain bins and will give you a standard service for years and repairing well for you. Superior quality, choose the repairer. Choose three prices methodically."
53. "Nicely exercised by profession for casual day wear. Beautifully embroidered black suede, with Calcutta crococrile. Cut above over the throat of the foot."
54. *Mantas lujuria*: lust blankets.
55. "Beautiful Pompous comfortable and that is rough scratchy around the back in miniature."
56. "New Zealand pigskin wool fabrics, maternal-blanket, in white, or in *casca-recto* stripe."

"Un nuevo artículo resbaladizo de buena con citara. La última está garantizada que no se deslizará llevando a lo alto. Lo está cortado alineadamente derecho afuera, con aberturas cerrando por dentro y los costados."[57]

"Unos encantadores cucharas plateado de plata, saborado para romper nueces."[58]

Eskimo cake pans:

"Para hacer pasteles culeratoras concreceta en las etiquetas. Remobable batir en brecha con sello en fondo. Los pasteles se reanudan afuera perfectamente en tamaños de 9 ¼ pulgadas."[59]

Dry cleaning:

"Usted afectúa una apariencia personal todos los días. Su presencia es tan elegante como de cualquiera de esas estrellas de cine... de sí mismo. Está seguro de producir una impresión favorable de elegancia... como nunca ofendida... con trajes de conservar con una apariencia de una inmaculada, por árido-desgrasamiento."[60]

Children's clothing:

"En tela impresa, alegre, brillante, en color de tupe, corimbo, pompón."[61]

Repair shop:

"Edificamos sus sitios oscuros o tejidos, techos de bóveda, de una casa, en buche o en cortadura, taburetes silicos, muy propiamente, justo, exacto para protección de abrigo y refugio en caso de tormentas."[62]

Mechanical coffee maker:

"¡Lo es irrompible, todo lustroso de cromio plateado! Y lo es un repleto vacío hacedor de café. ¡Es maravilloso! Simplemente ponga su café en

57. "A new slippery article of good with *citara*. The latter is guaranteed not to slide upwards. It is cut straight on the outside, with openings closing the inside and sides."
58. "Some lovely silver plated silver spoons, flavored for cracking nuts."
59. "For making culinary cakes with recipe on labels. Remobable beat in gap with seal on bottom. The cakes roll out perfectly in 9 ¼ inch sizes."
60. "You effectuate a personal appearance every day. Your presence is as elegant as that of any of those movie stars... yourself. You are sure to produce a favorable impression of elegance... as never offended... with suits to preserve with an appearance of an immaculate, by arid-degreasing."
61. "In printed fabric, cheerful, bright, in colors of toupé, corimbo, pompom".
62. "We build your dark or woven sites, vaulted ceilings, of a house, in crop or in cut, silica stools, very properly, precisely, exactly, for shelter protection and refuge in case of storms."

polvo en el más elevado vaso y agua en el vaso de disminuir, y olvídaselo de ello hasta que empiece a hervir. El restante estará hecho automáticamente; no hay necesidad de vigilar o de acción de hacer a propósito o cualquiera cosa que Usted haga."[63]

Bicycles:

"Niñas adultas del último modelo. Hermosos, luminosos. También modelos de manar curso, de fluir, que eso les dará a los chicos o niñas adultas la dicha y la felicidad alrededor del año. Con la luz delantera y con cadena de guía, acarreador de bagajes, chismes, con construcción de la lux trasera."[64]

Cotton dresses:

"¡Chistosos todos de colores para hacer ligero el corazón y el pie!"[65]

Before lunch we went to the Pastime Pool Hall for an aperitif, as Anduiza says. In this bar a hundred Basque men meet every day, although there is a sign on the wall that says "Ladys are welcomed," which translated literally and in Telleria's style means: "Ladies are welcome."

Pastime belongs to *Amoto*, and there the Basques play cards. In Idaho the Basques, aside from meals, drink nothing but rye whiskey (Canadian) and in large quantities.

Since gambling is forbidden in this state, the police sometimes will catch a poker game and fine the owner of the establishment and the players. The Basques here are quite fond of gambling their quarters.

Here's a detail that demonstrates the prestige enjoyed by the Basques in Boise. As soon as the police find a drunk in the street, they take him to the pound, where they oblige him to spend the night and impose a fine. A Basque, on the other hand, is picked up and taken home.

Simon Gandarias, from Ontario (Oregon), told me that as soon as the police arrest a foreigner for a nighttime scandal, they call him. If

63. "Its unbreakable, all shiny with silver chrome! And it's a full empty coffee maker. It is wonderful! Simply put your coffee powder in the highest cup and water in the diminishing cup, and forget about it until it starts to boil. The rest will be done automatically; there is no need to watch or action to do on purpose or anything else you do."

64. "Late model adult girls. Beautiful, bright. Also models of gushing course, flowing, that will give boys or adult girls joy and happiness around the year. With front light and with guide chain, baggage carrier, thingies, with rear luxury construction."

65. "Funny all incolors to lighten the heart and the foot!"

Train Slays Boise Basque

Lorenzo Garmendia Accidentally Killed On Tracks

Lorenzo Garmendia, 50, 124 East Jefferson street, was instantly killed Tuesday noon by the eastbound Union Pacific railroad train three and one-half miles east of Boise.

"Apparently Garmendia was struck by the eastbound Portland Rose as he was walking across the tracks," said Coroner J. T. McCann. "He was employed as a sheepherder by John Archabal, and left his home in Boise about 10 a. m. for the vicinity in which his body was found.

"Obviously, his death was an accident, and there will be no inquest."

The mangled body was found by J. N. Orr, railroad track walker, beside the tracks where they enter a deep cut. McCann said be believes Garmendia stepped from behind a pier of a bridge that carries a road across the tracks and did not see the on-coming train. The tracks make a sharp curve at that point, he said. Garmendia's automobile was discovered nearby.

Garmendia leaves his wife, Mrs. Fermina Garmendia, and three daughters, the eldest being about 12. He was born in Spain and came to this country about 20 years ago.

The body is at the Schreiber and McCann mortuary.

The Idaho Statesman, October 19, 1938.

he recognizes the detainee as Basque, they let him go, but if Gandarias confirms that he is not Basque, they keep him in jail.

Above the Pastime, a French Basque woman runs an inn—Empress Rooms—where some easy-living women are admitted.

We make the acquaintance of other important Basques.

Antonio Letamendi, from Ea, married to Leandra Ondarza. I also meet his children, Boni, Dionisio, Victoria, and Joe. The latter two are employed at The Golden Rule department store, where they serve you in Basque as if you were in Artecalle.

Boni Garmendia. He had a liquor business in Ogden, and is now a notary in Boise. He also trades in woolens. He has a son named Jose. Shortly before we arrived, Lorenzo Garmendia was killed by a locomotive, when he traversed a grade crossing in his car. He left behind a widow and 3 daughters.

John B. Anacabe, of Lekeitio. He has two sons: one in the automobile business and the other a clerk at the Boise Friendly Store. In 1917, there was a Lorenzo Anacabe, of Lekeitio, in Boise.

In the afternoon, Irala and I broadcasted a greeting to the Basques on the *Boise Capital News* radio.[66] Anton in Basque and I in English. The Basques were listening, gathered around the radio, in their homes and in the bars. We are told that in several bars at the end they applauded.

I have noticed the great emotion experienced by Basques when they heard Basque spoken on the radio for the first time. The women especially cried with emotion.

Then we were invited to dinner by two shepherds who are in Boise: Tomas Arambalza and Toni Laradogoitia *(Gitano)*. The latter is from Butron. They are very fine nationalists. When they found out that we were arriving in Boise, they quit their jobs and do not plan to work again until we leave. Since they are good workers, and also since Basques are very much sought after even by the Americans themselves as sheepherders, they are not worried about employment for the time being.

Before coming to Boise, Toni was sailing between New York and Bermuda. Most recently he was in the hospital injured by a bear, which attacked him when he went to steal her cubs.

66. The *KFXD* station.

We dined at the Ysursa's boarding house, at three long tables full of Basque sheepherders. There are some very curious fellows: a silver-haired old man with a sentimental face; a pug-nosed young man, always smiling, wearing a *café-au-lait* hat tilted to one side, in shirtsleeves and cowboy boots, who spent the whole night sitting backwards on a chair.

They all speak only Basque, and naturally their surnames are completely Basque: Paul Zugaza, Tomas Bizcarra, Pedro Cengotita, Jose and Juan Zorrozua, Juan Uscola, Timoteo Ursa, Juan Urionabarrena, Sebastian Salutregui, Jose Pildain. Canuto Otazua, Jose Cruz Oregui, Domingo Oñaederra, Antonio Olazar, Indalecio Muruaga, Nicolas Mugica, Juan Meabe, Antonio Malaxechebarria, Francisco Loyola, Raimundo Lotina, Juan Llona, Domingo Lejarza, Vitorio Lasuen, Martin Lariz, Luis Landa, the Iribars, Francisco Illagorra, Eugenio Idoeta, Homero Guinea, the Guezuragas, Nicolas Guerricaecheberria, Lorenzo Garmendia, Ben Goicoechea, George Gatica, Jose Galarza, Prudencio Elordieta, George Eguileor, Satur Echeita, Alejo and Santos Coscorrotza, Narciso Cortabitarte, Juan Chicumberro, Jesus Cenica, Simon Bildosola, Joe Berriatua, Telesforo Bernaola, Mateo Bastaieta, J. C. Barandica, Victoriano Baqueriza, Miguel Abaroa, R. Aberasturi, Paulo Acordagoitia, Gregorio Amuchastegui, A. Aranzamendi, Justo Arcocha, Ciriaco Areitio, Antonio Arescurrinaga, Pedro Armaolea, Jose Arostegui, Ramon Arrate, Pedro Arruzazabala, Pedro Arzuaga, Julian Aspiazu, Eugenio Azpitarte, and Eusebio Azumendi.

When we are all at the table chatting after the meal and the sheepherders are drinking rye whiskey, a new character enters like a star of the first magnitude. He is from Durango, surnamed Lupiola, better known as *Tabuyo* and *the Barber*. He is from Abadiño. He is one of those guys you see in every town, who makes a living without working and is always cheerful and drinking. He is in his fifties, has gray hair, the rosy face of a sacristan, and when he speaks he makes effeminate gestures. He is very funny, but for every word he says, he spouts two profanities. He has been a barber, has owned a bar and a dance hall, and his specialty is playing poker. At heart he is a good man who, as soon as he has money, spends it happily with his fellow revelers.

Then in comes another prominent figure in the nightlife of the Boise Basques. He is Jack Epalza, young, very gentlemanly, with a cocked hat and a vicious face. I am told that the American Government gives him a pass because he fought the war in Europe.

Jack picks up Benito Ysursa's guitar and sings some songs, among them "Pello Joshepe". Next to him *Ondarrukiño*, his inseparable companion, accompanies him playing the spoons, keeping the beat with two spoons held between the fingers of his left hand, with which he makes a metallic noise.

Jack, Lupiola, *Ondarrukiño* and some of the other sheepherders are going to a Basque woman's establishment to continue the revelry.

Irala and I have gone to Belaustegui Hall, to a benefit ball organized by the Society of Basque Ladies. At the door, the Committee, presided over by Casilda Archabal, welcomes us. When we enter, a string of women dance the *aurresku*[67] with true Basque flair, and they ask us to dance. After the *aurresku* the dance becomes generalized. Sometimes with a *txistu* and sometimes with jazz. The bar is also very lively.

I notice that there is a picture hanging on the wall, in the middle of which flies a monarchist Spanish flag, and I go home indignant.

The next day, Belaustegui's widow sent me a message to say that she had already removed the painting and that she had it there as a souvenir, without any political intent.

Belaustegui's widow has a son named Angel, who is a salesman at Falks department store, and two daughters: Marie, married to Uberuaga, and Petra. This Petra is a rather determined young woman with glasses. She recently ran off with a girlfriend to San Francisco, where they must have had a lot of fun.

This association, whose ball we attended, is called The Independent Social Organization, and in Spanish Organización Independiente Social de Instrucción y Recreo, a title that will bring together – according to the statutes – the Basques of this country who wish to help the needy, and to aid them in case of illness or death.

"This society", the statutes state, has as its purpose to foster union among all the constituents of the Basque community, to contribute to the enhancement and good name of VASCONIA and to provide its members with education, recreation, assistance, clothing, medicine and

67. *Aurresku*: ceremonial Basque dance.

other similar services if needed, for which purpose a special fund will be set up as soon as possible.

The statutes of this association include a series of definitions, which I have copied because they are written in the peculiar Spanish of the Basques here:

"Humanity: is a human kind with compassion of love."

"Friendship: is a benevolent, pure and interested affection with fine cross."

"Affection: is an affectionate will of love."

"Courtesy: is attention with proper liking and affection."

"Respect: is related to reverence, veneration, and observance."

"Kindness: is the first virtue of compassion."

"Sociability: is a doctrine constituted to fulfill all or some purposes of life with its culture and proper manners".

Before going to sleep I read the Basque edition of the *Boise Capital News*, and it reports the accident that cost the life of a Basque. I reproduce it exactly as it appears:

COUNCIL, Dec. 8 - They have told here the story of the accident that has happened to these four individuals who were going on inspection to explore the Alonso Goicoechea mine. They fell from a height of 1500 feet from the ravines of the Snake River heights.

The accident occurred on Sunday night. Those who died are: Alonso Goicoechea (alias Cale), aged 62, leaving his wife in Ea, Biscay, and Mrs. Anne Seigler, aged 28, and Mrs. Jane Siddonay, aged 74, of Boise.

But Goicoechea was killed instantly when he was caught by a rock on his way down. The oversight was that the brakes and bearings on the freight truck broke and that is when John Parson was unable to control his freight car that was going with 15 workers toward the Cuprum mine.

December 9

This morning we continued to meet more Basques.

Costan Ostoloza, who works at Spring Valley Ranch and lives with his sister, has a brother in Boise named Anastasio.

Anastasio Odiaga, another of the owners of the *Pastime Pool Hall.* I know other Odiagas: Joe, Juan, Genaro, Pedro and Santiago, some of them sons of a Domingo Odiaga, from Lekeitio, who had a beautiful ranch called Clover Flat.

I meet Agustin Abadia (who has two brothers in Boise, Ignacio and Victor), Damaso Amesti, Antonio Chacartegui, who has three brothers: Eusebio, Phil and John. (There is another Chacartegui named Lorenzo.) Gregorio Ligarreta, Antonio and Benito Garate, the Letes (Pedro and Manuel), Domingo Mugartegui, Aniceto and Martin Oar, etc.

The topic of all conversations is tonight's boxing soirée, in which the big event is the bout between Al Berro—*The Fighting Basque*—and Buddy Edwards—*The Knockout King of Nampa*—. Al Berro's name is Alberto Berrojalbiz, from Jordan Valley, where until now he has been a barber. The *Capital News* speaks of him in terms worth copying. It reads:

> We have a *fitelari*[68] among the Basquos today. Joe Cortez was the champion in the 20's and we haven't had any more until today.
>
> Today we have Al Berrojalbiz, from Jordan Valley.
>
> He's set to be one of the first middleweights to come from these parts.
>
> He had three fites to get people interested and made a name for himself on the Northern Nevada fight cards.
>
> In four fites he's lost one and that one lasted as long as ten rounds. He won three fites with knockouts at the Boise Athletic Club arena.
>
> The young man is a pure fitelari. By continuing his bouts he will be able to improve his time.

Simon Gandarias, in turn, dedicates the following poem to him:

68. *Fitelari*: from "fighting", with a trade suffix as in pelotari, a pelota player.

Alberto Berrojalbiz *Jordan Valleykua* *jokalari ederra* *pixu erdikua,* *tximistan jokaerakin* *begi argikua,* *neurturik ondo beti* *bestian jokua.*	Alberto Berrojalbiz from Jordan Valley, beautiful player, middleweight boxer, fast as lightning and bright eye, always measuring well the rival's game.
Indarraz eta joka, *Berro da benetan* *jokalari ederra,* *orixe oiñgutan.* *Euskaldunak arturik* *txapela eskutan,* *"Eskerrik asko" danok* *egin geuntsan esan.*	With force and hitting, Berro is really a beautiful player, that's why now we Basques, taking our hats in our hands, we all said to him: "Thank you!".
Lorrotz zuzenak dezuz, *Berrok, zuk ondiño,* *Gertzen badezu beti* *biyotzetik bero.* *Gorputz eta indarrakin* *goratu ezkero,* *ez zara iñon bildur* *orain ezta ez gero.*	You will still get straight victories, Berro, if you keep preparing with all your heart. If you grow in body and strength, you will fear no one neither now nor later.

We had dinner together as a large group of Basques and then went to the Boise Athletic Club to watch the boxing match. The place was full of Basques coming from Mountain Home, Nampa, Ontario, Jordan Valley, etc. Among them were many Americans who had come, curiously enough, to cheer on the Basque in his fight against the American. You hear nothing but talking and arguing in Basque. It seems like we are in Euzkadi.

Al Berro defeats Buddy by K.O. in the second round, and there is great enthusiasm among the Basques. During the show I could not help but stare at all those men from Bedarona, Natxitua, Garai, etc., who, with their hats, rolled-up overalls, and high boots looked like Americans from the Far West.

Berrojalbiz Es Buen Fitelari

Tenemos un fitelari entre los Basquos hoy. Joe Cortez era el campeón en los '20's y no hemos tenido mas hasta hoy.

Hoy tenemos Al Berrojalbiz de Jordan Valley.

El está apuntado para unos de los primero medio peso que ha venido de este parte.

Tuvo tres fites para que interés el gente y cogió buen nombre para el en los carteles de northern Nevada.

Entre cuatro fites el he perdido uno, y aquel agunto hasta diez vueltas. El fite era con el veterañ Truman Harvey en Winnemucca, Nevada.

Ganó tres fites con nockouts en el arena del Boise Athletic club.

El joven is puro fitelari. Continuando sus bouts podrá hacer mejor su tiempo.

Boise Capital News, October 1, 1938.

Juan Cruz Anduiza and Juana Gabiola. *Luis Babe Anduiza Collection. BMCC.*

December 10

Today Manu Anduiza—Jack's third son—and his wife have arrived for a two-day stay. Manu has broken the Basque tradition by marrying an American woman, who is also divorced. She is tall, slim, pretty, and dresses very well. She has that lack of ceremony and formality that makes American women so pleasant. Without pride or pretensions, she is very different from European women. I notice that she treats the barbarian Jack and the foolish Juana with great affection, and that she helps Matilda to clear the table with great naturalness. She must be a woman of merit, since she is secretary to the director of the mining company where Manu works.

The latter is a young man about 28 years old, who is handsome, strong and friendly. He is quite a character, and he's one of those men who doesn't mind getting slapped in the face when he has to. An American by upbringing, he is liberal and detests fascism. He dislikes small towns like Boise because there is a lot of gossip in them and everyone knows their neighbor's business. In Montana he has been working as a foreman or something like that in a remote gold mine in the mountains, living a life like in the movies.

Tonight we attended a banquet held for us by John Orbea, an old man from Biscay, who, in spite of his good position, is still a perfect Basque villager. He has with him two young sons, very gentlemanly, very elegant and very American, but who speak Basque perfectly. They have an automobile, a car as they say here. His daughters are in San Francisco, one studying painting and the other, medicine.

Attending the dinner are Archabal, Zenon Izaguirre, John Anacabe, John Luqui, Juan Odiaga, Damian Telleria, Hilario Arguinchona and M. G. Funke, editor of the *Boise Capital News*. The latter's wife, an American, and Telleria's wife are the only women at the table. The others do the cooking, wait on the table, etc.

The dinner, like all of them, was excellent in every way: rice soup full of morsels, cod in red sauce, lamb chops, stuffed chicken, and venison in sauce that was caught by one of Orbea's sons. Lots of desserts, coffee and brandy.

Jack Epalza and his inseparable Ondarrukiño come for dessert. The former plays the guitar and the latter accompanies him playing the spoons. Then the wives of the diners come to take part in the party, and a big informal dance is organized. It is amazing to see how these ladies, all of them over 45 years old, jump, dance and shake as if they were on a pilgrimage in Euzkadi. Then we wear costumes and do a series of *chirenadas*.[69]

At about two in the morning I go with Epalza and Ondarrukiño to a Basque bar called Merino Pool Hall. There are a few Basques and Americans who cannot be distinguished by their clothes. The owner, Sotero, has gone to the funeral of a Basque in Winnemucca, and his daughter, a slim, pretty 21-year-old girl, dances with the patrons to the jukebox. He is a very American guy, but speaks Basque very well. Her brother, a 24-year-old boy, is leaning against the bar sitting on a tall bar stool. With his big hat and tall boots he looks like a cowboy.

69. *Chirenadas*: mockeries.

December 11

Early in the morning Archabal came to pick us up in his car, accompanied by Zenon Izaguirre. It is a cold and clear day, like almost every winter day here. Archabal wants to show us how the Basque sheepherders live as well as their flocks, which are scattered (each comprising about 2,000 sheep) all over this immense desert.

From morning to night we drive through it. It is an endless plain a thousand meters above sea level. In the distance you can see the snowcapped mountains. On the bare ground, small bushes with hard, ashen-colored leaves grow. This same vegetation, which is what the sheep eat, is made up of different varieties: yellow sage, white sage (it has a very intense oily taste), sage brush, salt brush (its taste is extremely salty), grease nook and button brush (they pronounce "bóton," but I don't know how to spell it). The Basques call all this *chamizo*.

Occasionally there are small lakes, where sheep water, which are now completely frozen over. Further on, the Snake River zigzags in the abysses of an impressive gorge of dead rocks as if it were a moonscape.

All day long we have traveled miles and miles, and we have found only Basques. This is explained by the fact that even the Americans have no other shepherds than Basques. The Americans, it seems, are no good at this trade. The Basques are the shepherds who are paid the most and the ones who bring the most profit to the owners as well. Archabal tells me that he would gladly pay for five hundred young Basques to come and work with him. But immigration laws don't allow it.

I am moved by this immense ashen-colored desert, between the snowy ridges of the mountains, which shine as if they were white patent leather. In this infinite plain, it is very difficult to spot a herd in the distance. But Archabal looks with half-closed eyes at the horizon, like our fishermen at sea looking for a shoal of sardines, and soon says "There it is". And the car takes us off road to the herd.

Soon we run into the shepherd with his three or four dogs. We talk in Basque with him while Archabal carefully examines the sheep. Each flock

Jose Villanueva, unidentified sheepherder, Antonio de Irala, Manu de la Sota and John Archabal, during their visit to the camps.

of two thousand head has a shepherd, who walks all day long with the sheep, until nightfall when he arrives at the camp. They give this name to the spot in the desert where the camp tender—who cooks and maintains the camp site and sheepherder's wagon—has settled, at least for the night, with his *ardi-karro*,[70] his horses, etc. These wagons, which are sort of a small caravan, have a kitchen, a pantry with all kinds of foodstuffs, an endless number of pots and pans, and two beautiful bunks where the shepherd and the camp tender sleep. To eat, they lower a plank attached to the wall that serves as a table. Almost all of them have a radio.

We eat inside one of these sheephereder's wagons and the food could not be better: red beans, *tortilla*,[71] lamb chops, peach compote, sweets, cookies, coffee and *txitxiparra*.[72] We also enjoy delicious fresh bread, made by the camp tender. They tell us that they always eat so abundantly and so well. The sheep owner is obliged to provide them with food every week. Their salary, clear of all expenses, is $60 to $70.

During the meal, the shepherd and the camp tender tell us how pleasant their life is in the summer months, because up in the mountains, where they don't have to be so closely tied to the sheep, they fish for trout and hunt all kinds of birds. They also kill quite a few bears. During the heat wave there are many rattlesnakes, but they don't fear them. The animal they detest most is the *azeria* (coyote), because at night it kills sheep. Since the government pays for each coyote skin that is turned in, they catch them with traps.

In the afternoon, Domingo Aldecoa *(Katua)* driving his truck has joined the expedition. We visit the camp where his son Angel is working as a camp tender. We find him with a swollen face, a big wound on his forehead and a bad leg. He tells us that yesterday, on horseback, the horse threw him and dragged him a long way. Thankfully, the boot that had become entangled in his stirrup broke in two. Anything else would surely have killed him. But discreet, like a good Basque, he did not attach much importance to the accident.

Dusk falls as we leave the vast American wilderness where the Basque

70. *Ardi-karro*: sheepherder's wagon.
71. *Tortilla*: potato omelette.
72. *Txitxiparra*: aniseed brandy.

shepherds roam. The sun sets behind the immense rocks of the Snake River Canyon and the whole sky is tinged with reddish hues. We lose sight of the last Basque shepherd in the distance.

Why is it, I think, that the profession of shepherd fits so well with the Basque character? Because of our individualism and our way of being independent, I think. The shepherd, in a certain way, is the leader of his flock, and apart from the orders he receives from the owner when the latter visits him from time to time, he is master and lord of the sheep. He exercises his spirit of initiative without consulting anyone, and from morning till night he is the master of the desert or of the solitude of the mountains. The dignity of one's race is also distinguished in one's occupations. It is rare to find a Basque who is a shoeshine boy. On the other hand, even in the American Far West, the shepherds are Basques, and like Jesus, they are honored with that name.

Before dinner we go out for highballs at Pastime. I notice that all Basques, even speaking in Basque, use the refrain "You bet your life" when they want to state something categorically. For example, if I say to someone: "Would you give me a cigarette?". Instead of answering "Of course" or "With pleasure," he says, "You bet your life." But this expression is not exclusive to the Basques, because in this part of America it is used by everyone.

December 12

When I went down to breakfast, Jack Anduiza was talking to a Basque man about sixty years old, who was thin and strong. His name is Florencio Corta y Zaracondegui, and he is from Bedarona. He came to the U.S. when he was eighteen and settled in Eureka, where he made quite a bit of money as a herd owner. He now owns a ranch near Boise.

I also meet Hilario Urresti, from Berriatua, who owns a boarding house in Boise, Domingo Eiguren, from Mendexa, and John Urlizaga, son of Juan Urlizaga, from Errigoiti, who died. He was married to Gloria Bermensolo.

Tonight we were treated to a banquet by the editors and publisher of the *Boise Capital News*. Also in attendance were some 10 important Basques from Boise. It was held at the Boise Club owned by Dan Bilbao and John Legarreta *(Juanillo)*. This club has beautiful rooms with pool tables and a nice restaurant. The central painting among those hanging on the walls depicts a lady with her back completely nude. It is like a symbol of the spirit that animates these establishments.

During dessert the innumerable and absurd speeches of Damian Telleria could not be avoided. I spoke to thank the newspaper.

As Lupiola also came with his guitar, there was a frantic freewheeling dance with the girls who serve in the club, who are all Basques. With Lupiola came a young cowboy and his sister. They dance waltzes and tangos doing all kinds of fanciful things to the beat of the *jotas* and *porrusaldas* played by Lupiola. The cowboy introduced me to his sister, who by the way is very beautiful. He told me that she is a very nice girl, that she doesn't drink or smoke, that he wants her to learn to dance Basque dances, and that since he has been told that I do it very well, he asks me to teach her. Americans are naive and child-like that way.

At night, when I go to bed, I think about the lively personality of this Basque group in Boise: a colony in the style of immigrants from La Rioja or Palencia in Bilbao? No, it is a national minority, with a strength that distinguishes it perfectly from the world around it.

Here the spirit of our race is thriving, without obstacles or ties that impede its free growth, as happens in our country. A piece of Basque democracy, the oldest and most perfect known, has managed to become entrenched in the exuberant American democracy. Consequently, the most modern democracy in the world wears on its bosom, as if it were an ancient jewel, a vibrant piece of the oldest democracy in Europe.

The Basques who live here are, in these tragic times that Euzkadi is going through, the happiest of all our race without a doubt. Democrats by tradition, they have found fertile ground to work and live freely and respectfully in this blessed land of freedom and possibilities.

In order to give the reader an idea of the opinion of the Basques among the Americans of Idaho, I will translate the main points of some articles about our people that appeared in April 1937 in the *Boise Capital News*.

> The strength and sturdiness of the Basque nation, the character and discipline of the Basque community, the continuity and stability of the Basque family... all these virtues have their foundation in a primordial rule that lies at the very core of Basque life: self-respect. [...]
>
> They act on the assumption that, when one respects oneself, one respects the rights of others and the law. And when there is respect, harmony exists. This principle emanating from their political and legal conception presides over all their social functions, and even their conduct when they dance or walk down the street. [...]
>
> Basque family life is a prototype of harmony. The important thing is the family, and not the individuals in the family. A well-ordered private life creates citizens who behave in an orderly manner in public life. From a local point of view, this is reflected in the peaceful and vigorous citizenship of the Basques who live in southwestern Idaho, always law-abiding and respected by their neighbors. The Basque is essentially conservative, both in his business and social life. He is economical, tenacious and enterprising in his work, but cautious in his private life. He is fond of playing cards, but is not a gambler; he likes to drink, but rarely degenerates into vulgarity and scandalousness. [...]
>
> Family life is characterized by respect, almost veneration of paternal authority over things in general, and of maternal authority

over matters relating to the home. The Basques preserve an intense devotion to tradition, the main factor that structures all Basque life. Some of their family customs are soon revealed to have very remote origins. The Basque family is essentially patriarchal. The law of primogeniture generally is applied to the family. These two facts underlie the characteristic features of the Basque family: stability, permanence and family dignity. The home is the family trunk, the tree of Basque life. [...]

The two main features of the Basque race are its independent spirit and its reserved character. It is very difficult for an outsider to break through the Basque reserve. Practically all the Basques of Idaho belong to the Catholic religion. Some of the younger generation are drifting away from the faith of their fathers. Basque history shows us that religion and democracy go hand in hand. The Basque is calm and serene in his religious life, as well as in his economic and social life. In all these aspects he shows a balanced reserve that characterizes all his actions. [...]

From humble beginnings as shepherds, Idaho Basques have extended their activities into all branches of economic life. But raising sheep still continues to be their chief occupation, not only in the Boise Valley, but also in Malheur and Harney counties, in eastern Oregon, and in northern Nevada. At first, the Basques began raising sheep in their American *Basqueland* because they outnumbered the locals in that occupation. But there was a deeper motive that prompted them to embrace this kind of life. [...]

The new emigrants barely understood English. This fact, together with their reserved character and their innate tendency to isolation, made their coexistence with the locals difficult. Herding was a life of solitude, where contacts were scarce and language did not matter. So they chose a nomadic life, working alone with their herds in the beautiful mountain pastures of Idaho.

The Basque population of Idaho, confined almost exclusively to its southwestern part, is estimated at about seventy-five hundred. Of these, sixteen hundred are found in Boise and its environs. Here in this region of Idaho-Oregon-Nevada, the Basques have found

> peace, happiness and prosperity, resulting in the most important Basque settlement abroad having been established here. [...]
>
> Preceding the great tide of Basque emigrants who settled in the U.S. in 1899, there was a small group of Basque pioneers who began arriving in Jordan Valley before 1845. Since the Great War, emigration of Basques to the U.S. has declined because of the restrictive quotas, which has deprived our homeland of the invigorating virtues of the Basques, who have always been ideal settlers because of their bold, enterprising and peaceful nature and their adaptability to American life.

Throughout Northwestern America, Basque food enjoys a great reputation, to the point that when Americans want to treat themselves to a banquet, they turn to a Basque innkeeper. Let's see what the aforementioned article says on the subject:

> Basque food is like the Basque temperament: hot and well seasoned. Basques enjoy good food and are epicureans of the highest order. Among the best cooks in Boise are Basque women, who through daily practice have learned the secrets of Basque gastronomy. As far as the famed Basque potato is concerned, the Basques do not value it highly. In contrast, they prepare rice in different ways, each one more delicious than the last. [...]
>
> Basques like very seasoned dishes. In spite of the American belief, Basques do not eat a lot of garlic. They use it only to season delicacies, but remove it before serving the dish. They use garlic, onions, cloves, cayenne pepper and other ingredients to produce a stimulating flavor. A Basque meal is a gourmet's paradise. The Basque table is stocked with masterfully cooked and skillfully chosen delicacies. An American with a normal appetite could not eat all the dishes that make up a Basque meal without feeling bloated. [...]
>
> Most Basque meals—at least those this writer has enjoyed—consist of the following menu: two soups, one with rice; a fish dish, preferably seabass; two meat dishes, one of which is lamb or mutton; two or three desserts, delicious pastries, compotes and fresh fruit. Red wine is never absent. And to top it all off, coffee with a cigar. The Basques are people of excellent appetite, and they eat abundantly

> while talking animatedly. The table is one of the great institutions of Basque life; in this they differ from the Americans. [...]
>
> While the American eats a light lunch at noon, which he consumes quickly, the Basque indulges in two or three courses. The Basques' love of long, meticulously prepared meals, probably depends on the fact that Basque women are essentially homebodies. Home is everything in the life of the Basque woman. She is seldom engaged in business as American women are. All her time is spent at home, and she tends the kitchen with real devotion. The preparations for a Basque meal are profuse and elaborate. The Basque cook differs from the American cook in that she uses fresh, not canned products. That is why Basque food surpasses American food by far.

I believe that the preceding lines give a fairly accurate idea of the gastronomic activities of the Basques in the state of Idaho. It is interesting to note that, while Basque mothers in America continue to assiduously cultivate their culinary art, their American-born daughters neglect it and practice it much less, for all of them, in imitation of the American woman, are employed in banks or offices. I noticed that in Boise homes where the *etxekoandre*[73] is young and American-born, the food is bland and unremarkable as in American homes.

One cannot help but think: What is more important, that the wife take care of the household or that she help her husband earn money by taking a job? Julio Anduiza, for example, is married to Matilde Archabal. They both hold important positions at the First National Bank. So when they return home in the evening after working all day, she is not in a position to cook. Hence Julio's desire for Matilde to leave her position and devote herself more to the household, since here there are no maids in the houses.

But I will continue translating some paragraphs about Basque social life, written by the same author:

> The Basques of Boise and vicinity gave a party a few days ago in honor of John Archabal, the king of Basque sheepherders. The party brought out the effusive sociability of the Basque when he meets

73. *Etxekoandre*: housewife.

with his countrymen. It took place on one of Archabal's ranches and began at sunset. There were long tables set out on the grass in the shade of the trees. The table was literally covered with meats, fish, salads, omelettes, pastries, sweets, fruits and wines of all kinds.

The picnic was extraordinarily lively, full of laughter and conversation. As soon as the meal was finished, the tables were removed and a bar was set up in a corner, stocked with all kinds of drinks, an orchestra composed of three instruments played Basque airs and everyone began to dance on the grass. They also danced American dances, marking the steps with grace and rhythm. The party was a new joy for me, typically Basque.

Basques, in spite of the very sober side they show to Americans, are of a cheerful and expansive race, especially when they get together among themselves. They are very fond of dancing and singing. A spectacle that delighted the inhabitants of Boise some years ago was the Basque street dances, which unfortunately for some time have ceased to be performed. Another Basque spectacle that the inhabitants of Boise like to see is the parade that they organize on Christmas Eve, in which the Basques, losing their traditional shyness, present themselves just as they are.

Typical Basque festivals are slowly disappearing in southwestern Idaho. The new generation prefers American festivals and dances. However, on the 4th of July—U.S. Independence Day—Basques hold a festival near the Boise River that is worth seeing.

December 13

This afternoon we had a rather unpleasant visit with the Bishop of Idaho, Bishop Kelly. As soon as we arrived in Boise we telephoned him telling him that we had a letter of introduction from Bishop Ready and that we wished to visit him. This morning he told us to come and see him this afternoon at 3 o'clock.

He lives in a small chalet, close to a very charming little chapel—the Chapel of the Good Shepherd—built by the Basques from community fundraising. According to the Basques here, that chapel belongs to them and they built it to hear Mass. But this bishop has taken it away from them and turned it into a private chapel for himself. This is one of the reasons the Basques do not like this bishop very much.

The door was opened by a very serious lady, who did not ask us any questions and ushered us into a small room which was well-appointed, but not luxurious. After waiting five minutes, the bishop appears. He is dressed in street clothes, and if not for the pastoral ring, he could be mistaken for any other priest. He is of average height, with a clean Irish face and an authoritarian and unfriendly expression. We present Ready's letter to him; he reads it, but does not seem to attach much importance to it.

I begin by telling him that we find that the Basques here, in spite of being good, religious people, live apart from the Church. He cuts me off by saying that the Basques are all good, religious people, and he asks me what credentials we have to come and discuss these matters with him. I explain to him who we are. He asks me insistently if we have presented Ready with documents that vouch for our character, and he emphasizes this point. Undoubtedly, he does not trust us.

I tell him that, in our humble opinion, if there were a Basque-speaking priest here, Basques would go to church more. And that there are many Basque women especially who do not go to confession because they do not understand their confessor.

He answers me saying that it is not necessary and that the Basques of Boise do not want a Basque priest to come. I don't say anything to him, but that is false. Besides, he adds, he has no reason to discuss these things with us.

We talked a bit about the war. He seems to understand the problem without obfuscation. He tells me that the best thing we can do is to leave the Basques in America alone, let them become Americans and leave Spain's troubles behind them once and for all.

And he stands up, which means we're supposed to leave. His closing words give a full-length portrait of him:

> Don't worry about the religiosity of your compatriots, after all, they all die on the right side.

I come away disgusted from the interview with this barbaric episcopus. I have a dismal opinion of the U.S. Catholic hierarchy; I think it is one of the few impoverished institutions in America. But after the interview with Kelly I emerge even more convinced of my opinion. If it is true that there is a hell in the next world, it will be full of American bishops and other mitered men.

In the evening, when we are having dinner, Lupiola appears with a stranger with glasses and an owlish face. He tells us that this gentleman wants to meet us, and that, although he does not know him, he has brought him to us because men can understand each other by talking. The owl-faced gentleman turns out to be a certain Malaxetxebarria from Markina, who lives here in Sacramento (California) and is called Malax. He happens to be from the Democratic Center, and he comes to organize who knows what committees and hand out some anti-fascist membership cards. He is coming to Boise because he thinks this is not a "progressive" town. We tell him something similar to what the bishop told us: to leave the Basques of Boise alone and go away.

I stay talking to Lupiola and he reveals sensational things to me. He tells me that several years ago he devoted himself to forging banknotes with an Italian. The Italian is in jail and Lupiola has ended up with a suitcase full of counterfeit bills. He is looking for an opportunity to unload some

74. *Matsa*: bunch of grapes.

of them. Lupiola calls drunkenness matsa.

I have noticed that the most popular saying among the Basques in Boise is: "Mountains never meet, but men do." Lupiola has said it to me several times, Archabal too, and others. What fascination can this saying have for the Basques here?

Lupiola tells me about Jack Epalza and tells me that he smokes marijuana. I had already guessed that Jack had some unspeakable vice.

Lupiola picks up his guitar and sings his favorite song:

"All my life I have been a drunkard,
What shall I do with my unhappy vice?
If at my death they gave me a drink
I'd go up to glory happily...

Where are those half-bottles?
Where are they? I can't find them.
We'll drink with them, friends,
we'll drink till we're drunk.

I tell all my friends:
when they go to bury me,
the fists of earth they throw on me
should be filled with wine and mezcal.

My little box has to be tiny,
tiny and made of pure crystal.
And after they put me in it,
they should fill it with whiskey and mezcal.

Here the stars no longer shine,
I can never return to my land.
Let them bring me bottles of wine,
and drunk I'll be able to forget".

It is regrettable that when the Basques have such great musical treasure, the Basque speakers here prefer to sing tangos and nonsense like the one transcribed above. Because, the truth is that the Basque speakers here, as soon as they start singing, they forget that they are Basques. The *Pello Joxepe*, the occasional *Boga Boga* and that's it.

These Basque speakers are Basques by birth and Americans by citizenship. And yet they call themselves Spanish. It seems absurd to me.

Could it be true that the only unique thing the Basques have is that they speak Euskera? I don't know; but by the third generation Basqueness has ended in Idaho. When they sing, they generally sing Spanish or South American songs, and at school dances they dance stereotypical Spanish dances. How right Sabino was when he said that the Basque language without a national soul is useless!

In Boise there were some Basque policemen, but they had to be replaced because their compatriots did not respect them. The Basque has never understood the fundamental meaning of a uniform. That's why he doesn't like uniforms: from the porter's uniform to the general's uniform. For the Basque, everything that is not everyday clothing is a disguise. I remember once when a Spanish military man who was summering in Lekeitio had to put on his uniform to go to Bilbao; the kids pointed their fingers at him and said, "Ene, barrigoberde!" Meaning: puppeteer.

Today, the American insurance agent whom the sheepherders call Montes told me:

> In the states of Idaho, Oregon and Nevada alone I have written $500,000 worth of insurance policies for Basques. But they are going to drive me crazy with their nicknames. Pedro Allorta, for example, is sometimes Pedro, sometimes *Ispister* and sometimes *Prakatxiki*. And Juan is *Amoroto* or *Zorristo*. When one Basque dies, it seems that three have to be buried.

This nickname thing, I think it's a privilege of ancient peoples. The same thing happens with the Indians here. One is called Eagle Head, another Partridge Paw, and so on. Undoubtedly, the Basque preserve a very deep spirit and carefully retain the nicknames of their elders. Moreover, it should not be forgotten that the Basque family structure is eminently patriarchal. In Basque families, the father is venerated, and the son, no matter how many feats he performs, is unlikely to overshadow his father's name. People give the father's nickname to the son, and if he does not have a nickname, he is called "the son of So-and-so." For example, for the Basques of Boise, I am *Sota'n semie*.[75]

The issue of nicknames among the Basque people may be a return to primitive paganism, and a subconscious desire to prefer names deriveded from nature rather than from saints. The Basque, in this regard, unconsciously thinks in this way: To a one-eyed or lame man, why call him Luis if it is more natural to call him *Okerra* (Gimpy)? Besides, it is well known that the Basque does not choose a Christian name out of devotion to this or that saint, but because it sounds better to his ear or because it is the name his father bears.

Sabino's mistake, in my opinion, in inventing Basque first names, was to continue with the routine of the book of Roman Catholic saints, instead of going to the source from which the Basque draws everything: nature. *Kepa* or *Pedro* has little appeal for the Basque; *Arri* (Rock) would have been more popular.

In spite of the years that have passed, we Basques continue to possess a strong pagan legacy in the mysterious arcana tarot deck of our soul, and in spite of everything, we will continue to be named based on our homestead, our hair color or our physical defect, rather than by the name we were given on the day we were baptized.

Thanks be to God and to all the saints of the Sanctoral in this matter of differentiating ourselves from the Latinos, and blessed are all the differences that separate us from the Spaniards, even those that bring us a little closer to the devil.

I think it is worthwhile to speak a bit about the degree of religiosity of the Boise Basques.

In general, the men care very little about religious matters. There are very few who go to Mass on Sundays. They are religious, but they are not clerical. What happens deep down is that they are a little disenchanted with the Catholic Church, which lately is becoming more and more detached from Christian values. It bothers them that all the priests who come to visit them start talking to them about God and end up asking them for money. Moreover, with the belligerent position that the Catholic Church has taken in the current war in Spain, everyone sees that it is guided more

75. *Sota'n semie*: Sota's son.

by political and ambitious aims than by human and religious ones. The Basques are still with the apostles; it is the Church of Rome that has sided with the Scribes and the Pharisees. And the Basque does not go to Mass because what he wants is to go to a church, and not to a Sanhedrin.

Besides, the Basque by nature feels an innate repugnance to getting close to foreigners, that aloofness to which the British refer. This being so, how is a Basque from Idaho, who speaks English badly, going to confide his private affairs to an American confessor?

If the Bishop of Boise were a human being and if he had been offered a course in popular psychology at the Seminary, he would immediately understand the spiritual dilemma of his Basque parishioners and would send for two or three Basque priests. But the Bishop of Idaho, apparently, is not very concerned about the souls of the Basques.

Basque parents who were educated in Euzkadi still keep the faith; the children, born here, and not Americanized, are losing it in general. And I say in general, because those young people who have been educated in Catholic schools thanks to the economic position of their parents – a minority – still practice the religion.

In addition, it must be taken into consideration that the sheepherder lives most of the year in the solitude of the desert and the mountains, where, of course, there are no churches, not even hermitages. The Basque sheepherders could say with the cowboys in the famous poem: "Lord, I've never lived where churches grow…".

I would consider the presence of Basque priests in the states of Idaho, Oregon and Nevada to be absolutely necessary from a spiritual and patriotic point of view, and they could do very productive work from every point of view. For we must not forget that we are fortunate to have the best clergy in the world, the most Christian and the most self-sacrificing. And therefore, a Basque priest would be able to reach Basques with whom the American priests achieve nothing.

As for the women, they can be divided into two groups: the mothers, who come from Euzkadi, and the daughters born here. The former keep the faith of their elders, although there is the disgraceful fact that they go months and months without going to confession because they do not have a priest who speaks Basque. They hardly speak English and barely speak

Spanish. As for the daughters, educated in the utilitarian environment of America, they are quite unconcerned about religious matters. I have come across many, many Basques who wear a necklace with a cross but who do not go to Mass. Besides, as they have to do housework, they easily find an excuse for not going to church on Sundays, since, as they say, obligation before devotion.

For all these reasons, as I say, the presence of Basque priests among these Basques, who would show them that our Catholicism, at least, is not as corrupt and materialized as that of the Americans, would be highly desirable.

I hope that what happened to me—coming to America to convince Catholics, who are the ones who are convincing me by their example to leave Catholicism—will not happen to them.

Salutationes de la Natividad

a

Nuestros Muchos Suscriptores Vascos

de

Pacific National Life Insurance Co.

Salt Lake City, Utah

Earl Gustaves (Montes)

Boise

Paul Arruti (Artia)

Boise

Antonio de Irala, Tomas Arambalza, Tony Laradogoitia, Manu de la Sota and Jose Villanueva at the Idaho State Penitentiary.

December 14

This afternoon after lunch, taking advantage of the beautiful sunshine, we walked with Arambalza and Toni to the Idaho State Penitentiary. It is on the outskirts of town, in a barren landscape of bare mountains. There are several large buildings, surrounded by a high wall with battlements. We passed a truck with four or five inmates in it; we could recognize them by the numbers on their backs. They are among those who work on the construction of canals.

In the Penitentiary there is a Basque serving his sentence. His name is Pedro de Arescurrinaga, a native of Nabarniz. He is forty five years old and must have been something of a brawler and a drunkard.

Working as a camp tender in the desert all alone, a young man and his mother came to rob him. The son hit him on the head with a stick and the mother was going to finish him off, but he took his rifle and killed them both. The Basques here collected $3,500 from donations to pay for a good lawyer to defend him. The court sentenced him to 6 years, which was helped by the good conduct observed by the Basques here, among whom there have never been any convicted of blood crimes.

We Basques also have a nice population of the dead in this region. Buried in the Boise cemetery there are about five hundred of our compatriots. During that great flu epidemic there was a day when sixteen died.

Basque funerals are reputed to be the most lavish in Idaho. There once was a burial of a Basque to whom his compatriots sent flowers worth $2,000. In his lifetime, however, he was ignored. The Basque has always attached great importance to the dead. By tradition, he has always liked to be at ease with those who have passed into immortality. That is why he bids farewell to the departed with pomp. For the Americans this is mere superstition; for us, religiosity. The cult of the dead is characteristically Basque.

I have learned that American ranchers killed about twenty Basques back in the days when Basques were called *black Basco son of a bitch*. Our young men came from Euzkadi without knowing a word of English and started out as sheepherders. Unwittingly, they would herd their flock onto someone else's land. The owner would tell them to stop, but the Basque didn't understand and kept going. The American, then, believing he was doing it on purpose, took out his rifle and shot him.

The Spanish vice-consul in Boise, who, at that time was Arregui, the priest, never wanted to speak out against these crimes. So I am told.

December 15

Tonight the editor of the *Boise Capital News* and his wife have invited us to dinner at the Owyhee Hotel. Bradford is a blond American of Scottish descent, who is intelligent and friendly; he is one of those men whose age you can never guess. He speaks Spanish very well. She is young and pleasant.

While talking about Europeans' lack of knowledge of American customs, I tell them that in Europe they think Americans are a collection of shameless men who change wives on a whim, and that it is not true. Then I found out that Bradford has been divorced five times and that this is his sixth wife. For heaven's sake!

We talk about the Basque page published by his newspaper, and he agrees with us that Damian Telleria writes it in a Spanish that not even Esperanto speakers can understand. He tells us that, as of next month, he will dispense with Telleria's services, since several university professors of Spanish have written to him protesting that in Boise the language of Cervantes is mistreated in such a ruthless manner. We feel sorry for Damian, who is a good person, but it seems to us that this is the best thing to do. We promise to send him material for the paper every week from New York.

After dinner he introduces us to the new governor of the state of Idaho, Clarence Alfred Bottosfsen. He congratulates us on the fine reputation the Basques have here, and tells us that, in the last election campaign, he met some of them who helped him on the campaign trail, and that they are true gentleman. Moreover, as a member of the Republican Party, he has great sympathy for the Basques, as they always vote for the Republican candidate. The fact that the Basques in the U.S.A. are unanimously Republicans and not Democrats is one of the mysteries that I do not quite understand. Could it be because the word Democrat is discredited in Euzkadi because of the immigrant riffraff? Maybe that's the reason.

Manu de la Sota (right) and Antonio de Irala, during their visit to the Idaho State Capitol in Boise.

December 16

Tonight Al Berro, the Basque *fitelari*, boxed again and we went to see him. The event took place in a large hangar with a low ceiling and large wooden beams. All the bleachers around the ring are full of Basque ranchers and sheepherders. Our *fitelari* wins by knockout in the second round.

After the fight we greet Al Berro, the Fighting Basque, as they call him here, who is an unassuming, strapping lad, a noble kind of guy. He speaks to us in fluent Basque.

His father, Jose Berrojalbiz, is from Gernika and is established in Jordan Valley (Oregon), where he has a Pool Hall and a barbershop. He is very Basque and tells us about his daughter, who is a refugee in France, and who, although born in America, does not want to come back, as she prefers to follow the fate of the other Basque nationalists.

Agustin Azcuenaga and Jose Navarro, at their hotel in 213 S. 9th Street, Boise.
Picture courtesy of Paul Azcuenaga. BMCC.

December 17

Today I am going to write about Jordan Valley, a small village in the state of Oregon, which is one of the most Basque towns in America. It is about a hundred miles from Boise, a relatively short distance in these parts, for here you can make a trip of a hundred miles by automobile with less effort than traveling twenty-five kilometers in our land.

The state of Oregon has about 960,000 inhabitants and is bordered to the north by Washington, to the east by Idaho, to the south by California and Nevada and to the west by the Pacific. The climate in the part inhabited by the Basques is dry and cold and the terrain has the same characteristics as those of Idaho. Jordan Valley is a city of about three thousand inhabitants, located in the center of the valley with the same name, guarded by majestic mountains. It is a modern little town, advanced like all those of America.

This vast valley, where thousands of sheep, horses and cattle are raised, owes much of its development to the Basques. Antonio and Agustin Azcuenaga, Jose Navarro, Pedro Arritola, Luis Iturraspe and Cipriano Anacabe were among the first inhabitants of Jordan Valley. I will briefly review the principal Basques of this city, not touching on some of those whom I have already mentioned previously because they currently live in Boise:

Agustin Azcuenaga. Native of Abando, married to Agustina Urquiza. He came to America in 1890, and with his brother Antonio, whom I already mentioned, operates the Cow Creek Ranch, employing about twenty five men, all of them Basque. His wife runs the Jordan Valley Hotel.

Juan Acarregi, from Lekeitio, married to Paula Anchustegui, from Berriatua. He came to Jordan Valley in 1899 and owns sheep.

Timoteo Lequerica, from Ereño, married to a Zabalabeascoa. He owns sheep and horses.

Rufino Arritola. He is from Ispaster and came to the United States at the age of fourteen. He owns the Jordan Ranch and is married to Maria Elordi. He has another brother in Jordan Valley named Dionisio.

Marquina Boarding House. In the background, Joe Eguiguren, Joe Marquina and John Lequerica. In the middle, Pascual Arritola, Tim Lequerica, Victor Acarregui and Domingo Yturri. In the foreground, Iñaki Sarra «Billy George», Sotero Marquina and «Txakurri».
Paul Araquistain Collection. BMCC.

Luis Iturraspe. He was from Lekeitio, married to Natalia Acarregi. He had herds and several ranches. He died and left three children, named Jesus, Jose, and Maria.

I will speak of Domingo Iturri, married to Maria Elorriaga, when discussing Ontario.

Lazaro Urquiaga, of Arteaga, married to Josefa Aldecoa, has sheep and a ranch.

Pascual Eiguren, married to Catalina Elordi; Jose, with Jacoba Navarro, Felix, and Bonifacio, married to Luisa Bermeosolo, are sheep owners. There is another Jose Eiguren from Mendexa, married to Carmen Uberuaga.

Their brother-in-law is Blas Telleria, from Gipuzkoa, who is also a sheep farmer in Jordan Valley.

Antonio Bermeosolo, married to Petra Yturrieta, from Lekeitio.

Sotero Marquina, from Durango, married to Eustaquia Yturri. He has a hotel.

Eulogio Madariaga, from Ibarrangelu, married to Trinidad Arriola. Owner of the Hotel Madariaga. There is another Madariaga named Sabino.

Simon Acordagoitia, of Lekeitio, married to Mercedes Eiguren. His brother's name is Alejandro.

Ignacio Chertudi, married to Gabriela Iturri.

Jose Zabala, from Ispaster, married to Maria Madarieta.

Justo Corta, from Ispaster, owner of the Dairy Ranch, married to Maria Ocamica.

Jose Aramberri, from Elgoibar.

Ventura Bengoechea, of Ispaster, married to Juanita Goitiandia, owner of the King Ranch.

Damaso Elordi, from Ereño, sheep owner.

Simon Icaran, from Ispaster, has livestock.

I have not been able to get the names of all the Basques in Jordan Valley, but here are some more: Manuel Aburusa, a rancher known as Benta, Juan Calzacorta, Joe Laca, Pedro Larrinaga, Sebastian Larrucea, a fellow named Lazaro, Juan Mallea, Galo Mendieta, Santiago Mendieta, Eusebio San Cristobal, Simon Faratica, Joe Zatica (about whom I will speak later) and Pedro Zumaeta, whose wife, by the way, died a few days ago.

In other towns in Oregon I have met more Basques. Leaving for later those in Ontario, I will cite the names of those I have written down:

In Adrian, Enrique H. Moral.

In Andrews, Victor Onaindia.

In Bates, Luis Bidasolo, Damian Gabiola, a fellow named Isarsagosa.

In Burns, Casildo Asteasu, Jose Lizundia and Marcelino Osa, who has a hotel.

In Crane, Claudio Mugarza.

In Folly Farm, Juan Coscorrotza.

In Frenchglen, Juan Ibarzabal.

In Klamath Falls, Joe Uzcudun, owner of the Crater hotel.

In La Grande, Felix Asla.

In White Pine, Gervasio Mendiola.

I consider the opinion that Americans have of the Basques here to be more interesting than that of their compatriots. Therefore, I am going to translate an article precisely about the Basques of Jordan Valley written by a lady in the *Christian Science Monitor* of Boston (September 23, 1938). It reads as follows:

> We wives of engineers who have to run around trying to arrange a makeshift home often go through many an experience, and one of the most curious I have had was during the season I spent among the Basques in the little town of Jordan Valley, in the broken desert that stretches into the southwestern region of Oregon.
>
> During a long, cold winter we took up comfortable lodgings in a two-room apartment of a certain hotel, and from the window, which looked out over the main road, I amused myself by watching the picturesque characters as they passed by. There were Pinte Indians; cowboys of both sexes, who sometimes just for fun rode up on the sidewalks on horseback; the horse-drawn sleigh that brought the mail when the road was impassable for cars; and through it all the Basques, talking giddily among themselves in their strange language, which is harmonious in the way that castanets are.
>
> I was very interested in the Basque people, who, in spite of coming from the French and Spanish Pyrenees, are neither one

nor the other, but a different race that has preserved its language and customs for many generations. Our eldest daughter, now five years old, was born in the home of Basque friends, and our maid, a dark, slender girl, who was always well groomed and well behaved, had arrived from Bilbao a few years before, and sad to say, several of her relatives have suffered greatly in the present war.

Although the Basques' house did not have many amenities, it was kept with immaculate cleanliness: gleaming brass beds, admirably ironed linen, and refreshingly white children's clothes. Everyone in the family cooperated in the housekeeping, and even the children had their assigned chores.

Basque women are excellent cooks, and from them I learned to cook both well and economically, because with the most ordinary ingredients they make exquisite dishes. With a few simple beans or rice they work true gastronomic wonders. They usually serve different kinds of meat at each meal, accompanied by different types of sauces. They are very fond of vegetables and salads, and their desserts are generally simple.

Basque hotels have a reputation in this region, and in addition to indulging in good food, guests are entertained by watching the ancient Basque dances. They like to have fun and enjoy themselves, and the children learn to dance as soon as they start walking.

I had to change some of my previous ideas about raising children, when I saw our maid dancing a fandango holding in her arms my daughter, who was not more than a week old. Perhaps that is why Basque children are raised to be healthy and cheerful and don't seem to mind being treated like dolls. For my part, I felt a great relief during those days I spent among the Basques, outside of my own traditions and rules of education, but living in the manner of this primitive people. I shall never forget that charming experience in which I learned to live pleasantly.

Jordan Valley Basque pelota court in 1938. Colorized photo. *Oregon Historical Society*.

December 18

The big event of the Boise Christmas season is coming up. I'm referring to the ninth annual Basque Shepherders Ball, also called "the one with overalls and aprons."

Today's newspaper announces it in a letter signed by the secretary of the Dance Committee, Zenon de Izaguirre. This Committee also employs a Spanish invented by the Basques of Idaho. It reads:

> The grand ball for the ninth year of the Basque shepherds' overalls will be held on December 22, 1938, in the Riverside Pavilion Hall, with the magnificent orchestra of the Merril Farming band, with the best musicians of the locality composed of 10 instruments.
>
> With the best and famous and renowned Basque guraris of the locality, with their typical instruments and traditional Basque music, they will play in the same hall, in another separate room alternating with the orchestra, the instruments of the tamboril, txistu, tambourine, accordion and guitar.
>
> In the intermission of the dance there will be a very interesting auction which will please and interest the public, a magnificent, colossal lamb, the best you have seen, and a turkey chosen from the best ranches in the locality.
>
> And according to what Lorenzo Mendiola tells us, in these days he has been in charge of arranging the lamb as if it were a Tancredo doll, or a real baby in the style of Leon; and this lamb will be decorated better than in previous years, as if it were shorn with such fineness, its woolly body of the lamb, and so well shorn it will be, that the public will like it with the mastery that this lamb will be shorn and decorated, as if it were the white puppy in the style of Tancredo.
>
> During the evening Mrs. Antonia Zubizarreta will dance the auresku and Mrs. Eladia Goicoechea will dance the *atzesku*.
>
> Typical music will be played in the style of our native towns by

the famous tamboril drummer Ambrosio Apariasi, who will be accompanied by Joe Anacabe as tambor drummer.

The Organizing Committee has agreed that all the money collected from this Sheepherders Ball will be sent to Basque refugees, poor people who are currently in foreign lands. The American member of the International Red Cross will supervise and arrange for the delivery of this donation to the refugees from our beloved homeland Euzkadi who are currently in foreign countries, these orphaned children, women without husbands, those disabled for work, and for the wounded gudaris who are in hospitals.

And do not forget to come to this bidding contest that will bemore festive than previous years, which according to the public opinion of the locality will guarantee the greatest that you have seen in this dance of the shepherds, with their typical Basque manners, with their typical Basque music, and with their dances of the most interested that dance to the sound of the drum, choosing to your taste in the selection of the dance, to choose with the nice and pretty, kind young ladies of the locality that they are, and who will gladly accompany you in the selections of the dances, to give satisfaction of kindness to the strangers from outside, and from the locality in Boise, these pretty girls (of pure Basque stock) who have always merited their dignity and pride to the Basque population of Boise.

In addition, in the same newspaper, the committee publishes the following "Notice", which is not to be missed:

The good ladies of the household are requested not to bring small children of minor age to this dance, because it is for the benefit of the health and risk of their mothers, and at the same time they are also in danger of catching some sickness with this cold weather, and it is best if they please do not bring on this day and they will avoid the cold they may catch.

And at this dance, dear reader, it will be obligatory as the traditional custom of the colony that you come please with overalls pants, and the ladies with ordinary house clothes. These regulations will be very strict in this classic dance, and you will not be allowed without being with these regulations as their strictness details indicate.

> We sell men's pants and simple ladies' clothes for this day of the ball. And also ladies and young people will be received with typical clothes as from our beloved homeland Euzkadi.

This morning, being Sunday, we went to hear Mass at the Cathedral. We were accompanied by Johny Anduiza, Jack's youngest son, recently arrived from Portland, where he is studying at a Catholic university. He is a very good boy and very religious, without hypocrisy, in spite of being educated by the Jesuits. He spends all day at home, with his mother and sister, helping them with the housework, because with the upcoming Christmas holidays the house is full of shepherds who have come from all over.

After the Gospel, our friend the bishop climbed up to the pulpit and in a dry and inexpressive sermon that lasted 45 minutes, he put us all to sleep. On the way out I spoke with several Basque girls, among them the Totorica girls, who had just arrived from France after having escaped the bombing of Gernika.

Until lunchtime I have been dictating to Margari Madarieta several texts in English. She helps me not to make mistakes. She is a lovely girl, blonde, with a green bow on her head and a schoolgirl's collar. She speaks only English and Basque. She happens to be the girlfriend of Al Berro, the Basque *fitelari*. Margari had lunch with us.

In the afternoon we went with Archabal, Zenon and Mendiola to a ranch belonging to Archabal to inspect the lamb to be auctioned at the Sheepherders Ball on the 22nd. Last year a Boise banker paid $350 for the animal, to show the affection he felt for the Basques.

Archabal takes care of the lamb, which by the way is magnificent, as if it were a baby. He keeps it separate from the others and gives it special food. He puts on his gloves, takes a large pair of shearing scissors (which, according to Azkue, are called *arbaiza* in Basque) and spends an hour trimming the lamb's wool. Here I find out that Archabal was a champion at castrating male lambs with his mouth: seven per minute.

We also visited the herds of bulls (rams) that Archabal has for breeding. There are some wonderful specimens.

In the evening Arambalza, Toni Laradogoitia and Jose Villanueva Amezketa, who works in a shoe store in Emmett, came to dine with us.

Margari Madarieta and Alberto Berrojalbiz, on their wedding day.
Kathy Berrojalbiz Wilcox Collection. BMCC.

Jose is a full-bodied nationalist, cultured and intelligent, and he writes quite well. The trouble is that he talks too much.

Then we went for coffee with John Garechana and his family. Garechana is a good man from Aulesti, married to Romana Uberuaga, a domineering, gossipy and pretentious Basque woman. The highlight of the family is his daughter Toni, who is tall and slim, with a very expressive face. Aside from speaking Basque, she is completely Americanized. This girl was declared Boise's beauty queen in a contest held at the Elks Club. She is employed at the Golden Rule. Her other sister, Josephine, ran away with a young man and then returned to the parental home when he tired of her.

It is immediately apparent that Garechana, the poor guy, is overwhelmed by his wife and daughters, who insist on living to the dizzying rhythm of avant-garde American women.

Toni leaves because her boyfriend is waiting for her to go to the movies. However, tomorrow her other boyfriend, who is studying in Reno, will be arriving. When her mother hears this, she says with great satisfaction:

—"You have to follow American customs. Here every girl has at least two boyfriends."

The mother ends up showing us the Basque flag of the Independent Association of Basque Women. It is a very beautiful flag, which was embroidered by them.

I leave this house saddened. I have seen a Basque home torn apart by the stupidity of a mother and by a misguided idea of adapting to American customs.

<u>bari</u> vasco que hay en los Estados Unidos, voy a incluir las poesias suyas, mas o menos malas, que tengo en mi poder.

Empezaré por "<u>Mendigoixalen askatasunez</u>" en la cual relata algo de su vida:

Milla sortzireun lau ogei-ta
amasaspikko urtian.
Sortún nintzan itxasondoko
etxe-txipitxuan batian.

Orregaitikan jarraitu nai det
euzkaldunaren bixia.
Gabiltzan toki danetan beti
zabaldurikan egia.

Zerutik bera jatzi yatazan
edur matasa guztiak.
Alkar laztanduz zuritu dabez
nere lepoko jantziak.

Jesarririkan mendi ganian
aurritutzen naiz pentzatzen.
Nere oraingo bizi modua
zelan duten nik pasatzen.

Mendirik mendi edur artian
lorrotz guztiak bildatzen.
Eu bildotzik juan eta edan
aitziekin olgatzen.

Nere janari eta jantziak
ofe ta denak hostirik.
Iru egunek pasatu ditúz
arto ganian loturik.

December 19

Today Simon Gandarias, from Ontario, Oregon, came to visit us. He is a young, handsome and intelligent man. He is a Basque nationalist. He has a bar in Ontario and in his spare time he composes Basque poetry which he prints and gives away to others for free.

Since I consider these works by the only Basque *bertsolari* in the United States to be of interest, I am going to include the more or less bad poems of his that I have in my possession. I will start with *Mendigoixaleen askatasunez*, The Freedom of the Mountaineers,[78] in which he tells a bit about his life:

Milla zortzireun laurogei eta
amazazpiko urtean
sortu nintzen ni itxasondoko
etxe txikitxu batean.

Orregatikan jarraitu nai dot
euskaldunaren bizia,
gabiltzan toki denetan beti
zabaldurikan egia.

Zerutik beera jatsi jatazan
edur mataza guztiak,
alkar laztanduz zuritu dabez
nire lepoko jantziak.

Jezarririkan mendi ganean
aurkitzen nozu pentsetan
neure oraingo bizimodua
zelan doten nik pasetan.

78. *Mendigoixaleak*, or high mountain enthusiasts, was a Basque sportive-political movement that emerged in the 1920s. They advocated for the independence of the Basque Country, following the Irish example. Manu de la Sota was one of the movement's founders.

Mendirik mendi edur artian
lorratz guztiak bilatzen:
ene bildotsak jan eta edan
ardiekin olgatzen.

Neure janari eta jantziak
oge eta danak osturik,
iru egun bai pasatu ditut
asto ganian loturik.

Zortzi egunez bakardadian
mendi-basoen ganian
txakurtxuaren laguntasunez
gau eta egun lanian.

Koutxadurikan ezin kobratuz
iru illerik batian,
holaxe nabil leloturikan
nagusientzat lanian.

Promes onekin itxadoteko
bildotsak saldu artian,
gorantziekin bildur gabere
segiduteko lanian.

Pagatzen duten koutxaduakin
asiak dira larririk,
ludi onetako batzar-etxian
nagusi denak baturik.

Su-burdiekin batzar etxean
porra aundiak pipatzen,
artzain gaixoen koutxadu denak
irutik bira bajatzen.

Modu onetan bajatzen bada
bi ogeitara illian,
Errusia aldeko txapel gorria
ipiniko da ganian.

Azkartasunez asi behar dau
mendi goikuak lanian
nagusi denek paga daiela
artzain guztiak illian.

Modu onetan nai ezpadabe
segidutia lanian
asto eta ardi itxiko doguz
berekin naaste mendian.

Goi-zaleen azkartasunez
eginik danok lagunak
argiko doguz geure buruko
samintasun hotz illunak.

Gorantzi asko zabaldu nai dot
neure lagunen artian,
euzko odola dauen danori
agur bat gero artian.

1932 garren urtian, Elko,
Nevadan Euzkaldun
batek jarriak.

See this other one dedicated to his mother: *Kanta daiogun danok Euzkadiko neure ama Karmengoari.* Let's all sing to my mother Karmen from Euzkadi.

Mundu onetara ekarri nauzu *argituz zeure sabelian,* *maitasunakin hasirik gero,* *Ama, or zeure bularrian.*	You brought me to this world illuminating me in your womb, to raise me with love, Mother, at your breast.
Urte askuak hemen pasaurik *ordutik ona bitartean,* *amodioa zuretzat, ama,* *beti izan dot bihotzean.*	Many years have passed since then, but I have always had love for you, Mother, in my heart.

Lo asko galdu dozu zuk, ama,
neugaz sarritan gabian,
ipuin gozoak neuri esaten
arturik zedorren altzuan.

You lost a lot of sleep, Mother,
with me during the night,
telling me sweet stories
taking me on your lap.

Itxaso baltzak pasatu dodaz
urontzitan lau kurtzetara...
Europatikan Afrikara eta
Asiatik Amerikara.

I crossed black seas on ships
towards the four cardinal points,
from Europe to Africa
and from Asia to America.

Amodioak izan dodaz nik
neure ustean aundiak,
baina zureak, ama maitea.
denen gainian jarriak.

I have had wonderful loves,
in my opinion,
but your love, dear mother,
I have held above all others.

Zure moduko edertasunik
ez dot aurkitu munduan.
Goiko Jaunak tokia dauka
zuretzat gordeta zeruan.

Beauty like yours
I have not found in the world.
The Lord above has a place
for you in heaven.

Amets aundiak egiten dodaz
zugaz sarritan gabean,
pozgarriekin eukiten zaitut
jarririk neure aurrean.

I usually have great dreams
of you at night;
it is with great joy that I have you
sitting in front of me.

Holango jazokizunik, ama,
leenau zer zan enekian...
bihotz bigunez, Ama liraina,
neronek ezautu artian.

I didn't know what that was,
Mother, until I experienced it
myself, with a tender heart,
beautiful Mother.

Eguzkiaren argia zara zu,
mundu onetan garbia,
eta ondo irabazi dozu
goiko zeruko atia.

You are the light of the sun,
the purity of this world,
and you have well earned
the gate to the high heavens.

Zu zara aingeru, neure amatxo,
goiko zerutik jatsita,
Ama Karmengo izenarekin
bihotz gozotik hasita.

You are an angel, dear mother,
descended from heaven above
with the name of Mother Karmen
and with a sweet heart.

Maitemin onek dodaz nik, Ama, *orain zeuri eskatzeko* *parkazino apur bat zedorrek* *orain neuri emateko.*	These pains of love I have, Mother, lead me to ask you now to forgive me a little.
Nik zu bai maite zaitudala, nik *ez dizut, ez, ukatuko,* *eta zeurea ere nai dot izan,* *Ama, Eternidaderako.*	I do love you; I will not deny this love, and I want to have yours too, Mother, for all Eternity.

The next one is interesting because it relates the life of the Basque shepherds of Idaho.

As you can see, Gandarias's poems are no work of art, but they preserve that roughness and freshness of the poetic improvisations of our bertsolaris that make them very appealing.

Gandarias is the emigrant who sings to his homeland from this side of the sea. He is an American Iparraguirre, a bard, although not as bohemian as the original, since he runs his "Cigar Store" in Ontario, which provides him with handsome profits.

But we have to thank him above all for being in love with Euzkadi, the Basque Country, for never forgetting it, and for proclaiming it to the four winds, thus setting a beautiful example to some American Basques who are ashamed of their Basque ancestry.

Idahoko Artzañan Bixia. The Life of Idaho Shepherds. By Simon Gandarias. Ontario (Oregon).

1 *Mila bederatzireun* *ta ogei ta amalauan* *zabaldu nai det nik* *neure liburuan,* *zelan artzain ein dodan* *ainbeste urtian,* *Idahoko estaduko* *ardian atzian.*	1 In the year nineteen hundred and thirty-four, I want to show in my book that I have been a shepherd for so many years, following the sheep of the state of Idaho.

2

Gazte gaztetxutatik
eldurik onantza,
orain artue daukat
mutil zarran antza,
ardiakin lanian,
urdaila ere utsa,
olaxe pasatzen det
biximodu beltza.

2

Having arrived here
very young,
now I look like an
old bachelor.
Working with sheep,
on an empty stomach,
that's how it goes,
my black life.

3

Edurrak etortian,
bedar metetara
juaten gara danok
osozko pozera,
bertan janak egin ta
ekartzen maira,
ola pasatzen dogu
emengo denpora.

3

When the snow falls,
on the hay
we all feel
completely happy,
we prepare the food
and bring it to the table,
that's how we spend
our time here.

4

Batzuk ibiltzen gara
bedarrak zabaltzen,
beste batzuk berriz
bildotsak sartutzen,
beste bi edo iru
jan ta edan ematen,
eta beste batzuk
zarrenak bildatzen

4

Some of us go
to spread the grass,
while others
put the lambs in,
two or three more
give them food and water,
and others gather
the older sheep.

5

Sarri egoten dira
bildotsak nasturik,
zulo txipietatik
bertarantz juanik,
sarri askotan, berriz,
amakin galdurik
eta apaindutzeko
lan asko emanik.

5

Often, the lambs
get mixed up,
escaping
through some hole.
Other times, however,
they get separated from their mother
and it takes a lot of work
to fix things.

6
Lania kentzen gero
artazi batzukin
ardia egoten da
bildur aundiakin.
Lania kendu eta
errebañuakin,
errukarriak dira
denporaliakin.

6
Then we have to shear
the wool with scissors
from a sheep
that is scared to death.
Once the wool is removed,
it returns to the flock,
and they are worthy of compassion
if there is a storm.

7
Gero kanpora berriz
errebañuakin,
bi txakur atzian da
latx zar batzuekin
euraren atzetikan
bildur aundiakin
atzera eingo duten
pentsamentuakin.

7
Then we have to go out again
with the flock,
followed by two dogs, and
with some old sheep
you have to stay behind
fearful
that they
will be left behind.

8
Atzera juatian
ekarten bierrak,
ortxe izaten dira
artzaiñaren lorrak,
arinka ibiltzeko
belaunak gogorrak
olaxe eltzen dira
gaubeko izerrak.

8
Going back causes
hardship, and
that's what the shepherd's
tribulation consist of,
if his knees are too stiff
to walk fast, and
this is how the stars
of the night arrive.

9
Mendirantz urten eta
bedarrik bat ere ez,
urera juan eta
urikan ere ez,
kanpora juan eta
janaririkan ez,
alderdi guztietan
miseri gogorrez.

9
We go out to the mountains and
there is no grass;
we go to get water and
there is no water either.
We go to the camp and
there is no food,
there is so much
misery everywhere.

10
Kanpua ipintzen du
tontortxu batian,
azeriak zaintzeko
ideia guztian,
artzaña ibiltzen da
umore txarrian
azeriak gaitikan
gau ta egun lanian.

10
He sets up the camp wagon
on a hill,
to watch out for coyotes,
because the shepherd walks
all over the place
day and night
in a bad mood
because of the coyotes.

11
Pozik ibiltzen dira
denbora txarrian,
iñok ikusi gabe
ardien aurrian,
bi edo iru il ta
hor laga mendian
urdallak zabalduta
soñu ederrian.

11
Because when the weather is bad
they walk happily
among the sheep
without anyone seeing them;
they kill two or three
and leave them there
in the mountain, with their stomachs
open and howling.

12
Gora urten artian
ekin eta ekin,
au oba izateko
esperantziakin.
Bidian asten gera
geure txakurrakin,
eta mendi gorriak
edur aundiakin.

12
We walk and we walk
until we get to the top,
with the hope that
everything will get better.
We start walking
with our dog
and the red mountains
are covered with snow.

13
Mendi gorriak berriz
guztizko [mortuak],
errebañuarekin
[leku arriskutsuak];
artzañan zanguak
guztiz kantzatuak,
ikusten juateko
mendiko zuluak.

13
Plus, the red mountains
are completely deserted,
and very dangerous places
for the flock.
And the shepherds' legs
are already too tired
to detect the gaps
in the mountain.

14
Udan goiko mendirantz
bildots ardiakin
gizendu ta azteko
esperantziakin,
au be naiku zer egin
gaur otsuakin
ardiak ill ezteisen
bildur aundiakin.

14
In the summer, back to the mountains
with the lambs and the sheep,
in the hope that they'll
fatten up and grow up,
but it's not an easy task today
with the wolves,
and the terrible fear that
they'll kill the sheep.

15
Ipintzen du kanpua
erreka onduan,
bi egur ebakita
zutunik gañian,
iñor ikusi gabe
amar egunian
txakur ta zaldiakin
ardian atzian.

15
The camp wagon is set up
next to the river,
standing on
two pieces of cut wood.
With the dog and the horse,
taking care of the sheep,
you won't see anyone
for ten days.

16
Udan egoten gera
arbola azpian,
bildotsak saldutzeko
abisu artian.
Bildotsak saldutzian
asirik bidian,
bazkaldu izendu sarri
autsekin atzian.

16
In summer we usually
hang out under a tree,
among notices for
lambs for sale.
As soon as we sell the lambs
we start walking,
and often we have lunch
with the dust of the road.

17
Kortetatik urten da
eun bat buru falta,
orduan egiten du
nagusiak bota.
Ardiak galdu eta
gañera konduta:
onela egoten da
artzain sobranta.

17
Leaving the stable, about
a hundred head of sheep are missing,
so the owner
fires the sheperd
for losing sheep and,
furthermore, for misconduct,
And that's how the shepherd
ends up fired.

18
Majada eiten dute
kamporen onduan,
baina juaten dira
sarritan gaubian,
ogetik jaiki eta
baruko utzian
ardiak bildu nairik
txistuka mendian.

18
They graze
near the camp wagon,
but sometimes they leave
during the night,
you have to get out of bed
and, without eating anything,
walk whistling through the mountains
to gather the sheep.

19
Asko gabiltza emen
jornalak galduta,
onlango miseriak
mendian pasauta.
Lenago egon ziran
uzabak kebrauta,
gero diruak ein ta
zorrakin aztuta.

19
Many of us are here
with lost wages
living in the mountains
in such a misery.
Our employers
previously were bankrupt,
but then they made money
and forgot about their debts.

20
Amerikan beti dot
izan suerte txarra,
eta argituko dot
zelan dan aurrera.
Holaxe pasa dogu
gazteko denpora,
neure ixena Simon
Gandarias-tarra.

20
I have always had bad luck
in America,
and one day I'll tell you
what happens next.
This is how I spent
my youth.
My name is Simon
Gandarias-tarra.

Amerikako gaztiak, The Youth of America:

1
Goixian goixko mendigoizale
Eusko gudari matiak
arakatuten dozuezenak
uri, baserri, mendiak,
Egal danetan erein ondoren
Euskal-erriko aziak
nagi bagerik lan eiten dute
ameriketan gaztiak.

1
Mountaineers who rise
very early in the morning,
dear Basque soldiers who watch over
cities, farms, and mountains…
After having sown
Basque seeds everywhere,
the youth will work
tirelessly in America.

2
Jarraitu bada bide ortatik
Euzko gudari maitiak,
zabiltzan txoko danetan
zabaldurikan egiak.
Maite izanik guraso zarrak
eta Euskera garbiak,
erakutziaz egal danetan
geure Amaren berriak.

2
Continue then along that path,
dear Basque soldiers,
spreading the truth
everywhere you go.
Continue loving your old parents
and your clear language,
bringing to every corner
news of our Mother.

3
Abertzaliak erakustendu
nai nun beroren biotza,
lan ein ondoren aberri aldez
maite izanik izkuntza.
Iñor badago gudari aldran
loitutzen dunik lorotza?
Esan denari nola ixan den
ama Euzkadin bixitza.

3
The patriots show their heart
wherever they are.
After working for their country,
they love their language.
Is there anyone among the combatants
who tarnished their reputation?
Tell everyone how it was
in our mother Euzkadi.

4

Oitura onari abegi ona
txarrari begi illuna
ipiñi eta goguan beti
ibili goi maitasuna.
Beste guztian bildurrik gabe
atzera eta aurrera,
Euzkadigaitik Jaunan bitartez
maite dugu ba euskera.

4

A warm welcome for good customs,
a dark view of bad ones,
and always carry
pure love in your heart.
In everything else, without fear,
forward and back
for Euzkadi, God willing,
because we love our language.

5

Munduan geran euzko guztiak
onelanguak bagiña,
laster litzake geure aberria
askea lengo modura.
Denpora gutxiz idabazirik
juango giñan aurrera
gazte guztien azkartasunaz
geure Euzkadiko lurrera.

5

If all the Basques in the world
were like this,
our country would soon be
as free as before.
We would win in no time
and move forward;
we would go to our land of Euzkadi
with the strength of our young people.

6

Argitu gaizan orain guztiok
baina benetan argitu,
geure amaren berbeta zarra
egin baño len amaitu:
Ezkertarraren lanari utzi
eskumatikan jarraitu,
aberri onak aman esanez
ez daitezen gelditu

6

Let's get this clear now,
but let's get this clear for real,
before our mother's
old language disappears.
Stop working with your left hand,
continue to the right,
so that the good homelands
spoken by the mother do not stop.

7

Arakatuten asi biar dugu
uri, baserri, mendiak…
Ameriketan lana egiñez
Euzkadi gaitik gaztiak.
Agur aundi bat neure aldetik,
neska ta mutil guztiak,
urrez ta diruz ezin pagatu
zeuen biotz adoriak.

7

We have to start watching over
cities, farms, mountains...
We young people should work in America
for the Basque Country.
A big farewell from me,
to all boys and girls;
the passion of your hearts
cannot be paid in gold or money.

The following is a poem of deep patriotic feeling. It is difficult to find in America a Basque who speaks as Gandarias does of his homeland and of Sabino. It is true that most of them do not even know who Sabino is.

[The text gets interrupted here, on page 121 of the handwirtten diary, and continues on page 124. Two sheets are missing which would include the aforementioned verses.]

The following poem uses a completely Basque sense of humor. *Apostoluak aingeruakin.* The Apostles with Angels.

Amabi mutil apostoluak *alkarrandurik etxian* *amar botella ardu edan doguz* *jokaturikan musian.*	Twelve boys, apostles, gathered at home, we drank ten bottles of wine while playing mus.
Orregaitikan juan biar dogu *ego laburrak bilatzen,* *urdail legorrak ondo bustirik* *broma eder bat pasatzen.*	That's why we must go in search of short-winged beings, dry stomach well soaked having a nice joke.
Barrutik urten kanpora eta *goitikan bera kalian,* *erreka ondoruntz asiak giñan* *gelditurikan bidian.*	We went from inside out, up and down the street, walking toward the river, stopping along the way.
Konziertuak asiak ziran *argi gorridun etxian,* *tirrintadia atian jota* *sartu giñian bailian.*	The concerts had begun at the house with the red lights, we rang the doorbell and joined in the dance.
Apostoluak asi giñaden *esperimentuak artutzen,* *amar soseko fonografuan* *aingeruakin dantzatzen.*	We apostles began to gain experience, dancing with angels with the ten-coin phonograph.

Erreka ondorantz elduak dira
aingeru gazte lerdenak,
San Pedrorekin asarraturik
zeru aldetik eginak.

Aingeru onek ziran gaztiak,
amasei otsailekuak.
Begi beltzakin lerden ta zuri
labur jantzirik eguak.

Apostoluak asi giñian
aingeruakin olgatzen,
edariakin ondo berotuz
gona laburrak neurtutzen.

Izarrik izar asiak giñan
aingeruakin batian,
ego laburrak gora zabalduz
egaka zeru aldian.

Izar batetik urten genduan
beste baterantz bidian,
dantzaldi batzuk lenik eginik
Jupiterreko bailian.

Zeruko argiak iluntzen ziran
geure begian aurrian
apostoluak aingeruakin
seigarrenera eltzian.

Esango dabe aingeru onek
gu gariala zantarrak,
baña eztabe geiago esango
gu garianik makalak.

Young and tender angels
had reached the riverbank,
surely escaped from heaven
after getting angry with Saint Peter.

These angels were young,
sixteen years old.
Black-eyed, slender, and white,
wearing short wings.

We apostles began to flirt
with the angels,
getting excited with the drinks,
measuring the short skirts.

We began to walk from star to star
together with the angels,
expanding our short wings upwards
flying through the sky.

We left one star
on the way to another,
after dancing a little
at Jupiter's ball.

The lights of heaven were going out
before our eyes
when the apostles and the angels
arrived at six o'clock.

These angels will say
that we are clumsy,
but they will never again say
we are lazy.

Egunsentia eldu zanian *zorionakin batera,* *urrengorarte despedituez* *urten genduan kanpora.*	When dawn arrived, along with happiness, we headed outside said goodbyes until next time.
Aingeruakin jolastutzeko *gogorik inok badauko,* *gaba sartzian erreka ondorutz* *juana baño eztauko.*	If anyone wants to play with angels, just go to the riverbank when night falls.

The following one, a mixture of Basque and Spanish, although quite vulgar, is still funny: *Gabon Gabeko Buruko Miñak*, meaning "Christmas Headaches." It has an introduction:

Iduzkiaren dirdira argia mendi ertzian urre koloriakin edoi bitartez egun onak emoten eldu zanian, urten nuan etxetik neure lagun bat ikustera. Jakin gura nuan ja nora juan zan bezpera gaubian alako arropa ederrakin neure barri gabe, eta etxe aurrera eldu nitzanian, arritxuan ganian jarririk, bi belaunburutan beso ukonduak ipinita, bi eskuakin buruari eusten, bere buruko uliak arroturik alderdi bijetara: bere gitarra albuen suela topa neban. Geldika, geldika, lepuan jorik esan notsan: "Manolo, gaxorik zagoz?" "Yes, they made me sick." "*Baña zergaitik edo zelan?*" "I don't know, but they always make me sick." "Esan ya neuri zergaitik gaixotzen zarien?"	When the bright glow of the Sun reached the edge of the mountain with a golden color among the clouds saying good morning, I left home to visit a friend of mine. I wanted to know where he had gone the night before, wearing that elegant suit, without saying goodbye. When I arrived in front of his house, I found him sitting on a rock, elbows on his knees, holding his head in his hands, his hair dishevelled on both sides, and with his guitar at his side. Gently touching his back, I said, "Manolo, are you sick?" "Yes, they made me sick." "But why, in what way?" "I don't know, but they always make me sick!" "Tell me, please, why you're sick…"

1
Por andar con las rubias
emen nau galduta,
como los solterones
gelditu z sobrauta.
Y ahora toco el tremolo
guitarra artunda,
porque me pongo enfermo
neskakin batunda.

1
For hanging around with blondes
I am lost here,
like old bachelors
I've been left behind.
And now, picking up the guitar,
I play the tremolo,
because I get sick
if I hang out with girls.

2
Cuando van al toilet
euren trastiakin
trabajan con el arte
bere lapizakin
formando el arco iris
zazpi kolorekin.
Y me ponen enfermo
denporaliakin.

2
When they go to the toilet
with their stuff
thay work on art
with their pencils,
drawing the rainbow
with seven colors,
and they make me sick
with the storm.

3
Ponen una pechera
bular bietatik
y luego la braguera
badakizu nundik,
refleccionan con seda
zer dagon barrutik
y me ponen enfermo
begituz ganetik.

3
They put a breastplate
on both breasts
and then the truss
you know where,
they fill it with silk
what's inside,
and it makes me sick
just looking at it.

4
Cuando vamos al baile
besotik artunda
[enseguida empieza]
jirata biraka,
y luego ella se ríe
neuri begituta
porque me pongo enfermo
burutik galduta.

4
When we go to the dance
arm in arm,
she suddenly
starts spinning,
and then she laughs
looking at me,
because I get sick
out of my mind.

5 Bailan ríen y cantan *bata bestiakin,* toman, beben y fuman *neure diruakin,* y bailan charlestones *bijurriarekin,* y me ponen enfermo *buruko miñakin.*	5 They dance, laugh and sing with one another, they drink and smoke with my money and they dance the Charleston with a twist and they make me sick with a headache.
6 Y luego de paseo *automobillakin,* yo siempre lo deseo *atzian neskakin,* y no me dejan quieto *euren eskuakin,* y me ponen enfermo *gorputz ta animakin.*	6 And then a ride in the car, I always want to do it in the back seat with the girls, and they won't leave me alone with their hands and they make my body and soul sick.
7 Cuando vamos a casa *goixian goixetik* ella siempre me abraza *alderdi bitatik,* y luego me repite *bijen erditatik,* y me deja enfermo *bakarrik kanpotik.*	7 When we go home early in the morning she always hugs me on both sides, and then she insists on the middle, and leaves me sick alone on the outside.
8 Se despide Manolo *neska lagunakin,* porque quiero estar solo *Jaun Goikuarekin* tocando el tremolo *neure gitarrakin,* porque me pongo enfermo *neska gaztiakin.*	8 Manolo says goodbye to his girlfriend, because I want to be alone with the Lord playing the tremolo with my guitar, because I get sick with young girls.
AGUR GERO ARTIAN	GOODBYE, SEE YOU LATER

The following is a Bacchic song, which the Basques are so fond of: *Mozkorra arrapatzen dok edan ezkero*, If You Drink, You Get Drunk.

Neuk irabazi dot *aposta aundia:* *Pedro Olarretari* *asto ta zaldia.*	I have won a big bet with Pedro Olarreta: a donkey and a horse.
Neuri esana arek *eztala egia,* *egiten dunik emen* *munduak bueltia.*	He told me it wasn't true that the world here is spinning around.
Siñestu egiteko *zelan den egia,* *beko tabernan deko* *Maritxuk kañia.*	I told him to believe it because it's true. Maritxu has her beer right in the tavern downstairs.
Pitxer txipia gabe *eskatu aundia* *ikusi nai badezu* *munduko bueltia.*	Don't order beer in the small jug, order it in the large one if you want to see how the world spins.
Iru txakur aundikin *pitxerra betia:* *Maritxuk deko beti* *kañia merkia.*	For a few cents, she'll fill your jug. Maritxu always has very cheap beer.
Iru pitxar edan ta *Maritxun kañia,* *juango zara egiten* *munduri bueltia.*	If you drink three jugs of Maritxu's beer, you will travel around the world.
Maritxuk emon zion *Pedro 'ri kañia:* *Pedrok lastertxu eukan* *eranda guztia.*	Maritxu gave Pedro a jug of beer, Pedro drank it all down in one go.

Neuri esan Pedrok *andik pasterian* *bueltaka ibili dala* *iru egunian.*	Pedro told me when I passed by there that he had been traveling around for three days.
Iru txakur aundikin *pitxerra betia:* *Maritxuk dauka beti* *kañia merkia.*	For a few cents, she'll fill your jug, Maritxu always has very cheap beer.
Eldu ona, mutilak *edaten kañia,* *ikusi daigun danok* *munduko bueltia.*	Come here, guys, and drink a beer; let's all take a trip around the world.

The following one is also quite vulgar, but it is interesting for being the only one, perhaps, that exists, written in Basque and English. There is no title.

We are plenty in here *Euzkadin egiñak* and we want to advertise *pasatzen den egiak.* *Tran la ran lara larai* *pasatzen den egiak.*	We are plenty in here made in Euskadi, and we want to advertise the things that happen. Tran la ran lara larai, the things that happen.
Today-*ko neskatillak* *jazten dira* pretty, powder *ipini eta* *enseguida* allready. *Tran...* *Enseguida* allready.	The girls of *today* dress up pretty, they put on powder and right away all ready. Tran... Right away all ready.

Sidewalk-*ien pasatzen dan*
people *guztiari*
begia giñatu eta:
Come on right in honey!
Tran…
Come on right in honey!

Sartun barrura eta
enseguida allready,
lenik erraten dabe:
Gimme first my money.
Tran…
Gimme first my money.

How much money *zuk*
kobratu orregaz,
besides the war taxes
bakarrik two dollars.
Tran…
bakarrik two dollars.

Two dollars-*engaitikan*
skirts-*ak altzatu,*
allright *erran eta*
chewing *gomie maskatu*
Tran…
chewing *gomie maskatu.*

Two dollars *juaten diraz*
kaltza barrenera:
Oh, sweety, *etorri berriz*
zure mamma *ikustera.*
Tran…
zure mamma *ikustera.*

They wink at
everyone passing
on the sidewalk, and:
"Come on right in, honey!"
Tran…
Come on right in, honey!

Go inside and
right away all ready,
they start by saying:
"Gimme first my money!".
Tran…
Gimme first my money!

"How much money will you
charge me for that?"
"Besides the war taxes,
only two dollars".
Tran…
Only two dollars.

For two dollars
they lift their skirts,
they say "All right" and
chew chewing gum.
Tran…
Chew chewing gum.

The two dolars go
in the underwear,
"Oh, sweety, come again
to see your *mamma*".
Tran…
To see your *mamma*.

Pretty soon *juaten dira*
begira looking glass-*ei*
euran munak gorriturik,
begi beltzakin pretty
Tran…
begi beltzakin pretty.

Laster juaten dira
window *ondora*
kaleko people-*ari*
begia giñatzera
Tran…
begia giñatzera.

Palo Zuri juaten da
kalian erraten
come on everybody
good time *pasatzen.*
Tran…
good time *pasatzen.*

Baltza zein txinua
we don't matter who it is
dirue dakartala
come on right in, honeys.
Tran…
come on right in, honeys.

Urten kanpora eta
atzera begiratu:
we can find tomorrow,
it is number fifty two.
Tran…
it is number fifty two.

They leave pretty soon
looking in the looking glasses,
with red lips and
pretty black eyes.
Tran…
Pretty black eyes.

They will soon be gone
next to the window
to wink to
the people in the street.
Tran…
The people in the street.

White Pole goes
saying down the street:
"Come on, everybody,
let's have a good time."
Tran…
Let's have a good time.

Black or Chinese,
we don't matter who it is,
If he brings money,
"Come on right in, honeys!"
Tran…
Come on right in, honeys!

Go out, and
look back:
we can find tomorrow,
it is number fifty two.
Tran…
It is number fifty two.

Juan Marvin's cafera ta
gimme piece of apple pie
orain au jan eta
we will be feeling fine.
Tran…
we will be feeling fine.

I had amalau berso
in this paper *jarriak*
Idaho-ko estaduko
euzkaldunen berriak.
Tran…
euzkaldunen berriak.

Let's go to Juan Marvin's café,
"Gimme a piece of apple pie",
now after eating this
we will be feeling fine
Tran…
We will be feeling fine.

I had fourteen verses
placed on this paper,
news from Basque people
from the State of Idaho.
Tran…
From the State of Idaho.

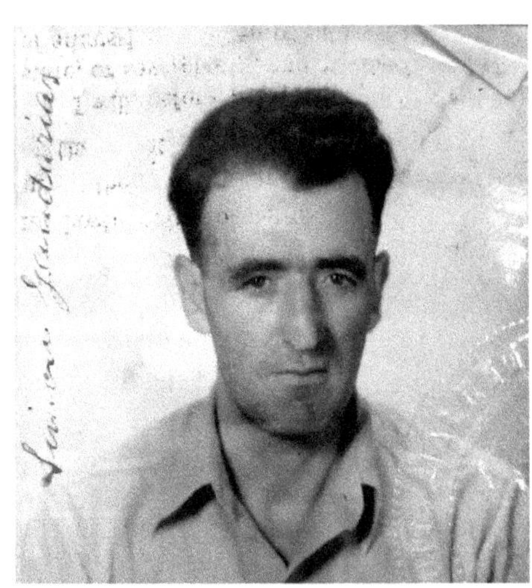

This evening after dinner we went to the home of Julio Anduiza, Jack's second son, who is married to Matilde Archabal. They don't have children. They have a very cute house on the outskirts of Boise. When we arrive, Julio and Matilde are coming from the bank where they work having just put up a Christmas tree. They also have their own little Christmas tree dotted with colored lights, set up by the window so that it can be seen from the street. This custom is very American. Outside, hanging over the door, a laurel wreath with red ribbons: it means that passersby are welcome to the house, and that they will be treated to a drink. Matilde fries us up some sausages and we eat them accompanied by wine.

Both of them, children of Basques, always speak English to each other, although they both speak Basque fluently. In their habits, in how she is not a stay-at-home housewife, etc., these two Basques constitute a completely American couple. This is the fate of emigrating races.

SR. DAMIAN TELLERIA

Silen, Samuel *Sol*, *La historia de los vascos en el Oeste.*
The History of the Basques in the West. *BMCC.*

December 20

Tonight we went to the Bristol Hotel to visit the foolish Damian Telleria. He is waiting for us in the lobby, very solemnly sitting in an armchair. He tells us that he has been fired from *Capital News*. We already knew this and the reason is that he can't write in Spanish. But he makes some wild speculations about his dismissal.

He tells us that he doesn't mind because two department stores have already offered him a job as a fabric salesman, and he also plans to edit a Basque-Spanish magazine for which he has many things written, among them the history of Basques in Aragon. That leaves us speechless.

Then we went up to his apartment to greet his wife Concha, or Conchin, as he calls her. She is also from Ea. It is stiflingly hot in the room, and Concha talks and moves as if in a dream. It seems as if she is under the influence of some drug. She talks loudly like a hysteric. She tells us that she is sick, that she has very bad lumbago, that after the heat of Manila she cannot get used to the cold of Boise. But it turns out that they came here because she couldn't stand the heat of the Philippines. After the marijuana wears off, she turns out to be a poor wretch, who is very kind, and she goes out of her way to be nice to us.

I feel very sorry for them, because, since Damian can't keep a job, these unfortunates are going to starve to death. Another tragedy of two Basque exiles.

Marcelino Aldecoa and Anastasia Arriandiaga, with their children.
Regina Aldecoa Bastida Collection. BMCC.

December 21

Today we were in Mountain Home, a small town of six thousand people one hundred miles from Boise.

A typical example of the Basque settlements that exist in southwestern Idaho is Mountain Home. Here the Basques have adapted to American life and have been important drivers of the town's progress.

As soon as the Basques arrived in Mountain Home, at the beginning of the nineteenth century, they gradually became part of the life of the community. A perfect example of a Basque settler was Jose Bengoechea—whom I have already mentioned—, who came to Mountain Home from Palo Alto, California. Another of those who first came to Mountain Home was Domingo Aldecoa (Katua), who now lives in Boise. He is from Ea and is married to Maria Pagoaga, whom I will talk about later. Katua, who now speaks English very well, tells an interesting story that shows the difficulties the early Basques had with the language.

Aldecoa, at that time, was young and had recently arrived from Bizkaia. Whenever he came down from the mountain where he was a shepherd, he ate in some of the restaurants in Mountain Home, almost all of them Chinese. "I didn't know a word of English," he tells me, "but I did my best to learn."

"And I started to learn what the people in the Chinese restaurant were speaking, until I found out that the Chinese couldn't speak English either and that what I had learned was Chinese."

Now it's very funny to hear Katua speak Chinese in his shrill voice.

Another of Domingo's brothers named Marcelino, married to Anastasia Arriandiaga lives in Boise. He has three grown sons: Luis, Domingo and Fermin.

Another Aldecoa or Aldecocea, Castor, from Ereño, married to Juana Beascoa, must have left years ago for Gernika.

The biographies of the Mountain Home Basques show the diverse directions taken by the new emigrants.

Teatro 

Starts Today—Thursday and Friday

"GUERNIKA"

Holy City of the Basque

See the destruction of Guernika and Bilbao during the Spanish War—See the evacuation of the Basque refugees. Extraordinary situations of the Children in England and France. This film is presented by the Basque Delegation to the United States by D. Manuel De La Sota, who will be present at each showing of these pictures tonight between 7 o'clock and 8 o'clock. A lecture from the stage will be given by the Basque Delegation.

DON'T FAIL TO HEAR THIS

Feature
Picture
Plus Disney
Cartoon

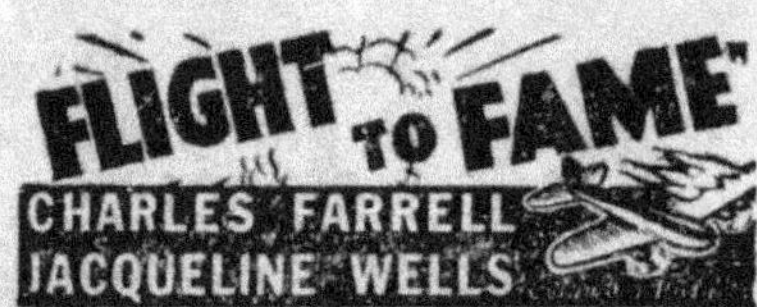

Prices:
Mat. 10c-20c
Eve. 10c-25c

Advertisement for the screening of the documentary *Guernika*, *Boise Capital News*, December 17, 1938

John Mendiola came to America as a sailor, landed in New Orleans, and sailed the Mississippi for a long time.

Juan Lugea, Higinio Cendagorta and Jose Laucirica, mentioned earlier, came from Ogden, Utah.

Pedro Gandiaga, Bengoechea's brother-in-law.

Vicente Guisasola, of Ea, came to New York at the age of ten, and most recently worked as a foreman in Shoshone for ex-Governor Gooding, who held him in high regard. He is married to Maria Camporredondo.

Domingo, Francisco and Victor Aguirre, Faustino Alzola, Norberto Ansotegui, Pedro Armaolea, Cleto Arostegui, Felisa and Mari Orbe (refugees from Gernika), Antero Arrillaga, Domingo Asumendi, Jose Barinaga, Juan Barrutia, Antonio and Andres Basteguieta, Felix Beascoechea, Luis Bengoechea, Agapito, Ignacio and Luis Bideganeta, Luis Bilbao (Bilbao Hot Spring Ranch), Juan Chacartegui, Pablo and Richard Cilloniz, Johny Cristobal, John Echebarren, Peter Echebarria, Felix Egusquiza, Jesus Elguezabal, Jose Elu, Jose Erezuma, Agustin Icazabal, Jose Idoeta, Benito and Jose Irazabal, Eulo Ituarte, Tomas Iturbe, Victor Iturri, Larre, Pedro Leaniz, Eugenio Legarreta, Leon Madarieta, Juan Mendilibar, Domingo Mendiola, Ramon Millan, Damaso, Pete and Vicente Monasterio, Blas Muniategui, Julian Olasolo, Candido Amias, Eusebio Oyarzabal, Tiburcio Pablogonan, Pedro Sengotita, Luis Solozabal, Pedro Totorica, Damian, Francisco, J.P. and Rufino Uriarte, Marciano Uriarte (a former captain who chairs the Idaho Basque Refugee Committee), Esteban and Juan Urizarbarrena, Andres, John, Jose and Juan Urquidi, Antonio, Ciriaco and Cristobal Urrutia, Justo Zabala, Gregorio Zubiaga, Joaquin and Cruz Mateo Zubizarreta, and others I don't know.

Annual Basque Dance Tonight

Prize Lamb To Be Sold At Midnight

Despite cold winds and a heavy frost Basques from as far south as Nevada and west as far as eastern Oregon arrived in Boise today to attend their annual Basque Sheepherder's ball at Riverside pavilion tonight. Because of the large crowd of Basques expected, the dance will be open only to them.

Music for American dances will be played by Merrill Tonning and his orchestra. A special attraction of the evening will be the presentation of the "aurresku" and "atsesku" danced by Mrs. Antonia Subisarreta and Mrs. Eladia Goichoechea, acompanied by Ambrosio Apariasi and Joe Anacabe.

Those attending this ninth annual affair must wear overalls or house dresses, and those not so costumed will not be admitted.

Advertisements related to the annual Basque Sheepherder's ball.
Boise Capital News, December 22, 1938.

December 22

Today there is a large influx of Basques who have come to attend the Sheepherders Ball and to see the movie *Guernika*. They are everywhere, and if not for their distinctly American outfits—not a single beret to be seen—Boise might look a bit like Durango, for instance.

We screened the film *Guernika* at the Rialto Cinema, in four showings. I gave a short explanation for the Americans. The Basques attended in large numbers and were very moved.

In the evening the Dance of the Overralls took place, the highlight of Basque social life in Boise. It has a great reputation, not only in the state of Idaho, but also in the states of Oregon, Nevada and Utah, and all the Basques make an effort to attend.

This ball, also called Sheepherders Ball is an annual celebration created by Archabal. It is obligatory for the men to wear overalls—that is the name given to the coveralls worn by the shepherds—and for the women to wear work clothes with an apron or Basque village attire. Only Basques are allowed to enter, and a few influential Americans, who are given different colored tickets, as if they were outcasts. It is worth seeing the interrogation in Basque that suspects are subjected to at the ticket office, to verify that they are legitimately Basques.

The proceeds from this dance—more than $1,000—always go to a charitable cause: to help a Basque who is laid up, for the hospitals, etc. This year the proceeds will go to Basque shelters. They usually auction a beautiful lamb and a turkey, which is always bought by a banker who has dealings with the Basques. Last year they paid $350 for the lamb and over $100 for the turkey. Archabal livens up the auction and always has two or three boys and girls ready to bid and drive up the price.

By 7 p.m. Archabal and Boni Garmendia were already going from bar to bar, dressed as villagers, encouraging Basques to come to the ball. Then, down Boise's main street passed the inaugural cavalcade of the ball: the camp wagon with Archabal in the lead and a swarm of Basques and

Sheepherder's ball at the Riverside Dance Hall, 615 S 9th Street, Boise. Ricardo Arriandiaga (with a cane), Ambrosio Apariasi (txistu) and Jose Anacabe (drum). In the background, Fermin Achabal (left) and Agustin Abadia (right). *Juanita Uberuaga Hormaechea Collection. BMCC.*

Basques with accordions and tambourines.

More than a thousand people attended the ball. The atmosphere was extraordinary. It was like Sondika on the feast of St. John.

Our friend Lola came up to us feeling very sad when we were having dinner. She told us her troubles in Basque.

"Since everyone in the house is going to the ball", she said, I have to cook dinner and take care of my nieces and nephews. I have no choice but to stay. *Jodiduta nago*.[79]

When we heard this we laughed, and she was very embarrassed, because she did not understand what was wrong. I have heard the term *jodiduta* used freely by other Basques who do not understand Spanish. By dint of using it without understanding it, it has almost become a respectable word in common parlance. It is funny to observe how the Basque assimilates incomprehensible words only by sound. Undoubtedly, the euskaldun[80] is onomatopoeic.

79. *Jodiduta nago*: I'm fucked.
80. *Euskaldun*: Basque speaker.

I am going to explain in a few words, this film of the Basques. ~~the mysterious race that lives since the most ancient times, in the French-Spanish frontier, between the Pyrenees and the sea.~~

A religious, working, peace-loving people, that have seen themselves involved in this civil war, because they have been attacked by the Fascists, in the things they most cherish: their language, their democratic institutions, their freedom. (a war that has cost our basque country the death of 50.000 persons; and the loss of liberty, property and exile to more than 200,000 people).

This picture is a vivid document showing the plight of the Basque population during this war.

Terrorized ~~tt~~ by the atrocious and mercilss

Manu de la Sota's notes for the presentation of the documentary *Guernika* in Boise.

December 23

Today the sheepherders continue with the euphoria of the binge (*matsa*, here) they started yesterday. *Arratia* played the accordion and there has been dancing.

In the evening, Anastasio Jayo and the shepherds who live in his house treated us to a succulent banquet. You can judge by the menu:

Olives and orange jelly
Noodle soup
Baked fish
Roast chicken
Squid in its ink
Beef tongue in sauce
Desserts

I continued explaining the film. In the seven o'clock showing, my attention was drawn to two young men, with crosses on their lapels, leaning back in their seats with a peevish air. Two Catholics, undoubtedly. When I finished my little speech, quoting the words: "and peace on earth to men, etc.," they uttered words of protest. They were taken to task.

Martina Bicandi's house, December 14, 1938. Clara Beitia, Jay Aldrich Uberuaga, Espe Alegria and Regina Madarieta. *BMCC*.

December 24

This morning Pete Anduiza drove us to Ontario, Oregon. First, we got gas at the Alegria Brothers Service Station. They are two brothers, Al and Henry, who speak Basque very well, although based on their uniforms and manner they are completely American. They employ one of Frank Aguirre's sons. I have not met a single Basque here who employs an American in his business.

Other Alegrias live in Boise: Espe, Felix, Ignacio, Santiago, and Simon.

The Basques of Oregon, according to data provided by L. S. Cressman, Professor of Anthropology at the University of Oregon, have settled mostly in the southern section of a line running west from Ontario on the border of Idaho and east of Steens Mountain. The Basque region of Oregon is situated on a high range that is watered by few streams, the main one being the Owyhee River. There are sparse Basque ranches scattered along its tributary, the Jordan River. The terrain is more suitable for grazing, although agriculture is also practiced along riverbanks and in areas reached by irrigation methods.

The first Basques arrived in Oregon around 1875, settling in the southwestern, rugged regions more in keeping with their character. Most came as shepherds. The Basques did not acquire ownership of the flock initially, because they had a stake in the herd. If they worked well, they earned the opportunity to come into possession of their own flock.

In eastern Oregon the main Basque establishments are in Jordan Valley and McDermitt, on the Oregon-Nevada line. There are scattered clusters in Andrews, Fields and other locations.

The Basques have contributed to the life of the nation with their herding expertise, with their honesty and tenacity, and to some extent with their architectural style. Although their houses are not the same as those of Euzkadi, they are somewhat similar. Some are made of stone, with red roofs and blue or green windows. This style is not typical of Oregon.

The language of an immigrant group is a factor that contributes to the greater or lesser assimilation of the group to the new environment, making it difficult when it is very different, as is the case with Basque. The Basques stubbornly preserve it, although they also speak English. And it should be noted that they avoid a conversation in English as soon as they believe that their pronunciation is going to be a cause for amusement.

When speaking of the difficulty Basques have with English, an anecdote is cited of a Basque who went to a neighboring ranch to buy chickens to start a poultry farm, but asked for hens instead. Once the deal was finalized, the rancher began to put the hens in a basket, and then the very agitated Basque began to shout: "No, No! Some bull hens! I want bull hens!"

The first occupation of the Basques in Oregon is that of farmer and the second, innkeeper. In any small town inhabited by Basques there are two or three boarding houses run by Basques. There is a great rivalry among these hotels, and the guests take part in the rivalry, forming as many factions as there are inns.

The second generation follows the norms of American life. Mrs. Kathryn Claypool, Malheur County school inspector, wrote to me:

> We have several Basque teachers in Malheur County who have been raised in this region, who have been educated in our teacher training schools and are working to our complete satisfaction. Nearly all of them teach exclusively in English-speaking places, displaying great empathy for the children, whether American or not.

Anthony Yturri, the Ontario lawyer, tells me that, in order to study criminality among Basques, he looked into the court records of Malheur County. He was able to deduce that in this county there is no lawbreaking problem involving Basques. Proportionally, the number of Basques arrested is very small. There are many Basques residing in Malheur County, but those booked for law violations are relatively few. The records do not show a particular crime involving Basques. Very few serious crimes have been perpetrated by them. Most are minor offenses as befits people who have various occupations, such as trespassing, speeding, illegal sale of alcoholic beverages, etc. The most frequently violated law for them is the one concerning the abuse of alcoholic beverages, but they do not exceed those of other nationalities.

When Basques have to stand trial, they do not present any difficulty, because they never try to defend themselves by inventing falsehoods. In general, they are frank, and do not try to evade responsibility.

Oregon Basques live more or less modestly and seem content with their lot. What Americans consider necessities are luxuries to them, although they appreciate the modern advances that make life more comfortable. They still remember when they worked in the garden, eating just enough to keep body and soul together. They realize how fortunate they are in their new life, and are content with simple but hearty food, and dislike ostentation in their clothing.

A very Basque quality, according to Yturri, is how jealous they are of the fortunes of other Basques. They will do anything to be considered on an equal footing with the richest. There is no sacrifice they would not make for their children to have everything that the offspring of wealthy families possess. This jealousy is only toward Basques, not toward people of other nationalities. If a merchant wishes to promote merchandise, the best thing he can do is to sell it to the richest Basque in the area, and soon the other Basques will come to buy it. It is this pride that motivates them to send their children to universities, even if they do not have the means to do so. As the English say, "They must keep up with the Joneses."

Another of the most salient characteristics of the Oregon Basques is their tenacious adherence to their moral traditions. The private code governing relations between the sexes, etc., is very strict, and a violation soon makes one an outcast. In this matter liberties and vagueness are not permitted. The older generation has accepted modern American ways with hesitation and out of fear of adverse comments. Basque women did not adopt the fashion of short hair until a long time had passed and most of them still keep the traditional bun. For a Basque mother, a woman smoking is cause for scandal. Young women who smoke never do so in the presence of their parents. Basque women do not like liquor; the most they drink is a glass of wine with a meal.

On the other hand, and this seems a contradiction in terms, the Basques are very free in their conversations with women. They have no qualms about saying things that would scandalize a foreigner. This is due to the fact that when they are said in Basque they are not considered rude.

The Basque in general, unlike the American, does not like to appear at society events with his wife; he does not believe that this is a demonstration of affection toward his wife. From the moment they marry, they accept as a *fait accompli* that the wife works for her husband. As the father dominates in the family, the son obeys as soon as his father says a word. The father's word is the household law for all.

Mr. L. S. Cressman, who has studied the customs of the Basques of Oregon, observes that since the Spanish war began, both Basque men and women have been going to church less, because, he says, they surmise that the church bears a large share of the blame for the Spanish tragedy.

The Basques of Oregon continue to maintain the culinary tradition of their elders. One of the most picturesque sights is to see a Basque family devoted entirely to making chorizo, which, by the way, has become very popular among Americans in this region.

The Basques are very sociable: when they get together they play the guitar and sing songs from their homeland, but especially Spanish and South American songs. Although they like to have fun playing cards, they are not gamblers; however, there are a few in Oregon who make a living at cards. Men play *mus* and women play *brisca* when they gather in homes.

There is a saying according to which one can be sure that if a Basque is asked to do something, he will do it immediately or will make every effort to do it. Basques are excellent workers. They work for the boss with the same enthusiasm as if it were for themselves. They are not of the opinion that they should do as little as possible to muddle through. A Basque would rather be accused of anything rather than of laziness.

Basques pay their debts religiously, especially when the creditor belongs to another nationality. They will rarely haggle over the amount of the debt. A Basque will rarely go into a business that is beyond his means.

The State employee in charge of paying relief allowances informs us that, during these past three years, only two Basques have filed applications for payment. One was a young shepherd suffering from spotted fever, who later repaid every penny spent on him. The other was an old bachelor who had to be given relief for three weeks.

During the last three years there were sixteen hundred applications for relief in that department, but none were Basque. There were two hundred requests for old age relief, but none of them from Basques. Out of forty requests for destitute children none were from Basques. There has not been a single Basque who has sought to enlist in CCC, the Civilian Conservation Corps, a government institution that employs unemployed young men in public jobs. The reason could be that Basques possess an incredible capacity for finding work.

The very idea of relief seems contrary to their concept of society. Very few need pecuniary help, and those who do need it get it from relatives and friends. The sense of responsibility of the Basques towards their needy relatives is deeply rooted among the Basques. In accordance with their sociological views, the duty to help the sick and elderly is incumbent on their relatives and not on the State. If relatives cannot, then it is their friends who take care of them.

At school Basque children are among the most advanced. Since they are accustomed to obeying at home, they are very disciplined at school. The American children treat the Basques in the schools with a certain degree of reserve. This is manifested not by demonstrations of contempt but by an air of protectiveness and condescension. The tendency of the Basques to group together with those of the same nationality also manifests itself in school life. And it is not that the Americans do not accept them, but that it is they who do not accept the Americans.

Second-generation Basques have become so Americanized that it is difficult to distinguish them from those of other nationalities. Young Basques who still speak Basque do so with a different accent. They have lost the rigid conventions of their elders.

Anthony Yturri, the Ontario lawyer, cites the following people as representative of the Basque race in Oregon:

Domingo Yturri

He was born in Errigoiti in 1882. He was one of the children of a humble family of five boys and six girls who worked daily in the orchards and fields, praying to heaven all the while that the grain would grow and that the fruit would be protected. At the age of six, Domingo entered the Errigoiti school. However, as he was one of the eldest in the family, from early childhood he was already considered one of the breadwinners of the family. Consequently, his education ended four years after it began.

By age ten, Domingo had learned all the farm chores and how to take care of livestock.

At the age of thirteen, the responsibilities that had weighed on Domingo had made him a man. Tired of working the land, he embarked on a ship as a kitchen scullian with the idea of sending money home to his family. Domingo worked conscientiously, saving every penny. At the end of the first year, the captain gave him $16, which was the amount agreed upon. One of the most transcendental moments of his life was the day he went to Bilbao to send his father the money, dressed in a new suit that the captain had given him. The father's pride was no less than that of the son. Domingo at the age of fourteen was already a hero among his siblings.

In the following years he slowly worked his way up until he became a cook. But, tired of the sea and wanting to try his luck, he landed in New York, thinking of the gold mines in the West that he had heard about from the Basques in his town.

Always thinking of sending money to his family and with seven dollars in his pocket, he came to Delamar and walked eight miles to find work in Silver City. There he started as a shepherd and then worked in the mines for four years.

And then the time came to get married. The decision was a difficult one: either to marry an Irish woman he liked or to marry a love he left behind in Errigoiti. But, always obedient to his father who admonished him at the idea of marrying a foreigner, he returned to Euzkadi in 1907 and married the Basque woman, both of them returning to Silver City, from where they went to Delamar, establishing a hotel there, which provided him with some money, as there were quite a few Basques in the mines.

In 1910, when the Delamar mines closed, they moved to Jordan Valley, Oregon, where they opened a boarding house and a store.

In 1918 he lost his wife at the same time that he took up arms to serve his new homeland in the war.

By 1919, Domingo is already a prominent citizen of Jordan Valley and his good name is known throughout the surrounding states.

A few years after the death of his first wife, he remarried. The children were proud of their father, but the stepmother entered the family without friction and became a real mother. Domingo, a naturalized citizen, raised the family in a modern way; the children, educated in colleges and universities, occupy important positions. His dealings with people of different nationalities and the success obtained in his new American life positioned him with a different attitude from that of his ancestors in relation to his children, whom he was pleased to see leaving home to follow different professions.

As for marriage bonds, since his life was associated with that of American citizens, he wanted his children to marry people from this country. Since they were not educated in the Basque way, Domingo believes they would be considered strangers in the land of their ancestors.

Had he been a Hispanic citizen he would have sided with the Loyalists; as a true American, he has democratic leanings and ideas.

English is spoken predominantly in the family, because he wants to educate his children in an American atmosphere; but also Basque and Spanish, and he does not want them to lose touch with their Basque ancestors, whose virtues of modesty, industriousness and sobriety he wises to transmit to his family.

Joe Zatica

He was born in Ispaster, August 1st, 1893. The son of farmers, he dedicated himself to the family occupation in the first years of his life.

When attracted by the news that his friends sent him from Jordan Valley, he set out to come to the USA. He obtained the permission of his parents, on the condition that he return home very soon, and with the promise of employment made by Justo Corta, a friend of the family.

Justo Corta and Maria Ocamica with seven of their children at the Soldier Creek ranch, near Jordan Valley (Oregon).

Soon the boy was in New York, where he left immediately for Jordan Valley, and from there to the countryside, with the responsibility for 2,000 sheep at the age of eighteen. Fond of the trade, he did not go down to the small town for four years, saving all he earned. When the owner decided to grant him a vacation, he stayed only three days in Jordan Valley and did not return for another two years. During this period of six years, he did not have the opportunity to learn much English; he did, however, acquire the wealth of expressions with which the cowboys used to scold him, when he was careless about entering their property with his sheep.

Determined to establish himself on his own, he said goodbye to his employer and bought twelve hundred head of select sheep with the savings accumulated over six years; but the general economic conditions of the country were not favorable to him, and after three years he found himself without sheep and with a debt of $10,000, thus ending his career as a shepherd with this unfortunate event.

Intent on repaying the debt—aggravated by the additional burden of a wife and child—he obtained from friends the money to open a poolroom, which proved fortunate. He supplemented the quaint English he learned as a cowboy with the lessons he received from a teacher and from his dealings with the patrons of his establishment. After nine or ten years he was the owner of a very prosperous business and the father of six children.

But as the children grew up, he felt he should leave the poolroom behind, with great regret indeed; he transferred the flourishing company, after he had settled all his obligations and debts, and started a new transportation business. Hauling sheep, vegetables, coal, wool, etc., was a resounding economic success, superior in profitability to his previous enterprises.

Today Joe has five children in school, two of whom are attending high school, preparing for university studies, and he has made a serious and attractive home in the USA, whose nationality he has acquired.

Long before becoming an American citizen he demonstrated his democratic sentiments; but currently he is an enthusiastic supporter of the Democratic Party, and reveals an astonishing knowledge of the politics and economic problems of the American government.

In the peninsular conflict, he considers himself a loyalist. As a Catholic, he dislikes the attitude of some members of the clergy, although he recognizes that he has not been very observant since his arrival in America. He says that his departure from religious practice is due to his lack of knowledge of the English language when he arrived here, which prevented him from understanding the Catholic priest. Moreover, his solitary life in the countryside made him accustomed to fulfilling his Catholic obligations privately.

With the Basque homeland, he retains no ties other than the sentimental ones of an indelible memory of the country's festivals and dances, views on religion, morals and family discipline—above all he is indignant that women smoke, drink and are so nonchalant—as well as loyalty to traditional cuisine.

Like so many of his brethren, who are not at all eager to get to know more American regions and have never left Jordan Valley, this Basque has only traveled in a very limited circle: he was once in Omaha (Nebraska) when he brought his first batch of lambs in a boxcar.

In his loyalty to the USA, Joe does not differ from the other Basques; but he does differ in his ardent adherence to the Democratic Party, since the majority of the others support the Republican Party.

Then we went to visit Tony Yturri in his office. Tony, who is the son of Domingo mentioned above, is a perfect representative of the young Basques of the new generation. He is a young man in his twenties, completely Americanized. He studied at the University of Oregon and is now practicing law. He has great enthusiasm for all things Basque, and has written some interesting articles about the Basques in Oregon law journals. He is proud to belong to our race and eagerly asks us for books and documents to brief him on the Basque question.

He speaks with indignation of some young Basques here who are ashamed of being Basque, and cites the case of a certain Egurrola, a wealthy rancher living near Boise, who does not even want to be called Basque.

"Spaniards," he says, "when they want to settle here, they say they are Basques. On the other hand, these Basques insist on saying they are Spaniards. It is absurd".

Next we visited Simon Gandarias whose poems I have already transcribed. He has a magnificent Bar called the Elk Cigar Store which is one of the best in Ontario. He runs some very funny advertisements for his business:

Txomin Bedaru eta Ezkerra *bi kiputza'kin gorratuz* *ibili dira iru urtian* *musian ezin apurtuz.*	Txomin Bedaru and Ezkerra competing with two Gipuzkoans, they have been for three years not being able to win at mus.
Ardau onakin ondo beterik *asi diraz bart gogoratuz* *bana kiputzak bete zituzen* *euren sabelak tzorizuz.*	Well filled with good wine, they started enthusiastically, but the Gipuzkoans filled their bellies with chorizo.
If you want to buy wine *Gabon egunetan,* we have imported klase guztietan. With Rioja and Claret maian ganietan, enjoyment with family *lengo legietan*	If you want to buy wine at Christmas time, we have imported all kinds of wine. With Rioja and Claret on all the tables, the family enjoys itself according to the old laws.

We all had lunch at Jack Echaniz's house; he has a small hotel, The Echanis Boarding House, exclusively for Basque sheepherders. We eat with them.

Here is a short list of some of the Basques living in Ontario:

Basilio Aguirre, Antonio Arescurrinaga, Domingo Corta, Benito and Ignacio Echaniz, Gaspar Ibarzabal, George Iturri, Cecilio Madariaga, Segundo Oar, Genar Plaza (Bedarona), Santiago Uriarte, Joe Zarraonandia.

We spent *Gabon*[81] quietly in our house having a sumptuous dinner and without longing for home too much. After dinner we went to Archabal's

81. *Gabon*: Christmas Eve.

Jose "Joe" Zatica and Ines Bilbao. *Julie Yzaguirre Moore Collection. BMCC.*

house where about twenty men of the family were gathered. Drinks, dancing, singing, and so on.

Later I went to Midnight Mass with Julio Anduiza and his wife. Then we went to the Ball that the Association of Basque Women held at Belaustegui's house.

199.

200.

201.

202.

203.

204.

205.

206.

207.

December 25

This afternoon we were at the beautiful ranch of Isidro Madarieta *(Urkiya)*.

In the morning there was a challenge pelota match that attracted a big boncho of Basques. Anton and Zabal[82] won.

82. Antonio de Irala and John Zabal (Zabalandicoechea).

Slayers Denied Release

The board refused to free Arley Latham, principal in the "Craters of the Moon" murder, who has served 14 years of a 25 year to life sentence. It marked the seventh refusal of a state pardon board. He was accused of killing a man and throwing the body in the Craters of the Moon in Butte county. H. A. Reed, with a similar sentence, who has served six years, also was denied freedom.

Pedro Arescurrinaga, charged with an Owyhee county murder, convicted of voluntary manslaughter, also was refused clemency. He has served a year of a 5 to 10 year sentence.

Pedro Arescurrinaga's picture of his police record. Below, brief news about his request for freedom. *Idaho Statesman*, October 1938.

December 26

I met a very picturesque Basque shepherd: Marcelino Maortua *(Garai Txiki)*, a famous *aurreskulari*, ceremonial *aurresku* dancer. Short, sallow, and old, he has a Charlie Chaplin mustache and a goatee. He talks wildly and it seems that he is a bit crazy. When I told him that he looks very handsome with his goatee, he went to have his portrait taken and sent us fifty photos. Apparently, despite his years, he spends his money freely and doesn't send a penny to his family.

In the afternoon we visited the penitentiary where Arescurrinaga is held. The prisoners could not be any better off; they have soccer fields, a band, cinema, radio. The cells are good; they go in at 4.30 pm and stay until 8 am the next day. The dining room is beautiful and is decorated with a Christmas tree and other Christmas accessories. There are also some religious pictures hanging on the walls. While some handsome young prisoners are arranging the tables, the radio is playing. Twenty-five prisoners are at home spending Christmas on special leave. The bakery is magnificent. There is a long, narrow stone building they call the dungeon, where they put the fractious prisoners who refuse to work. A Black man has been in it for two months. He has no light except what comes in through the vent, is on bread and water, and sleeps on the floor. They took him out for Christmas, and since he refused to work again, he is still in the dark.

They don't let us talk to the Basque, and we only see him from a distance.

After dinner I was talking with Anduiza and Aldecoa about the first Basques who came here. They tell me that the first was a captain, Jose Antonio de Erquiaga, from Ea, married to a Chilean woman, who landed in San Francisco. He brought Jose Manuel *Sendo* Ugarriza and Natxitxu Badiola.[83]

Damian Telleria Sr., *Atabal*,[84] also arrived around 1870. Erquiaga must have arrived around 1839.

83. Mateo Badiola Anduiza

84. Julian Telleria Aldamizgogeaskoa.

Delegates Return To New York

Basque delegates to the United States, Manuel de la Sota, Antonio de Irala and John Zabal, will return to New York within a few days after two weeks spent in Idaho.

All three came to Boise because of the large Basque colony here, most extensive in the United States.

"Few in Europe and in the east realize how many thousands of Basques there are in Idaho," de la Sota said. "They are perhaps the happiest and most contented Basques on earth now that those in Spain have been ravaged by war."

Zabal is connected with a travel agency in New York, the V. Aguirre Travel Bureau, 82 Bank street.

De la Dota and Irala are at the Hotel New Weston. They expect to be in France within a few months. The elder de la Sota was owner of Vizcaya's greatest shipping enterprise, operating out of Bilbao with 87 vessels. Most of these have been confiscated or destroyed by Fascists.

De la Sota brought to Boise the motion picture, "Guernika," seen by many Boiseans this week at the Rialto theater. It depicts life in Basque Spain, and the destruction wrought by war.

All three Basque delegates were guests Thursday night at the Sheepherders' ball at Riverside pavilion.

De la Sota and De Irala announce their return to New York.
Boise Capital News, December 24, 1938.

December 27

This afternoon we went to visit an Elguezabal who has been bedridden for eight years. She and her sisters are from Algorta. Here they claim that she got that way because of a scare "she took" one day when a burglar broke into her house; but it soon becomes apparent that she has ankylosing rheumatism.

All of them are very good patriots. The husband of one of them, Basilio Iriondo, from Gallarta, is one of the best Basques we have encountered here. When he sees us he weeps tears of emotion. He and his wife work together as sheepherders in the mountains and the wife shows us pictures of herself on horseback.

Mateo Arregui's Delamar Hotel, in Boise.

December 28

Tonight we attended the Ball held at Mateo Arregui's Hotel. As with all Basque dances, it was very lively.

55.
Barrena Eustaquio
C/o A. Belaustegui
Boise Idaho.
56.
Barrenechea Juan
Mendaro Gui, Spain
57.
Basabe Antonio
P.O. BOX 427
Emmett Idaho.
58.
Basabe Artia
Emmett Idaho
59.
Basabe Teodoro
P.O. BOX 543
Boise Idaho.
60.
Bastarrechea Hilario
202- therd St South
Twin Falls Idaho.
61.
Basterrechea Juan
C/o jack Boyle
Rupert Idaho.
62.
Basterrechea Toribio
Grand View Idaho.
63.
Ramon Bastida

December 29

Tonight we went to Emmett to attend a party in our honor organized by the Basques there, led by Jose Villanueva Amezketa. Here they call it a "card party" because you start by playing cards and end up dancing.

The festival venue is small, with a huge stove in the middle that gives off a blistering heat. There are groups of women, children, and men playing cards.

Irala, always a lover of the fair sex, sat at a table surrounded by girls with ponytails and played a Chinese game unknown to him. I played the role of *txartero*, dealer in a game of *mus*. Then, very ceremoniously, we were treated to sandwiches and coffee, which had the effect of lifting the spirits of the event. Two lively musicians, *txirripitas*, played the accordion and the dancing was unbridled. A prominent figure was the Guipuzcoan *Txartxa*, who laughed raucously. We met a Zabala, about twenty years old, who, although born here, is an enthusiastic Basque.

Here is a list of names of Basques in Emmett that I have been able to note down, in addition to others that I have mentioned above:

> Andres Arriaga, Agustin and Anastasio Arrizabalaga, Cipriano, Francisco and Felipe Barruetabeña, Antonio, Gregorio and Andresa Basabe, Eugenio Bicandi, Frank and Jose Bilbao, Luis Ciarsolo, Bonifacio, Fernando, Julio and Pedro Eiguren; Eusebio Foruria, Frank and Simon Galdos, Francisco Garechanaga, Escolastico and Felipe Jayo, Manuel Laradogoitia, Antonio Malaxechebarria, Juan Olabe, Eustaquio Sarriugarte, Jesus Ugalde, Domingo and Pedro Uberuaga, Jose, Tomas and Martin Zabala, Miguel Zubizarreta.

Founders of the American Basque Fraternity Auxiliary: Escolastica Arriandiaga Ondarza, Antonia Yribar Ysursa, Carmen Maruri Gabica and Carmen Jayo Luque.
Juanita Uberuaga Collection. BMCC.

December 30

Tonight's dinner was at Isidro Madarieta's house, a loyal and friendly man. A group of friends attended, all from Lekeitio and Ondarroa. His daughters, the eldest married to Pete Anduiza, served the meal. Isidro, whom everyone calls Urkiya, is from Ispaster and is married to Isidora Osa. It was the best served meal of all:

Sausage and olives
Rice with bits and pieces
Fried hake
Beef tongue in tomato sauce
Tenderloin
Stuffed turkey
Salad
Flan and pastry

After coffee and drinks there were nuts and lots of singing. Then we attended the ball organized by the Basque American Confraternity for the benefit of Basque refugees. The dance, which was the most elegant of all the dances we have attended, was in the ballroom of the Eagles Lodge. It is the first dance here where I have seen the Basque flag next to the American flag. They played some pretty good ladies' jazz, including three Basque women. Amoto's daughter sang American songs at the microphone with a lot of flair.

Basques Speak Saturday

Making a farewell address to the Basques of southwest Idaho Don Manuel de la Sota and Don Antonio de Irala will speak over KFXD Saturday afternoon at 5:45 o'clock.

De la Sota and de Irala, official Basque delegates to the United States, have been in Idaho for the past three weeks.

They will speak Saturday in English and Basque.

Boise Capital News, December 30, 1938.

December 31

This afternoon we spoke on the radio[85] to say goodbye to the Basques here. Once again they were greatly moved by the speech in Basque. Hearing the language they thought was confined to a remote corner of the mountains coming through the air and coming out of a device really amazes them. Moreover, it reminds them of their distant home, their childhood memories and, above all, their mother's voice. In addition, Anton delivers his speech with good intonation and speaks confidently into the microphone.

We celebrated *Gabon Zar*[86] with Txomin Aldecoa's family. There was Txomin, his wife, his three daughters and his two sons. The refined influence of his daughters was immediately noticeable. The food was not as "overloaded" as in the other Basque homes. In addition, the ladies were seated at the table with us. One of the boys first made a cocktail which was served to us in silver-plated goblets.

All the food revealed American influences; first a fruit cocktail, and one of those American salads composed of lettuce and a kind of jelly; then they gave us some very well prepared squids as a tribute to Basque cuisine. I noticed that the young ladies did not eat any and were disgusted at the sight of them. The first course was traditional turkey with all the trimmings. For dessert, ice cream and a collection of pastries and sweets that reveal the existence of a good pastry chef.

The table was tastefully decorated, and in the fireplace a special wood burned that produces colorful flames.

This family provides an opportunity to study the evolution of transplanted Basques. The father remains a Basque villager and the refinements he accepts at his wife's direction seem artificial to him. The wife, a Mutrikan, strives to be a lady of rank, but does so with a certain timidity, and although she figures in the social life of Boise, she hardly

85. The farewell message was broadcast on the KFXD station at 5:45 p.m.
86. *Gabon Zahar*: New Year's Eve.

knows any English. It is obvious that she is a woman of character and has become independent of the *fait accompli* that the Archabal clan is first among the Boise Basques. However, she is Archabal's sister-in-law.

Their daughters are refined, cultured and very pleasant. The eldest, Maurina, is a Spanish teacher in Buhl. Lately she has been traveling in Europe and it quickly becomes apparent that Italy has left its mark on her. However, she is interested in all things Basque and writes in Basque accurately. She is smart and with such an independent spirit. Another of the daughters is studying in Salt Lake.

The two sons in their twenties are very witty and are Americanized after having had an education. They work on their father's sheep farms.

Abarrategui and his wife also attended the meal. He is the son of a woman whom some call the Bascongada, who has a boarding house in *La Arboleda*. He has money, lives in a very nice house and is a patriot. He retains his independence from the rest of the Boise *andikis*[87] and criticizes them for their selfishness.

87. *Andiki*: big shot.

January 1, 1939

Today Jose Villanueva and Arratia from Emmett had lunch with us. Then there was a great challenge match: Anton and Pete Anduiza vs. Mallabia and Erquiaga. All the Basques from Boise came to the match and the court looked like the Astelena *fronton* in Eibar. There were bets, but Anton and Pete won the match by a landslide.

After the match we had a few drinks with Txomin Aldecoa, Marciano Uriarte and Lopez, the shoemaker. The conversation was regarding the Board of the Mutual Aid Society, of which Jack Anduiza is the secretary and go-to guy. All agreed that the two societies should be merged immediately. Suddenly Juana, Jack's wife, came out of the kitchen and with angry shouting started to insult Txomin Aldecoa, telling him that he is a henpecked husband and that his wife is the one who wears the pants in the family. We had to leave the gathering in haste.

In the afternoon, Lopez, the shoemaker, who is Villanueva's father-in-law, took us to his house to meet his wife, a former maid of the Goyarrola household, who overwhelms us by talking about the "aristocracy" of Bilbao. It is incredible how a woman who must have earned three or four *duros* a month, and must have been humiliated, still retains a true adoration for her "masters." The spirit of loyalty of the Basques is truly extraordinary.

In the evening we dine with the Ysursa family. The sheepherders continue celebrating the New Year and continue drinking whiskey in an incredible way.

Ezquerra is an old shepherd, a loafer who, when he is not working, gets drunk every day and dances like a spinning top. Ezquerra recounts the advice his father gave him when he left: "Never tell a lie, and don't always tell the truth."

Basilio Iriondo, the friendly fellow from Gallarta, who barely speaks Spanish, explains to me his work with the sheep. I will transcribe it below just as he explained it to me:

> I begin my information about our work on the sheep, from the day we gather the rams with the herds or flocks, which is approximately

EN HONOR DEL SENOR DE LA SOTA, SE CONGREGAN LOS VASCOS DE BOISE

Con motivo de la visita que hicieron a Boise Idaho, los señores de la Sota (Manuel y Ramón) y el Señor Irala, delegados vascos en Norte América, en diversos lugares hubo concentraciones vascas, que ofrecieron a nuestros amigos fervorosas expresiones de adhesión y afecto. En la fotografía aparecen rodeados por más de un centenar de vascos residentes en aquella zona.

Newspaper clipping about the gathering of Basques at the Anduiza's fronton (619 Grove Street) on December 31, 1938. *Juanita Uberuaga Hormaechea Collection. BMCC.*

the 24th of November, which is done in the lowlands, halfway between the desert (winter site) and the reserve (summer site).

To each flock of approximately nineteen hundred ewes we put forty rams, where we leave them for thirty five days, more or less. When separating the rams we usually separate from each band the ewes that are skinny, taking them to the dry grass of the ranch, where they are kept until the winter is over and spring begins to show its strength, growing vegetation.

The others stay in the desert during the winter, grouped in herds of about two thousand head, attended by a shepherd and another person we call "the camp tender," who is in charge of finding the best pastures and bringing water and provisions for the camp, that is to say, the place where he and the shepherd camp with the herd, once the day's work is over.

The camp tender is supplied by the company with a team of horses and a saddle horse, which are maintained with secate[88] and barley, which the owner arranges to provide. They use the cart-box as a manger.

The camp tender usually goes with the wagon to fetch water from the nearest river for their own use and for the horses. This is done in fifty gallon barrels, three or four of which the camp tender usually has. As the winter is usually very cold in these deserts, they load the wagon with chunks of ice which they then melt.

When it snows it is usually easier, because they melt the snow in buckets over the fire. In snowy weather the sheep also have a better time quenching their thirst, as long as the depth of the snow does not exceed four to six inches, depending on the size of the pasture. When there is no snow, the shepherd has to take the flock every two or three days to water at the nearest river, which is usually about three miles from the sheepfold, returning to it for the night.

The shepherd usually brings some food to eat at noon, which he prepares in the morning before the camp tender leaves, while gathering and chopping wood to make a fire.

The camp tender usually stays two or three days in each field, which

88. *Secate*: dry grass.

helps the shepherd a lot, because in addition to being very appreciated company in the solitude of the desert, he cooks in abundance to leave the pots full of food when he moves on to another field.

When the shepherd is in doubt as to whether any sheep have gone astray, he counts the bells, which number six or eight in each flock, and the black sheep, which usually number between twenty and forty. If any of these markers are missing, the camp tender will look for the stray sheep.

When the snow is too deep and prevents the sheep from grazing, the owners break up the roads by pulling horses or using trucks in order to herd the sheep along the roads.

Once the flock is on the road, with favorable weather they usually walk ten to fifteen miles per day, and at night they are usually brought to the dry grass.

We usually get our food in the morning before leaving and at noon, when there is time, otherwise we carry our provisions in our knapsacks.

Once we get to the ranches, our job is to bring the secate from the stakes (the name given in this area to the pile of secate, which consists of several tons) in specially prepared carts (generally eight- by sixteen-foot flat carts), in which we load about two tons at a time, and we widen the sheep away from the cart by pulling with forks, as the cart moves, and taking care to distribute the secate wide enough, so that the sheep can comfortably fit in the rows formed in this way.

We usually stay in the secate until spring breaks, as I explained before.

Shearing starts around the end of March. For this, our company has pens in the desert where twelve machine shearers shear about fifteen hundred sheep a day. This wool, in sacks of approximately three hundred metric tons, is transported to the railroad in trucks.

As they are sheared, the herds go out grazing to the spring hills, or hills where they lamb. This begins around April 20, and is considered the hardest period for the worker and the most costly for the owners. This is how we begin: As previously mentioned, the camp tender arrives with two flocks and each one with a shepherd (or sheepherder); the owners calculate beforehand or by experience where the lambing might begin; taking into account the abundance or scarcity of pasture, as well as the weather and the possibilities for changing weather, and forming an imaginary line between the two flocks, the camp tender sets the direction of each one of them and orders the camp to be placed approximately two miles from where the flocks are, to which he brings two or three more men to assist in the lambing and has someone there to cook for all of them. This camp is made up of sheep wagons and enough tents to house the personnel.

From that day on, each shepherd sleeps near his flock in a small tent, and his gear consists of a bed and some clothes to change into, in case he gets wet, and some kitchen utensils—in general, a coffee pot, a plate, cup, spoon and fork, a can of milk, sugar, coffee, (they are given a donkey with its proper packsaddle, saddlebags and rope to move this equipment); a saddle horse, a hook to catch sheep, and rope to tether any sheep that may need to be tied up.

The other workers all retire to the main field, which is conveniently located so that both sides can be helped equally, and therefore placed on the line mentioned above. In the morning, while the cook prepares lunch, her husband (for if possible they usually find a suitable couple) is in charge of giving grain to all the horses (in general, each man is provided with a saddle horse) and saddling them; he calls them in time so that all the workers can reach their respective flocks before they leave the sheepfold (that is, from where they have slept that night), for they usually leave at the break of day.

Once the shepherd has broken camp and loaded the donkey, everyone waits for the sheep to come out – those that have had lambs that night usually stay behind, since they cannot walk yet – and between two or three men we herd all the sheep that do not have lambs towards the flock, making sure to leave each sheep with its own little lamb or lambs (this is a job that requires a lot of experience). Once we have removed all the ewes that have little lambs from the flock, we join the flock and look carefully, since almost every time we remove them, we usually find some mother that abandons her young. So with the hook that each one of us carries, we grab one or more of them and, with a quarter-inch (thick) rope four feet long, we tie her to a bush by the front leg, and looking carefully in the lambing group, we find that one of the little lambs is neglected or orphaned, and, bringing this one alongside the ewe, tied up, after giving it a few suckles of milk several times, we usually find that she cares for it more. If she doesn't, having them together for a day and a night is usually enough for her to adopt the little lamb, and she can be released.

I forgot to mention that one of us is in charge of going three or four times a day to where they are tied up, and we make the lambs drink a little bit of milk and they get strong.

During the day, we take care of the flock so that it runs as little as possible and covers little ground; but, nevertheless, giving them enough freedom to graze as much as necessary, because that way those with lambs are kept closer together during the day and it is easier to take care of them and protect them from dangerous animals.

At about eleven o'clock in the morning, the shepherd who slept with the flock goes to the camp with his horse to eat and returns as soon as possible, so that his helper can do the same. At about 5 o'clock in the afternoon the shepherd goes to dinner, and when he returns he brings with him some food for breakfast the next morning. The rest of us, paying a visit to the lambs born to the ewes that are tied up, retire to the main camp after dark, and after grooming our respective horses, we have supper. And, it is usually 12:30 at night when we go to bed.

In the first few days few lambs are born, but the number of straggling lambings increases to one hundred eighty in twenty-four hours; so, as they are born and stay behind, the person in charge of them makes sure that groups do not mix with each other, until the lambs are four or five days old. For in too large groups it is difficult for some of the weaker lambs to find their mothers, and therefore, the most experienced man of the group, judging by the age, robustness of the lambs, and the needed shepherds in the vicinity, proportionally makes larger and larger groups, until the number of ewes reaches about five hundred, which he usually puts together to form half a summer flock. After completing two half flocks that are in lambing, leaving with the ewes that have just lambed, one man for each one thousand or eleven hundred with their respective camp and camp tender, so that the two are in charge of doing everything possible to fatten the lambs and protect them from dangerous animals.

Then comes the branding or castration of the lambs, which is usually done at approximately one to two weeks of age. It is usually one of the most interesting parts of the lambing, in which the lambs are counted, and all the workers strive to save the highest percentage, which is where our worth is appreciated. There are usually some who are experts and make a notable difference every year. But, as I said before, the groups that work with the other flocks put all their effort into getting closer to these experts in number of lambs.

The lamb marking is usually carried out in the following way: the company usually has corrals at appropriate points, where we take the sheep, which with their lambs are prepared in herds of about five hundred, as I have said before. There the owner or foreman, with two or three other men, bring in a group of sheep and lambs, which are prepared ahead of time; then on one side of this section, above the door—which is approximately three and a half feet high—we place a board that serves as a table and the castrator—usually the owner or the foreman—outside the door. The workers bring the lambs to the table one by one, while he, with his knife, castrates the males and docks their tails about an inch and a half from the body (some cut a mark on the ear, to distinguish them in case they get mixed in with those of other companies) and also stamp their backs with a stamp smeared with paint, on which one can read the number of the flock they belong to. Once the sheep in this section are also stamped, they are released to another adjoining pen, and the whole flock passes through group by group.

In general, it takes about two hours to mark a flock of half a herd—an average of five hundred to six hundred ewes with as many other lambs. It should be noted that the ewe lambs only have their tails cut off, their ears are marked and stamped with paint, as previously mentioned for the ram lambs.

Once the lambing operations have been completed, all the lambs have been marked and the flocks have been arranged in the way they are supposed to be (which is usually about six weeks from the beginning of lambing), each camp tender and his shepherds are in charge of fattening the lambs.

Since in early July we usually enter the reserve (that is, the mountains that the sheep-owning companies lease from the government until the beginning of October), we work with the flocks, and at the end of August we set aside the best rams, sending them to the railroad by truck, to drive them to market. These sheep usually weigh about seventy five pounds each.

The thinner ones are transported to the highlands of the ranches to fatten them up, putting them in suitable corrals to give them grass and grain.

The young ewes are usually better off, as they are not taken away from their mothers until the beginning of November and are not taken to the slaughterhouse. Around the 20th or 25th of November, we bring the rams into the flocks.

This concludes my brief explanation of our work.

We attended the New Year's Eve banquet held every year in Burns by the Harney County (Oregon) Basques. The banquet, attended by over 142 people, was in the Pine Room. The courses, all of them Basque, were cooked by the wives of H. B. Schroeder, Joe Lizundia, Felix Urizar, Martin Ramirez, Victor Azqueta, Marcelino Osa and Peter Obiague. The table was served by young ladies in outfits that sought to be Basque in style. Tío Antolin (Uncle Antolin), who now resides in Crane, was today's host. "Tío," as he is called by all Basques in this region, was one of the first Basques to arrive in this region.

Peter Obiague served as master of ceremonies and began the speeches. The mayor of Burns, a priest named Father Gregory, and a host of other people spoke.

At the request of the audience, Mrs. Edward L. Wells, who is Basque, sang, accompanied by Marie Obiague, a very corny song titled "Roses of Picardy" and, given the enthusiasm of the diners, she regaled us with an encore, the inevitable "The Dove" with all the requisite rhythmic movements when singing this work of art of musical cheesiness. To lend more solemnity to the song, John Madariaga and Peter Obiague did the background vocals.

The highlight of the party were the wineskins, from which the diners drank with all their Navarrese expertise.

Among the diners I remember Marcelino *(Blackie)* Osa, Peter Obiague, Felix Urizar, Martin Ramirez, Wm. Pochalu, Tribis Arrospe, Joe Madarieta, Frank Inda, John Obiague, Santos Arguinchona, Cecilio Exposito, Daniel Ramirez, Boni Fernandez, Joe Lizundia, Joe *(Big)* Abasolo, Steve Irigoyen, John Gogenola, Sabino Barainca, *Dot* Mugartegui, Peter Ebar, Simon Aramburu, John Madariaga, Ben Echaniz, and Victor *(Macarroni)* Azqueta.

All the Basques of this county celebrate a big dinner on Gabon Zar, and when the clock strikes twelve, they all congregate around a big Christmas tree, which the Town Hall puts up in Burns Square, singing and dancing *biribilketas*.[89]

89. *Biribilketa*: traditional Basque dance.

New Year's Eve dinner in Burns. *Urizar Family Collection. BMCC.*

January 2

Today we spent the whole day in farewell visits.

In addition to those I have mentioned, I have the following list of Basques living in Boise:

Abarrate (Anastasio, Domingo and Benedicta, the latter being Vice-President of the American Basque Fraternity); Abarrategui, Domingo; Carlos Achabal, Gregorio Alberdi, Domingo Alcorta, Aldape (Eugenio, Felipe, Florencio, Jose and Juan), Ansotegui (Antonio and Domingo), S. Ansotegui, Juan Arambarri, Pablo Aramburu, Antonio and Maria Arana, Eugenio Arano, Benito Arego, Donato and Juan Arriaga, Antonio Arrillaga, Antonio and Genaro Arriola, Leon and Meliton Arrizabalaga, Paul Arruti *(Artia)*, Francisco, Juan and Pablo Asla, Carmen Astoreca (owns a beauty parlour), Diego and Tomas Astorquia, Domingo, Felix and Juan Asumendi, Louis Azcuenaga, Francisco and Juan Barinaga, Manuel Basques, Juan Cruz Bastida y Ramon, Matias Bengoa, Juan and Teodora Berriatua, Tom Bicandi, Luis and Nick Bilbao, Joe and Jesus Egurrola, Jose Eizaguirre, Prudencio Elordieta, Luis, Jose and Martin Epeldi, Andres and Sabino Erquiaga, Eustaquio Garro, Francisco and Manuel Goitia, Guillermo Guerricabeitia, Joe Guisasola, Agustin Irazabal, Joe and Juanito Iturri, Julian and Leon Juaristi, Gregorio Landaluce, Pete Larrucea, Juanita Lejardi, Vicente Lizaso, Juan Lopez, Domingo Madariaga, Daniel Martinez, Gregorio and Hipolito Mendezona, Felisa and Pedro Mendieta, Pedro Mendizabal, Tony and Justo Murelaga, Dora Olarreaga, Julian Olaso, Antonio Olazar, Felix Olea, Victor Onandia, Escolastica and Richard Ondarza, Victor Orbe, Eustasio Ormaechea, Juan Osa, Ignacio, Manuel and Santiago Pagoaga, Santos Pastor, Abel, Alejandro, Angel, Benito, David and Joaquin Rementeria, Juan Samendi, Jose, Leandro and Segundo Totorica, Fermin Ugarte, Julian Uriarte, Antonio Uribarri, Felis Uribe, Frank and Jacinto Urresti, Carmen Urriola, Ignacio Urrutia, Esteban, Fermin, Juan Luis, Paul, Pedro and Tomas Zabala, Alejandro, Alfonso, Antonia, Juan, Julian, Mateo and Ventura Zubizarreta, Francisco and Juan Zugadi.

226.
Zabala Daniel
C/o Iribar.
Boise Idaho
227.
Zabala Francisco
C/o Herrero
Salmon C.Idaho..
228.
Zabala Juan
C/o Anduiza.
Boise Idaho.
229.
Zabala Justo
Metropol Hotel
Green River Utah
230.
Zallo José
P.O.Box 46
Twin Falls Ida.
231.
Zorrozua Raymundo
C/o John Achabal.
Boise Idaho..
232.
ALEJANDRO ZUBISARRETA
Markina, Espana
233.
Zubizarreta Luis
P. O. Box 5 4 3
Boise Idaho
234.
Zugari Francisco
P.O. Box I 8 2
Mt. Home, Idaho

January 4

Today at twelve noon we set out for Ogden, leaving this friendly town that we may never see again. Every departure is surrounded by a aura of melancholy. I don't know why whenever I leave a beloved place I seem to be leaving on the arm of death. Getting to know a new place only ends up helping me to collect memories that unintentionally turn into thorns.

Before leaving, Matilde left me a gift on the bed; a notebook and a pencil on a shoulder strap, wrapped in tissue paper and tied with a pink ribbon. And an Christmas card of flowers and birds with a tender farewell.

Poor Matilde. Two more men passing through her house about whom she may have indulged in some wishful thinking. She will continue making beds and serving food to the sheepherders until one day, a little desperate, she will let herself get married to some man who will be a lesser evil.

We are bid farewell by a group of Basques who leave with a melancholic air when we depart.

After Mountain Home, a small wooden village, the landscape becomes more mountainous, everything takes on definite shades under the winter sun. The grass has a tired yellowish color, dotted with dark rocks. A quiet river runs beside us and seems to be singing a hymn to sedentary life. No houses or people are visible. Occasionally, a deserted ranch, a cow grazing and a mound of secate.

At 10 o'clock we arrive in Ogden, Utah. Sam Maruri is waiting for us, bowlegged and with his café-au-lait colored hat. We go to his Royal Hotel, whose interior is very reminiscent of a friars' refectory. They gives us dinner as only Basque cooks know how. The Etchart couple and Valdés, an Asturian, make conversation with us. Valdés' criminal face contrasts with the placid faces of the French Basque couple.

Joe Bengoechea's hotel in Mountain Home.

January 5

Snowing. Sam has brought his sister-in-law home from the hospital where she had a baby. We have lunch with Sam, his wife, the Etcharts and three or four sheepherders. After lunch Sam took us to Salt Lake City, the headquarters of the little Mormon world, where 75% are Mormons.

We visited the Mormon tabernacle. A man from Navarre named Tony Olague, who is a Mormon, told us about the excellencies of his new religion. He tells us about the prophet Smith, the angel Moroni and the new gospel discovered by him on some mountain or other by divine inspiration.

Then we dined at John Landa's Hogar Hotel. He is an uncongenial, small man with pretensions of being educated. He greets us emphatically, like the captain of the thieves in *Captain Grant's Nephews*. His wife, from Ibarrangelu, is more pleasant than he is; she has that characteristic marital resignation, whether due to religion or because women consider all men equally calamitous, one does not know. Their daughter Mary is a dancer and is married to a Hawaiian guitar player named Bob True. The family consider themselves very proud because this citizen plays on the radio. This guitar-playing couple has a cabaret in San Francisco called South Seas. Landa tells us all this as proudly as if his daughter were a duchess.

We had dinner at a long table with several Basque shepherds. After dinner, in the midst of a heavy snowfall we returned to Ogden. We took with us one of Archabal's daughters who works in an office in Salt Lake.

Ogden. Eugene F. Darlilng, 1889.

January 6

After lunch at Sam's house, we went to have a few drinks at Domingo Ydo's house, owner of an inn called "La grande Cottage." Ydo's surname is Ydoyaga, but when he became a naturalized citizen, he adopted this name more in keeping with Americans' eagerness to shorten things. His wife is a beautiful woman from Arteaga, full of energy, who wears the pants in the family and talks up a storm. She is one of those who brandishes the political slogan of "peace and good food. And may lightning strike anyone who doesn't have money."

They know people in Bakersfield (California), where almost all are Navarrese and French Basque. In El Puente (California) they are all French Basques, and they have a Basque priest.

I note several names of Basques residing in Ogden: Juan Aberasturi, Micaela Aguirre, John Balan, Juan Bilbao, Florentino Goñi, Pedro Hualde, Julia Laucirica, Herman Mericaechebarria, Simon Nachiondo, Josefa Osa, Peter Ospital, Nicolas Totoricaguena, Tomas Uribe, Jesus Varela and Ramon Varela.

Here is a list of other Basques living in Utah County: Dionisio Irazabal and Manuel Susaeta, in Bingham Canyon, also Mrs. Victor Camara; Jose Arrillaga, in Garrison; Vicente Erquiaga, in Lucin; Eulogio Yzaguirre, Sebastian Lazaro, Justo Iriondo, Paco Alleni, in Park City; L. B. Aguirre, Frank Goñi, in Price; Hilario Landeta, in Woods Cross; Domingo Ayarbe, Martin Elizegi, in Wendover; Andres Beguiristain, Luis Eizaguirre, Jose Urrutia, Cirilo Zarrao, Segundo Estancona, Fred Otasue, John Harriet, in Salt Lake City.

At 5 pm we left for Elko (Nevada) with a magnificent day all the way and snowy mountains. We arrived at the little town of Elko at twelve o'clock at night; it is completely covered with snow and it is very cold. Calixto Laucirica is waiting for us. and he takes us to his Star Hotel. In the bar there is a group of Basques: Legarreta, the cook at the "Star Hotel," who sailed twenty three years in our company, and who was shipwrecked on the *Albia*; Canfranc, a Navarrese with all the clichés of those who consider themselves to be of pure stock; Garamendi, who works in the mines of Ely.

We sleep in a huge room, with a big stove, but it is still very cold.

Joe Anacabe'store: Jose Anacabe, Fabiana Guenaga and their son Frank.
Anita Anacabe Franzoia Collection. BMCC

January 7

This morning I had my hair cut at Arostegui's barber shop, a barber shop that looks like the ones in Mundaka. All the locals are Basques; some are chatting and others are getting their hair cut.

When I enter, Arostegui is serving John Orbea, a fur trader, a Basque nationalist, who immediately offers his services to me, and is going to drive us all around.

After lunch we visited the cinema impresario with whom we arranged the screening of the movie *Guernika*. We also visited the tiny editorial office of the local newspaper.

Elko is a town of about four thousand inhabitants. It is the second largest city in Nevada. It is located next to the Humboldt River, and two railroads cross the city.

We visited the Town House Club, which is a bar where people dance at night and play roulette. Its owners are Celso Madarieta and Pedro Jauregui. The latter is from Gernika, and in 1889 he came to California where he made money in the sheep business. With the savings he made he came to Elko, where he bought the Telescope Hotel with Guy Sabal. Later he built the Star Hotel. He is married to Matilde Eizaguirre.

Celso Madarieta is big, resembling the priest Domingo Abona, and is red-faced from the drink. He is always at the bar.

Then we visited Felix Plaza, from Berriatua, who has a bar at the Clifford Hotel. He is married to a very nice woman from Durango.

After dinner at a mixed table of Basques and Americans we go for a walk. I meet a brother of Eugenio from Laida, whom I met on that beach many years ago when he went with a very flamboyant doctor named Show.

Then we go to make conversation in Anacabe's store, sitting around the radio. He is Macues, as they call the people of Elantxobe. He is a Jesuit type, soft-spoken and silent, and blames everything on the Vatican's money. He is the enterprising Basque type; he has made and lost a fortune several times in as many places in the USA. Here he has a store that is thriving more and more.

Here's a case of racial hatred I hear about: the Spaniard Valdés shot Justo Urrutia to death and badly injured Jose Asteguia, because they were speaking in Basque and he thought they were making fun of him. It just so happens that he was executed recently.

January 8

Today, Sunday, we went to Mass with Balbino Achabal and his wife Hermenegilda Urizar. It is the anniversary of the death of their only daughter who was killed by the railroad that crosses Elko.

They are a very nice couple. He came to America when he was 18 years old; he has a ranch called Jack Creek, next to which there is an Indian reservation, some of whom have learned Basque. His wife is a little old lady racked with rheumatism who was raised in Bilbao in a home of a *maketo*'s family.[90] She talks about how she was paid a few duros and had to fetch the young master from *El Sitio*[91] when it rained. Now they have money and are happy in a free America.

In the afternoon we visited Jacinto Garteiz, from Bermeo, who is at his gas station. He is very American looking; he studied English before coming here and was on an American cruiser during the war. He is a lively and enterprising man who must have a lot of money, although he does not have a very good reputation. He has some tourist cabins with every conceivable convenience.

In the evening we showed the film.

90. *Maketo*: Spaniard who does not speak Basque.
91. *El Sitio*: A cultural, social and political society.

Basque pioneers pose in front of a bar-saloon in McDermitt, Nevada.

January 9

After making farewell visits, we boarded the bus for Winnemucca in the afternoon. We met the widow of Joe Sabal, Jesusa Guridi, a Lekeitian who was in Gallarta. Joe and his brother John, from Ispaster, came to America young. They ran their sheep business in the place known as Snow Canyon. They made a lot of money. She is a woman of years, clever and determined. She came to America abruptly because her family would not allow her to have a relationship with a sailor from the ship *El Riojano*, from the Arrotegi company. She has a beautiful ranch and a store on Battle Mountain. She has three daughters: one working in a bank in Elko, another in Sacramento and the third working with the senator from Nevada, who was a great friend of her husband's, and she goes with him to Carson City for the legislative session.

Other Basques from Elko:

Pedro Corta *(Pedro Txiki)*, from Ereño. He arrived in 1898. He owns a large ranch called Cedar Hill, where he employs several Basques. Married to a Gortari.

Juan Quintana, from Garralda. He arrived in 1891. He worked in New Orleans, on the Mississippi and in Montana. Sheep raising and farm management office. His whereabouts are unknown.

Pedro Orbe, of Ispaster. He owns property in Skelton. Married to Tomasa Arrascada.

Vicente Juaristi. Gizaburuaga. Married to Mary Walters. He now lives on the Huntington Ranch, Jiggs (Nevada).

Pete Olabarria. Markina. Married to Simona Bastida.

Andres Inchausti. Kortezubi. Herds and hotel business. He married Lorenza Urizar in Tuscarora.

Domingo Calzacorta. Markina. Sheep and hotel. Wife: Anita Marisquirena.

Domingo Zabala. Gizaburuaga. He had the Overland Hotel. Gregoria Garteiz.

Francisco Odiaga. Lekeitio. After having worked with Urquides, one of the pioneer settlers of the West, he worked with George L. Shoup, the first Idaho citizen to be a senator. He then went into the sheep business. Married to Concha Bedarona. Must have died.

Pedro Altube (Palo Alto) and his brother Bernardo fought with the Indians on more than one occasion. They established the famous Spanish Ranch in Independent Valley. One harsh winter they lost everything. But they recovered what they lost. Pedro died in California at the age of 78. They were from Oñati.

Grace Aldaya
Mike Arregi
J. F. Arrascada
Joe Berrueta
Esteban Bilbao. Nevada Hotel
Jose "Joe" Corta
S. Etchebehere
J. S. Etcheberry
Albert Garamendia
Celestino Garamendia
Domingo Garamendia
F. Goicoechea
Santiago Yrigoyen
Alberto Jauregui
Calixto Laucirica
John Leniz
Joe Marisquirena
Antonio Mendibe
Juan Muguerza
Emeterio Plaza
Tony Telleria
Isidro Urriola
Antonio, Joe, Juan and Ray Zabala
Juan Zubialde.

Speeches, letters, and report

[To the Basques of America][92]

MANU DE LA SOTA

Since I left our beloved homeland, Euzkadi, leaving it plunged into the horrors of war, I believe I have not experienced a more intense emotion than the one I have experienced upon my arrival in this capital of the state of Idaho.

Back in Biscay, in the happy days of peace, I had heard much about the Basques residing in this part of the United States. In any village in our homeland, who hasn't heard, over a succulent meal, stories and events about the Basques of California? (For our Basques especially, all North America is California.)

I knew that the Basque community here was a sample of Basque national life unique in the world, but I must confess that reality has surpassed all my hopes. Here, the spirit of our race lives vigorously and spontaneously, without obstacles or constraints that impede its free growth, as it does in our country. A piece of Basque democracy, the oldest and most perfect known, has managed to weave itself into the exuberant American democracy. In this way, the most modern democracy in the world carries within it, like an ancient jewel, a vibrant piece of the oldest democracy in Europe.

The Basques who live in these privileged places in the United States are, without a doubt, the happiest of our entire race at this moment, and they can thank heaven for having spared them all the horrors we, unfortunate brothers of the exemplary Basque family, have suffered.

Therefore, when considering this happiness in which the Basques here live, I cannot help but remember with sorrow the sad fate endured with admirable resignation by the children of Euzkadi, some in exile, others in hospitals and prisons.

At this time when our mysterious and ancient race is suffering the most barbaric and cruel persecution, the Basques who, having had the immense good fortune to escape this horrible tragedy, must turn their eyes

92. Manu de la Sota's message broadcasted in English on local radio station on December 8, and published in the *Boise Capital News*.

toward their unfortunate homeland and feel in the depths of their hearts the misfortune of their brothers, who whether right or wrong, at this very moment are suffering as no other people in the world has ever suffered.

I ask you to spare a thought for the thirty thousand Basques who suffer with heroic fortitude in the prisons of the Iberian Peninsula, and who are being taken to the prisons of North Africa, a large number having died along the way; for the other thirty thousand Basques who work as slaves in the concentration camps; for our mutilated youth, without arms, without legs, without sight, once beautiful specimens of the race, now transformed into true human wrecks, Basque women and children who drag out a life of sadness and misery in exile.

If any human being would feel compassion in the face of this picture of pain, how much more emotion will the Basque experience who, although far from his homeland, still deeply feels the brotherhood of blood?

Fly with your imagination to that wonderful piece of French Euzkadi called Lapurdi. Its smiling farmhouses, its singing streams, its little paths climbing through green groves... Everything continues to live in bucolic peace. Everything sings and laughs in Lapurdi, except for a few elderly people, women, and children, who walk lost in thought along the roads: they are the Basque refugees, people who lived in happiness and well-being, but who now live in exile, reduced to misery, struggling to find their daily bread, since French laws do not allow them to work.

I want to evoke the memory of Petra Uranga, that seventy-five-year-old woman I visited in the French Landes region. She lived happily in a small village in the Basque Country, with her husband and son, who worked. But the war came, and they followed the fate of the Basque souls.

She remained in her village, where she was imprisoned, and when the fascists issued that inhumane decree expelling all those with male relatives in the loyalist camp from their homes, Petra Uranga had to cross the trenches with her young daughters, "after having kissed—she told me—all the walls of my old farmhouse."

In Gernika, where she went to take refuge, she suffered the terrible bombing of April 26th and was one of the few people who survived in the shelter where she had hidden. She took refuge in Mungia, a town that was also destroyed by German planes, and from there she left for

Bilbao, suffering all the horrors of its siege. And from Bilbao, the poor old woman with her daughters left one night on foot, following that horrific exodus of belongings, carts, and people, who in endless lines fled from the fascist terror.

She walked to Santander, where she slept for two days in the open air, eating little. And from there she set sail on a refugee boat for France, where she has suffered all the hardships of penniless refugees. "Faith in God and the hope of returning to my homeland—she told me—keep me alive, otherwise I would have died long ago."

Now she lives very poorly in a lumberjack's cottage in the immense Landes Forest, where she and her daughters have been taken in out of compassion. In the middle of that gloomy pine wilderness, she prays night and day with her face turned toward Euzkadi and waits for the white doves that will one day come from Etxalar to announce peace and victory.

—I can't cry. I left all my tears in Euzkadi – she told me.

—And why do you want to return to the village? – I asked her.

And Petra Uranga answered me in a firm voice:

—To forgive those who have made us suffer so much, and because I want Basque soil to shelter my body forever.

And like this case, I could mention many others, of women who bravely endure all the bitterness of exile, and of others as well, whose grief has ultimately killed them, or whose pain has driven them mad.

Only by witnessing all these tragedies, only by contemplating those men, who after a life of work and savings, are reduced to poverty in exile in the final stage of their lives; only by seeing those homeless children, many without parents, only by knowing the life of pain our refugee brothers and sisters have been enduring, can one realize the magnitude of the ordeal the Basque people are suffering because of this inhumane war provoked by international fascism.

On behalf of all these Basques who suffer their exile in poverty but with dignity, on behalf of the hundreds of disabled Basques who remain resigned in the hospitals of France, we have come here to ask you not to forget them. You must not dispute these martyrs of the homeland, for whoever dies for an ideal ascends to the rank of hero. You must help them so that, comforted by your assistance, they do not falter in the midst of tragedy. At this moment, do not think about your political opinions; think only that there are 200,000 men, women, and children in Europe who share your blood, and who are victims of the bloodiest tragedy in history.

You, Basques who live in happiness, do not forget the Basques who live in pain!

[Tonight, my dear compatriots][93]

Manu de la Sota

Tonight, my dear compatriots, let us recall the most tragic and cruel moment of the civil war on our homeland: the destruction of Gernika. This monstrous event alone would be enough for every Basque with an ounce of dignity to revile the names of Hitler, Mussolini, and that macabre puppet, traitor in the name of the homeland and perjurer in the name of God, called Franco.

I am not going to explain to you what the name of Gernika represents to the Basques. Because of its national and sacred significance, because of the traditional spirituality with which its ancient stones are imbued, the murderous wings of the modern horsemen of the Apocalypse reduced it to ashes.

Gernika's only sin was that of being sacred to the Basques, of being the political capital and soul of Euzkadi: that's why the soulless and honorless leader decreed its destruction.

On April 26, 1937, Gernika had its usual population of seven thousand inhabitants, three thousand refugees, and two Basque battalions. Because of this population increase, the traditional Monday markets continued to be very lively, and villagers from the surrounding areas flocked to the town with their wares. One of these market days, a Monday, was chosen by international fascism to carry out the greatest mass murder in recorded history.

At 4:30, the church bell rang, and everyone took refuge in shelters, most of them of rather rustic construction. A few minutes later, a *Heinkel 111* appeared, dropping six bombs and a shower of grenades near the railway station. A short time later, another Heinkel appeared, striking the same area, but this time closer to the center of town.

The curate of Gernika, Don Eusebio de Arronategui, left the church carrying the Holy Viaticum, having been informed that there were some dying people near the station. Solemnly, he crossed the deserted streets,

93. Speech given by Manu de la Sota before the screening of the documentary *Guernika* in Boise.

carrying the body of Christ in his hands, from that God of ours, whom the fascists have tried to turn into an Antichrist of hatred and blood.

Fifteen minutes passed, and as people began to emerge from their shelters, the hoarse drumming of the *Junkers*, the heaviest bombing aircraft Germany had sent to the Peninsula, was heard to the east. They began to circle over the town, unloading their deadly cargo, one ton at a time. The roar of explosions began to be heard, and columns of smoke rose into the sky, growing larger as new bomber planes maneuvered through the air. In addition to the bombs they dropped, they also dropped large torpedoes weighing a ton, shattering houses from top to bottom and penetrating shelters. The people's morale had been good but now panic gripped them.

A squadron of *Heinkels* was waiting for that moment. Until then, they had been strafing the roads leading to Gernika, attacking flocks and villagers. But just as the terrified population tried to flee the town, the planes descended, mercilessly strafing them, leaving scattered in the rubble-strewn streets the corpses of women and children.

The twenty machine guns on the small planes continued their murderous work unabated, and the people, crazed with terror, threw themselves into ditches, took cover under trees, crawled into the smoking holes the bombs had opened in the ground, or fled with their eyes closed in a hectic manner.

And that was when the great bombing of Gernika began, when the soulless murderers of Germany erased the regional capital from the map of Euzkadi with fire and blood. It was approximately 5:15. For two and a half hours, squadrons of planes followed one another in quick succession, mercilessly bombing Gernika, targeting the center of the town. Around the hospital, located on the road to Bermeo, the bombs fell like a shower of stars: the windows shattered, the wounded were thrown from their beds, and finally the walls of the building collapsed, burying everyone beneath the ruins.

In the piles of rubble that had once been homes, where shreds of carpets and curtains and splinters of furniture awaited the flames, the planes dropped veritable incendiary sparks which were tubes the size of our forearms, loaded with a silvery, fire-spreading powder. Thus, while the buildings collapsed, burying the poor, defenseless people beneath the rubble, an exterminating fire descended from the sky, scorching alive those who had not yet died.

Every twenty minutes, the raids continued one after another, and people took advantage of these moments of calm to run between the explosions and jets of fire that the incendiary metal spurted everywhere, while a shroud of black smoke floated over the indescribable catastrophe. And the unfortunate women of Gernika—mothers who are listening to me—hurled themselves like wild beasts against the crushed doors of the collapsed shelters, trying to pull out their children who were already crushed and burned.

The whole of Gernika was one immense wail. Urged on by the cries of its wounded, its people worked desperately to recover the bodies of the wounded from the rubble before the new planes returned. And during those intervals of horror, our priests, those Basque priests who have given the world a sublime example of Christianity, and who, for being true apostles of Christ, have been shot and imprisoned by the abject Franco, those exemplary priests, I repeat, climbed onto the rubble, consoled the people in their enormous tragedy. The sacred village of the Basques was already being reduced to ashes, and the faces of the survivors were blackened by the ash, faces illuminated with a horrible hue by the glow of the immense bonfire. Only the dying uttered wailing moans. The men and women who were still standing did not cry, could not cry; terror had turned them into mute statues.

And again, and again the satanic planes returned, destroying what remained standing, burying more men, women, and children inside the shelters, and mercilessly machine-gunning those who fled in horror from the immense bonfire.

But the people could bear no more and exhausted by the scorching heat, the infernal noises, and the terror, they lay on the ground like piles of lifeless rags.

At 7:45, the last plane disappeared, and now, knowing of that indescribable desolation, all that could be heard was the creaking of everything burning in a state of turmoil, and the hoarse sound of collapsing walls and roofs. The great crime had been committed. Gernika lay destroyed, trapping beneath its ruins the corpses of two thousand innocent Basques, two thousand of our brothers and sisters, my beloved compatriots, who had committed no crime other than that of loving their land.

And when night fell, the entire sky of Euzkadi was dyed red, announcing to the world that the very soul of the Basque homeland was burning, and that the souls of the Basques who still existed were also burning with rage, promising heaven never to forget the criminal offense that international fascism had perpetrated with blood, fire, and shrapnel against the oldest and most genuine democracy in the world.

Gernika was left like an immense glowing ember on the historic night of April 26, 1937. And around its fiery corpse, some farmhouses burned in the neighboring mountains, like mortuary candles. It was because the German planes, their desire for extermination not yet satisfied, had dropped their remaining incendiary bombs on those humble dwellings as they departed.

Amid the reddish glow that dispelled the darkness of the night, a sublime shadow rose in the air: it was the silhouette of the holy oak, the tree of our freedoms that stood tall, announcing to humanity that the rebellious and righteous spirit of our race will never die, and that as long as the world remains the world, the Basques will continue to live and die for freedom and democracy.

Basques who are listening to me, the immortal ruins of Gernika the martyr will now parade before your eyes. Despite their silence, those charred stones will speak to you with eloquent emotion. Engrave in your hearts the great lesson of pain that emanates from them. May these holy ruins be a symbol for all of us, a symbol of unity among all Basques in misfortune, and a symbol of the common effort we must make to build with these martyred stones the magnificent edifice of our homeland when the sun of victory illuminates our mountains with rays of justice, brotherhood, and freedom.

The tree of Gernika continues standing, scattering throughout the world—as Iparraguirre sang—its fruits of wisdom. And calling out to you sons and daughters who live in distant lands, so that today more than ever you may remember those brothers and sisters of your race who have suffered so much, who have wept so much, and who have shed so much blood, and whose ordeal is not yet over, for they now continue to suffer all the bitterness of exile.

Brothers and sisters who are listening to me: *Gora, gora* forever Gernika, long live, long live Gernika, everlasting symbol of our immortal race!

Scan this code to watch the documentary *Guernika*.

1

Before leaving this beautiful city of Boise, where we have been treated with the most friendly ~~and~~ ~~simpathetic~~ kind hospitality, and where we have found (in these Christmas days) comfort and sinpathy for our sorrowful hearts, afflicted by the sufferings of our far-away country, ~~I~~ we want to say ~~some farewell-words~~ a few words of farewell to ~~my~~ our fellow countrymen, the Basques that dwell, happy and freely, in this noble american nation, the only democracy in the world that stands firmly against the ~~advances~~ evils brought upon ~~the~~ mankind by ~~of~~ the dictatorial states. ~~helping the people unjustly persecuted in Europe~~.

As delegates of the Basque Government, we have ~~come~~ ~~arrived~~ come to the United States to explain to our fellow countrymen, the distressing condition of the Basques that still remain in our subjected country, and the appalling situation

Draft of Manu de la Sota's farewell message.

[Before leaving this beautiful city of Boise][94]

Before leaving this beautiful city of Boise, where we have been treated with the most cordial hospitality and where we have found comfort and sympathy during these Christmas holidays for our hearts afflicted by the sufferings of our distant country, we want to say a few words of farewell to our compatriots, the Basques who live happily and freely in this noble American nation, the only democracy in the world that firmly opposes the evils that dictatorial states have caused to humanity.

As delegates of the Basque Government, we have come to the United States to explain to our compatriots the pitiful situation of the Basques who still remain in our subjugated country and the atrocious situation of the Basques who are exiled in France, enduring the wretched existence of refugees without a home or country, depending on the charity of good people.

At this moment, all Basques must realize that their ancient and mysterious race is subjected to the most cruel and atrocious persecution; that our people are oppressed with all kinds of punishments, ranging from confiscation of property to death; that our songs and dances have been banned; that our lives, liberties, and traditions have been destroyed; and that our mother tongue, the beautiful and beloved Basque, is banished from schools and churches, and even speaking Basque is considered a grave violation of the law.

And why all these punishments and penalties against us? Because we love liberty, justice, and equality; because history shows that we have built one of the oldest democracies in Europe and we want to continue along the same lines; because we have always fought against tyrants and oppressors, and even in the current war, we have preferred death to submitting to the rule of foreign invaders.

Some people, deceived by malicious propaganda, say we are reds, communists, etc. I emphatically assure you that this is not true. As Basques, we have always been a religious people, lovers of God, and wanting to

94. Original in English. Message broadcast by Radio Boise on December 31, 1938. Antonio de Irala spoke in Basque and Manu de la Sota, in English.

live in peace with all. Our colors are green, red, and white; they signify hope, faith, and charity, and our motto is *"Jaungoikua eta Lege Zarra,"* that is, "God and the old laws." We do not join the sword to the cross, as some so-called Christians do, and the cross on our flag will never yield to the swastika cross of modern autocrats.

We defend Christian democracy, and to maintain this doctrine of justice and peace, several thousand Basques died on the battlefield. And I want to repeat this plea to you in Spanish. These days we are celebrating the Christmas holidays, the traditional *Gabon* festivities that back in our homeland bring families together in the old homes of our race. Let us think of the Basque refugees who in these days will have recalled from exile, their hearts broken with sorrow, their mountains, their homes, all the memories of their beloved homeland; let us think of them, who perhaps spent the holy night of Gabon hungry, cold, and without hope of happiness, while all around them was song and laughter.

And you too will sing, laugh, and dance; but I am sure that in the midst of our joys you will not forget your brothers in misfortune, for if you did, you would commit the greatest crime against our blood, against our people, and against our God. Let us make this profound humanity you feel toward them reach them so that those poor exiles realize that the Basques of the United States have not forgotten them, and that you comfort them with actions more than words, so that they do not lose heart in their misfortune.

Goodbye, Basque brothers! May the church bells of Euzkadi soon ring out in the new year that begins tomorrow, proclaiming the triumph of justice, and may bonfires be lit on the peaks of our mountains, announcing the victory of Basque ideals, so that from now on we may know how to love and forgive one another under the protection of Jaungoikua, the only Lord of Euzkadi.

[Euzkaldunak, Agur][95]

"Because all good things in this world come to an end, so too do the good days we have spent among you. We will never easily forget the Basques of Idaho; we will keep your brotherhood forever in our hearts.

The hands of the Basques here have shaken our hands, your doors have been open to us, and you have always been willing to help us. Thanking each one of you for all this is not enough; we would like to do more for you, and we ask God for this with all our hearts. What you have done for us will not be forgotten by us, nor will it be forgotten by the Basque people.

We will continue throughout the world working on behalf of the Basques, for the good of our beloved Euzkadi. And when we go to meet our brothers, we will take with us the best we have learned from you: your Basque soul, your true Basque personality. The eyes of the Basques of Idaho have shed many tears when talking about our brothers, and we will not forget that either, nor will our brothers.

Farewell, farewell, brothers. Always remain on the side of the Basques, as honorable Basques, on the side of our people, on the side of Euzkadi. Goodbye to all. Farewell."[96]

"Before leaving this land of peace and work, we would like to write a few words of farewell, dedicated to our Basque brothers and sisters who are fortunate enough to live in the state of Idaho, protected by the democratic laws of this magnificent American nation, far from unfortunate Europe, which has been transformed into a hell of persecution and death because of the satanic policies unleashed by soulless and dishonourable dictators.

To all Basques, we would like to say that you should continue to love your homeland, Euzkadi, generously and without intransigence, remembering it fondly today more than ever, because the more unfortunate mothers are, the more worthy they are of being loved. May they keep our

95. *Goodby, Basques.* Message from Manu de la Sota and Antonio de Irala, published in the Boise Capital News on December 31, 1938, page 10.
96. Speech given in Basque.

language alive, the ancient and admired Euskera, passing it on to their children with the same devotion with which our mothers taught us, and speaking it with pride, especially at this time when it is persecuted in our own homeland, as if it were a cursed language.

There are no people in the world that have more beautiful songs and more original and evocative dances than ours. For this reason, and because they are the artistic expression of the soul of Euzkadi, Basques who live far from your homeland, you should use them in your moments of joy and teach them to your children so that when they dance and sing, they proclaim with their melodies and pirouettes that they belong to one of the strongest and most spiritual races that God created.

And to you, Basque mothers, who have brought all the virtues of our *etxekoandres* to these distant lands, we ask you to instil them especially in your daughters, along with the holy religion of our elders, helping them understand that the Christian customs of our parents are a more sure source of happiness than all the pagan modernisms that surround them. May the fashion of Basque women always be inspired by the virtues of the race and may their main adornment be exemplary behavior rather than luxury.

And to the young people, in particular to those born here, we want to say that they should proudly proclaim their Euzkaldun ancestry everywhere, for they must not forget that they are of noble lineage and pure blood, thanks to their parents who gave them Basque surnames. By being staunchly Basque, Basque in body and soul, they will become worthy citizens of this great American nation, to which they owe so much.

And to all Basques in Idaho, we wish to express our hope that you will always live united, brothers and sisters of the same family, without allowing petty political squabbles to sow hatred and enmity among you. During this unforgettable *Gabon*,[97] we have shared with you all the joys that Gabon Christmas festivities bring to Basques. Amidst the natural joy, we have not forgotten to remember the Basques who are suffering misfortune, our brothers and sisters who are suffering in body and soul the consequences of a great injustice. For the future, let us not forget our

97. *Gabon*: Christmas season.

unfortunate brothers and sisters, and let all of us Basques unite forever in a desire for love, which will seek to repair the current ills of our homeland and work to make it happy with all its children.

With these words we bid farewell to you, Basques of Idaho, which we convey to you with the utmost emotion, because they have been sent to us expressly for you from Barcelona, where our President, Jose Antonio de Aguirre, is currently dealing with the situation of our brothers and sisters living there.

Agur, Basques of Idaho! Engrave these words of our President in your hearts, the man who has sacrificed everything for the freedom and well-being of Euzkadi, and may *Jaungoikua*, return our homeland to us, free and good, as it was from the beginning of the world."

Antonio de Irala riding a sheep. On the left, Manu de la Sota.

[Letter from Antonio de Irala to Jose Antonio Aguirre, December 9, 1938]

Your Excellency, Mr. Jose Antonio Aguirre
Paris

Dear President and friend,

I am writing to you from Boise, Idaho, where we arrived on the 5th, after a four-day bus trip. We are delighted, and our first impression could not be better. Patriotically, it is difficult to imagine a greater emotion than that experienced in this Euzkadi, the true Euzkadi. The capital, Boise, where we reside, has about twenty five thousand inhabitants, a charming, clean town with no factories, and a climate much better than that of a city like New York; it is not harsh. The geographical environment of this place chosen by our men to establish their residence is the best we have seen during our trip through the United States.

We have been received very well and with enormous interest by everyone, not forgetting the Americans, who greatly appreciate the Basques. Without our having asked, the press announced our arrival; it has been published in both local newspapers; I'm mailing you some different issues separately. We have two planned visits to each of the newspaper editors; we've already seen them, but they want to treat us. We'll also be with the State Governor; he has already expressed this desire. We have a letter of introduction for the bishop, provided by the Catholic Committee in Washington, so we will definitely visit him; he's been away these days. Yesterday, Manu and I spoke on the radio for fifteen minutes, in English and Basque; the people are happy.

I think the case of the Basques here is the greatest example of the vitality of the race. The life of our brothers and sisters here is unexpectedly interesting. We have often thought about what a Basque Country without models would be like; in this environment, one can get an idea. There are no Spaniards; everyone speaks Basque, but with greater ease and fluency than in our small towns. The Basques, who are especially dedicated to sheep, occupy positions throughout the entire population's life, from banks to hairdressers and taxi drivers. Talking to the children of Basques from the Basque Country makes a great impression. Many of them are educated men who have never been to the Basque Country and speak Bizkaian Basque like any farmer from Nabarniz, not a word of Spanish. And don't think these are isolated cases; it's the rule. You should see them, with an American-style dress and manner, speaking Basque. Naturally, they tend to be elegant and well-off, but they differ from ours in that they don't disdain Basque—quite the opposite.

These past few days, we haven't had a free minute. They don't leave us for a moment, always waiting for visits to Basques and invitations to lunch and dinner. By the way, they are even more advanced in gastronomy than ours; they serve you truly enormous quantities amidst an astronomical number of dishes.

We haven't yet, naturally, learned every detail of our people's lives. We'll be preparing a comprehensive report with everything of interest we find, which is a lot. There's no shortage of picturesque details; Manu will do up something nice for you. In this letter, I'll omit telling you about our projects; I'll keep you updated on what we're doing, mainly because by the time you receive this letter, I'll have already communicated something by telegraph. It's a shame how in such little time we must carry out such in-depth and extensive work; we'd need several months, and we'd fall short; we must not forget that there are also many Basques in other areas. I think it would be a good thing to bring two or three of our priests here who are zealous and patriotic with personal charm. I made some arrangements in Washington, and now I'm going to raise the matter with the bishop, taking the spiritual problem of our people as a starting point. If we're lucky, the trip and stay will cost us nothing, and the benefits of every kind will be great. I'll let you know what I find.

I'm enclosing a note from Ramon[98] in New York. Frank P. Walsh, whose visit I told you about at the time, has once again expressed his desire to work for us in the political arena. He is Catholic, Roosevelt's friend, leader of the Irish who worked in the United States for Irish independence, hints that he would like to present our problem like that of Ireland and work in a similar way. For the moment, through his mediation, the

98. Ramon de la Sota McMahon, nephew of Manu de la Sota and member of the Basque Government Delegation in New York.

report on our persecution is being presented to Roosevelt. Afterward, we will speak with him in detail and submit everything he proposes to us for your consideration.

At this moment I have received a telegram from Ramon Sota announcing the arrival in New York of Arritola[99] and Urresti;[100] once they arrive and inform us of your instructions, we will prepare the distribution of the work according to your wishes. The duration of our stay here will also depend on this; as I said, there is much to do before then and the area is very extensive.

I have not yet received any information from New York on how things are going there; I assume there will be nothing in particular and that they will proceed as normal. The letters from the Archbishop of Bordeaux and the Bishop of Dax are truly beautiful and will surely have a great impact on American Catholics.

I will write to you again one of these days; in the meantime, receive a very affectionate greeting from your good friend and servant.

Antonio de Irala

99. Eustasio Arritola, nationalist priest.
100. Jose Urresti, brother-in-law of Manu de la Sota, was treasurer of the Delegation in New York.

Visit to the Idaho State Capitolio: Manu de la Sota, in front; behind him, from left to right: Tony Laradogoitia, Jose Villanueva, Tomas Arambalza and Antonio de Irala.

[Letter from Antonio de Irala to Jose Antonio Aguirre, December 14, 1938]

His Excellency Jose Antonio Aguirre
Paris

Dear Jose Antonio,

I am attaching a note on the interview with the Bishop of Idaho. The results, so far, have been entirely null. He is an extremely unpleasant person, despite his youth. The way he spoke to us will give us even more sympathy in Washington. It turns out that the bishop's statements about the spiritual situation of the Basques are false. It seems to me that he has absolutely no idea about the state of our compatriots, and even the very few in Idaho. Saying that we shouldn't worry that they will eventually die well sounds like un-apostolic language, especially when it is possible to achieve a general religious practice. Everyone has a religious background; Everyone, even the girls, is seen wearing medals, but religious practice among men is arguably nonexistent and very limited among women, due to various causes, especially the lifestyle they lead and the lack of the slightest incentive to go to church, nor anyone to tell them so. It is also completely false that everyone understands English; many, most, if you will, understand it superficially, but not sufficiently to express or understand the full range of ideas and feelings that spiritual life requires.

In short, the idea of bringing in a priest is impossible for the moment. We will see the Bishop of Reno, Nevada; if we also fail, we will have to follow another path to obtain what cannot be denied us for any reason. It would be ironic if our people were forever more miserable than the Black people in Africa to whom we preach in their own language. A great deal of political misgivings will have influenced our administration against it.

Otherwise, we are doing very well. The day before yesterday, the editorial staff of the newspaper that publishes the Basque newspaper invited us to dinner. You'll see from the latest issues we've sent you how we control the entire publication. We follow the tactic of letting locals write in our direction; we provide them with material.

On the 22nd, the Shepherds' Ball begins at 10:00 p.m., and the premiere of the film *Guernika* takes place in one of the best theaters here. It will run for at least two days, from 1:00 p.m. to 10:00 p.m. as a general program, with 35% of the ticket sales going to us. The profits from the dance will go entirely to us. Now we have to organize the committee and the general collection. We've decided against speaking at a public event; we think it's better to organize the event and then speak on the radio as we did before. Everyone hears it, and it's a more accommodating approach to what people here are used to, especially considering, as I said, the general sympathy. We're jotting down a good number of addresses for the future. Here we can have a permanent organization and do really good things; once we've finished reviewing everything, we'll address this point in the general report, including the possibilities we believe exist for action.

We've arrived at a very opportune moment. Yesterday, an envoy from the Confederated Hispanic Societies,[101] from California and unfortunately a Basque speaker, showed up in town to set up shop. I saw him once he arrived and I already told him he has nothing to do here. I think we have the means to keep things going normally, but it probably won't do us any good anyway.

In other Basque areas, it will be worse, because these envoys from the Hispanic Societies have already passed through and have some people working for them.

ONE IMPORTANT THING. It would be advisable for a Basque chronicle of the week to be written from Paris. It would be very effective: in Basque and Erdera,[102] initially more so in the latter, with short news items and commentaries in the same style and format, with short paragraphs; the Basque language must be Biscayan and without neologisms. The person writing the leaflet is a poor man who cannot write, and if we don't help him, we're in danger of him dying. Receiving something from Paris would give him "prestige." We would have to send by air mail to: Damian Telleria (name of the newspaper) Boise, Idaho, U.S.A. We must and can

101. Confederated Hispanic Societies (SSHHCC), coordinator of various Spanish associations in the United States supporting the Spanish Republic and refugees.
102. *Erdera*: Spanish.

ensure that the leaflet is completely ours. We will continue collaborating as we have been.

Juan Zabal, Valentin Aguirre's son-in-law, who is accompanying us, has left for California. This will save us time, as he prepares the way for us by informing us about the situation in the towns along the way. He arrives in Boise on the 22nd.

And that's all, Jose Antonio. I wish you a very happy Easter, and let's hope *Jaungoikua* makes 39 the year of our victory. *Agur.*

Antonio de Irala

Boise. 17 Dic. 1938.

Mi querido Presidente:

He leido la carta que le diriges a Irala, y como supongo que en ella tambien te dirigis a mi, voy a contestarte punto por punto, los parrafos mas interesantes, argi eta garbi como a mi me gustan ~~hacer~~ decir las cosas. Cuando termines de leerla, ya se que me vas a achacar de pesimista. Pero me voy a permitir hacerte una observacion: Es obligación nuestra no mostrarnos nunca pesimistas con la gente, pero es tambien obligación nuestra el decirte siempre la verdad a ti, aunque esta no sea de color de rosa. Lo contrario seria engañarte, y eso no lo podemos hacer. ¡Cuanto mas facil seria para nosotros el comunicarte todos los dias grandes proyectos, diciendote que los dollars van a venir a nuestras manos como el pan, que esto es jauja para los vascos, que todos los empresarios quieren traer Eresoinka, etc. Esto – que es una forma indirecta de la adulación – no podemos hacerlo; a ti no podemos comunicarte mas que realidades, precisamente porque eres Presidente del Gobierno Vasco, en Paris y no en la Luna. Asi es que con todos los respetos debidos, vas a tener que apechugar con las verdades que voy a decidirte.

Empiezas tu carta diciendo: "que no te gusta nada lo que te deciamos relativo a la nueva Comision. Que observas en nosotros indecision, que variamos de criterio, que antes pediamos a Alejandro y a Urresti, y que ahora ya no te interesa nadie".

Si relees las cartas que se te escriben desde aqui, veras que en ninguna de ellas te hemos pedido mas gente. Unicamente, en la carta que yo te escribi hace algun tiempo te decia que de mandar personas, no mandeis gente que no sepa inglés. Luego por dos veces os hemos rogado por telegrama y carta que

First page of the letter from Manu de la Sota to the President of the Basque Government from Boise.

[Letter from Manu de la Sota to Jose Antonio Aguirre]

Boise, December 17, 1938

My dear President:

I have read the letter you addressed to Irala, and since I assume you are also addressing me in it, I am going to respond to you point by point regarding the most interesting paragraphs, *argi eta garbi,*[103] as I like to say things. When you finish reading it, I already know you're going to accuse me of being pessimistic. But I will allow myself to make an observation: it is our obligation never to appear pessimistic with people, but it is also our obligation to always tell you the truth, even if it isn't rosy. To do otherwise would be to deceive you, and we cannot do that. How much easier it would be for us to inform you every day about major projects, telling you that dollars will flow into our hands like bread, that this is a godsend for the Basques, that all the businessmen want to bring *Eresoinka,*[104] etc. This—which is an indirect form of flattery—we cannot do; we can only communicate the facts to you, precisely because you are the president of the Basque Government, in Paris and not on the Moon. So, with all due respect, you're going to have to accept the truth I'm about to tell you.

You begin your letter by saying that you don't like what we're saying about the new Commission. That you notice indecision in us, that we're changing our minds, that we used to ask for Alejandro and Urresti, and that now you're no longer interested in anyone. If you reread the letters written to you from here, you'll see that in none of them we have asked you for more people. Only in the letter I wrote to you some time ago did I tell you that, if you send people, don't send anyone who doesn't speak English. Then twice we have begged you by telegram and letter not to send more people, but unfortunately you haven't listened to us. Regarding the specific case of sending Onaindia,[105] we have always informed you of the desire of those who carry the propaganda of loyalism here (Jay Allen,

103. *Argi eta garbi*: loud and clear.

104. Music and dance group founded in 1937 by de Basque Government in exile to represent the Basque culture around the world.

105. Alberto Onaindia, priest, delegate of the Basque Government to the International League of Friends of the Basques (LIAB, in its French acronym) in France.

for example, and the ambassador as well) to have a Basque priest come to influence the Catholic clergy.

Recently, we telegraphed to you the request of several prominent loyalists who considered it essential that an intelligent Catholic priest come on the same ship as Cardinal Mundelein to work for him. If we mentioned Onaindia, it was because he seemed the most suitable, and we can't think of anyone else. But Arritola, whom I know, seems very good to me, and I think he can do a great job.

I remain firmly convinced that the Basque Delegation in New York City only needs three lay people and a priest. The rest is just throwing dollars into the wind. In the project we concocted in Paris, we included the salary for an office worker we would hire here. Since we felt we could do this job ourselves, we took it on as well, and we only employed a young lady for a few hours.

When you told us Aramburu[106] was coming, we telegraphed you not to send him. However, you ignored us, and Aramburu is in New York City. He's an excellent man who gets along very well with us, but his work is extremely meager. First, because given the organization of the journalistic world here, he has no access to this protected area for foreigners (we already knew that), and second, because articles must be sent in English, and Aramburu doesn't know it. The only articles that can appear in the newspapers about our cause are those we, through influence, get written by American journalists, apart from the letters and press releases we send as delegates of the Basque Government, which Aramburu cannot write because, as I repeat, he doesn't speak English. Furthermore, since Aramburu hasn't been raised on nationalism, he lacks the enthusiasm that compels us to work with gusto all day long. Left to his own devices, he does very little, and unless he's pushed, he stops. This may be influenced by his health, which in my opinion isn't very strong. This is the pure truth, and I'm not getting discouraged. I repeat, Aramburu is unnecessary, and having him here is a waste of money.

While we were in Boise, Urresti arrived in New York, so I don't know what he's doing, but I know him and believe he'll work well, because he has the presence and the nerve to get into places. However, my point

106. Juan Aramburu, journalist, contributor to the French news agency Havas.

of view is this: currently, the Basque Delegation in New York consists of six people, almost as many as the Basque Embassy in Washington. This is excessive; three and the priest are enough. This number of people can very well live in New York without asking the Basque Government for a room, and on top of that, send a few dollars there. The six-person Delegation is a disaster. And if we continue with this issue, we'll soon have to send you an SOS for financial help. (As I'll explain later, Arritola can't come to Idaho.)

You sent Ramon, Irala, and me for three months to prepare the ground for the Great Commission. The ground is already prepared; now, in my opinion, you should choose three of us to form the Delegation, and the rest should go home. I'm going to give you my opinion on how this commission should be formed.

Anton does great work among the Basques and among Catholic figures who speak Spanish. He's also the financial helmsman of the expedition, the cheapskate who complains about the expenses (something very necessary), and the most capable of all at getting money out of people.

Ramon, although a bit of a codger, is the only one who writes English correctly, which is essential, and, thanks to his connections in London, he has access to the most important families in New York. He knows many people from the diplomatic and academic world, and since he's smart, worldly, knows how to present himself and speak, he plays an excellent role. It's a shame he has such a childish face.

Urresti, I suspect he'll do very well, with his aristocratic appearance, his Oxford English, and his nerve, which nothing intimidates.

And now I'll digress to quote a conversation that might take place:

—OUR FRIEND: Mr. Hull, I'm going to introduce you to these members of the Basque Delegation.

—MR. HULL: Oh, what a pleasure! And who are these gentlemen?

—OUR FRIEND: This is Manuel de la Sota, son of Sir Ramon de la Sota; this is Ramon Sota, grandson of Sir Ramon de la Sota, and this is Jose Urresti, son-in-law of Sir Ramon de la Sota.

Mr. Hull says nothing, but he thinks "Oh, in Euzkadi everything belongs to this Sir R. Sota!" Or, in another case, "these Sota people are more connected than the Trujillo family."

The result is that I am the one who should leave the Delegation with

Aramburu. Reasons:

1. All the work on filing, archiving, etc. is already underway, and anyone can continue it.
2. I consider the *Eresoinka* case a failure, either because it can't be done or because of my clumsiness. In both cases, someone new can try it again, perhaps with more success than I had.
3. The equipment is fixed (as I'll explain later). And it will remain fixed even if Doña Elvira Arozena de Belausteguigoitia insists on ruining it.

So, I think you should send me back to Europe to work in Paris, Barcelona, or wherever. And if not, home, to Biarritz. You don't know how much I long to be quiet in my corner of continental Euzkadi to write a couple of plays about the war I've been thinking about! But, anyway, you'll decide, because at the moment there's no room for selfish thinking.

Then you say in your letter: "Well, I want to ignore you, and Urresti and Arritola will be there this week." Well, I'm also very sorry that you ignore us, because it seems to me that being here, we can know better what's happening in this country than those in France. And, therefore, advise you with a greater chance of being right. Besides, it seems to me that's why we're here, to keep you informed about what's best for this country, which, naturally, you can't know through spiritual revelation. Believe me, when we tell you something, we don't do it lightly or on a whim, but rather weighing the pros and cons.

I fully agree with you that, both here in Idaho and in Nevada and Oregon, a Basque priest is needed. The Basques here are religious like all their fellow Basques, but very few Basque men go to church. The women go to church but are quite indifferent when it comes to religious matters. The girls, especially the young ones, aren't concerned about religious issues. A Basque priest would do a world of good in this regard.

Furthermore, the Basques here are truly Basque in that they keep the language alive and use it constantly, although their children are losing it, and their grandchildren, almost completely. Outside of Basque, you don't hear a Basque song here, nor do they dance any of our dances. And when they talk about our homeland, they always say Spain. In this regard, the work of a Basque priest could be enormous, as he would unite them, teaching the catechism to children in the vernacular, as well as our songs, creating organizations like the poxpoliñas, etc. But...

There was a Basque priest here named Don Bernardo Arregui (from Tolosa) who arrived in Boise in 1911, as a result of a letter written by the then Bishop of Idaho, Monsignor Glorieux, to the then Bishop of Vitoria, José Cadena y Eleta. The Government of His Catholic Majesty also appointed him Vice Consul of Spain in Idaho in 1916, in that most Christian zeal the Spanish monarchy always had for blending the human with the divine. From what I have heard, the good Don Bernardo was quite self-interested and did his best to extract everything he could, which must have been quite a lot, from his parishioners. However, in Arregui's time, many more Basques went to church.

But protests arose from American priests who wanted to receive what Don Bernardo charged for burials, baptisms, etc., and the bishop at that time sent Arregui to who knows where in California, taking over the beautiful Chapel of the Good Shepherd, built by the Basques through individual contributions and still known today as the "Basque Chapel".

The other day, Anton and I paid a visit to the Bishop of Idaho, carrying a very kind letter of introduction from Monsignor Ready, a very important Catholic figure in Washington. He received us coldly. He told us flatly that he wouldn't admit a Basque priest in Idaho, that we were no one to discuss this matter with him, and finally, he turned us out. Under these conditions, how do you expect us to bring Arritola to Idaho? If we did, we would only make things worse. The only thing left to do is talk to Mundelein, explain the absurdity of a Basque community not having a pastor who speaks their own language... and then see what he decides.

When we go to Nevada, we'll talk to the bishop there, for whom we have letters of introduction. We'll see if this illustrious person isn't as narrow-minded as the one from Idaho.

But, for now, Arritola has to stay in New York.

You mention a misgiving in your letter: that there's no unity among us. I can assure you that it will be very difficult to find a group of four men who get along better than we do, always acting without hiding anything, always walking together, and without having quarreled even once. On this point, I assure you we're exemplary.

Eresoinka: We have many businessmen, and good ones… but once the group is on American soil. But *who* is going to pay the transportation costs? We cannot find anyone, and until someone emerges, *Eresoinka* won't be able to come here. This is the naked truth, and the rest is wishful thinking. You see, the Russian Ballets have been in New York, but their arrival was financed by twenty American millionaires who have formed a society. From this, we deduce that bringing a company here is very difficult.

Soccer team: This one, as you know, due to the many injuries and illnesses, has been forced to play in the Mexican Championship, which isn't bad. Then it will tour South America and will end up in New York in the spring—during the World's Fair—where we are working to arrange for it to play against a professional Scottish team that is coming. Afterwards, it will probably go to Canada. But don't get your hopes up about these games; there's very little support for professional soccer here. We see it through the championship matches. Much less than in Bilbao. However, we're assured that the team won't lose and will surely earn a few thousand dollars. If not, it won't come. The professional association teams here are of the same quality as those in the second division of the Basque Country. Association football is not played at the universities; only American football, which is all the rage and sells out eighty thousand people.

The committee formed by Irazabal, Alegria, Regueiro, and Rezola[107] acts well, by mutual agreement and in perfect harmony. They depend entirely on our Delegation; they send us the accounts, they consult this Delegation on everything they do, etc. Therefore, I don't think I should go there, as this would only increase expenses.

In New York this winter, I spoke with Patxo[108] and his wife Elvira. I was able to deduce that she is the one causing all the trouble. She told me two or three very unpleasant words here. She's a politician in the manner of our local bosses, and all she wants is for everyone to join her side against her political or economic enemies. Unfortunately, she's the one who wears the pants in this marriage, and she interferes in all of her husband's affairs, deciding everything. If we want peace within the team, we must keep this woman out of his business. And I warn you that neither

107. Members of the Basque Country soccer team.

the players nor the management have said a single word to me about this. When she was in New York, I could see that she detests me. She says of Regueiro that he's a rabid anti-nationalist, which is completely untrue. Let's see if you can get Patxo, who's good, to get back the pants he's lost.

Salaries: None of us had the slightest idea about that salary scale you're talking about. We don't get any salary here. We record every expense we incur, even the newspaper or bus fare, meticulously, and at the end of the month we compare it with the amounts we've been given. We spend only what's strictly necessary, and that's why we've been able to save quite a bit of money. You'll be able to see this when you review the accounts we each submit. I prefer not to receive a salary while I'm in this Delegation. When my mission is over, and I return to Paris, then you can pay me whatever salary you wish, and if you wish, deduct any expenses I have incurred that you consider personal. I consider this best to avoid gossip. I am at your service, and I have too much to thank you for: the positions you have given me, and for the pleasant life you have allowed me to live traveling while others suffer, to remember salaries.

I will soon write you a lengthy memorandum about the Basques here, which I hope will be very interesting.

And finally, I will tell you that before the end of the month, about $1,500 will be sent to you from here for the refugees.

Goodbye, a hug, and may *Jaungoikua* enlighten you.

Manu

108. Francisco Belausteguigoitia, delegate of the Basque Government in Mexico, footballer for the Bilbao Athletic Club between 1918 y 1922.

9/

Sueldos. De esa escala de sueldos que hablas, ninguno de nosotros teníamos la menor noticia. Aquí no cobramos ningún sueldo. Todos los gastos que hacemos, hasta el del periódico o el bus, los apuntamos minuciosamente, y al fin de mes los confrontamos con las cantidades que nos han sido entregadas. Gastamos lo estrictamente necesario, y por eso hemos podido hacer bastantes economías. Esto podrás verlo tú cuando revises las cuentas que presentamos cada uno.

Yo prefiero no cobrar sueldo estando en esta Delegación. Cuando se termine mi misión y retorne a París, entonces me podéis pagar el sueldo que os place, y si lo queréis, deduciendo los gastos que he hecho que consideréis personales. Esto considero que es lo mejor para evitar habladurías. Estoy a tus órdenes, y bastante tengo que agradecerte los cargos que me has dado, y la vida agradable que me has hecho pasar viajando, mientras otros sufren, para que yo me acuerde de sueldos. Lo que decidas estará bien hecho y yo no lo discutiré.

Pronto te escribiré un profuso memorandum sobre los vascos de aquí, que espero resultará muy interesante.

Y para final, te diré, que antes de fines de mes se os mandarán desde aquí para los refugiados unos

$1.500.

Agur, un abrazo y que Jaungoikoa te ilumine.

Manu.

Last part of Manu de la Sota's letter to the President Aguirre.

[Letter from Antonio de Irala to Jose Antonio Aguirre, December 19, 1938]

Your Excellency, Mr. Jose Antonio Aguirre
Paris

Dear President and friend,

I received your letter of the 5th; from it I see that in my last letter I gave you the impression of two things that are not in our hearts: disunity among us and discouragement from work. You can rest assured regarding how we get along; we have not had the slightest difficulty or difference; we act without any kind of mutual reservation; if anything else were the case, I would clearly tell you. And this harmony is self-evident in our actions with others; we have had no disagreements with anyone with whom we have interacted: with the Basques in New York and here, we have been perfectly well received, we enjoy general sympathy and also respect; our relations with the Embassy are unbeatable, as is the case with the Consul. A good impression has been made among the Americans, both among friends of the Republic and among Catholics. And what I'm telling you isn't merely our assessment, but rather information that has reached us through various channels.

I'll tell you the same about our spirit for work. We've always acted with intensity and enthusiasm, which has grown as new horizons have opened up for us. We've undoubtedly been fortunate in our work; overall, I don't think things could have gone better for us. It was precisely for this reason, among other reasons, that I wrote to you the way I did in my letter of the 13th. We have general sympathy; the Basque problem, in its national aspect, is much more widely known than we could have hoped, and since this is a momentous moment, we urgently need political action on our behalf that coincides with other actions being taken there, but in a concrete and immediate manner, all planned and directed by you. To achieve this, it's essential to know the details of the situation there and the means of action here. The latter, to be perfect, is difficult to convey in a letter, because it doesn't allow for the dialogue that may be essential.

With the instructions you give us, both religious and political, we will continue to act with all intensity. In the Catholic field: organize economic aid and support for the political endeavor you propose. The letters from the French bishops are bound to have a great effect.

Attachments. Notes from the recent visits made to New York. From now on, they will be sent directly to you to gain time. Don't be surprised by Baldwin's statements; he is the "top dog" of the American Committee for Aid to Spain; he is useful to us, but due to excessive enthusiasm for the "cause," he is sectarian in the political aspect. He sees nothing but the Republic and its triumph.

More interesting is the conversation with Father Walsh. I have indicated to New York that it might be advisable for them to see him again and propose drafting a plan for our mission that he could direct; all with the purpose of submitting it for your consideration. On the other hand, since he wants *something* official, which would have to be remunerated, the answer seems obvious. Of course, he doesn't need this; he's a wealthy person with great prestige in all circles, both political and religious.

Friends of Euzkadi. In the United States, there are many societies that are friends of everything imaginable. Most of them do nothing in practice; "friends" societies are somewhat discredited. It seemed better to us to make friends of Euzkadi without specifically raising the issue of forming a group at first. According to what Mr. Manuel Intxausti told me before leaving, he believed the group should be composed of a few names, but carefully selected ones. Since we already have friends who are helping us at this point, forming the entity should be easy, especially with the precedent in Paris. Perhaps it would be advisable to wait a bit until our relationships are more extensive so that the selection is more precise.

In his letter to you, Manu tells you about other matters that concern us. From the press I've been sending from here to Basaldua,[109] you will see that our arrival has had a positive effect. We completely control the Spanish-language page. The last one I'm sending you doesn't have an entirely national feel to it, but is interesting that, so far away and in a newspaper not ours, a purely Basque publication is coming out, with

109. Pedro Basaldua, secretary to the Basque president Jose Antonio Aguirre.

many mistakes, but Basque, nonetheless. The day before yesterday we had lunch with the managing editor and his wife; we're on excellent terms with him; he'll be traveling to France in May. He is, naturally, unhappy with the section editor since he cannot write; the problem is that there is no one here to replace him. The managing editor talked about doing away with this section because Telleria is paid quite a lot. We proposed creating a page for the Basques in English, with some Spanish and Basque: for this doesn't need a special editor. This has the advantage that more Basques will read it (most of our people cannot read Spanish), and at the same time, Americans will read our work. He liked the idea, and we agreed to finalize it. Therefore, what I mentioned in my last letter about the Paris chronicle, in both Basque and Spanish, is not necessary.

We met with the Governor: a courtesy visit. He loves the Basques, they are good people, and they also vote Republican, the party to which he belongs...

I'm also enclosing a letter I wrote to Ramón Laguardia regarding an event that is about to be held in support of oppressed minorities.

Idaho. Aside from what Manu tells you in his letter, I'm not going to write anything to you about things here for the time being. Since it's not an urgent matter, we'll wait until everything's finished to give you the report; it will be more convenient for you to have a broad overview.

Salaries. I'm referring to what you told me in your letter about this. None of us get paid here. We don't have the salary scale you mention in your letter; this is the first time I've heard of it. You verbally indicated to Manu and me the amount of francs you mention in your letter. I think I heard Aramburu say that you indicated you would give him 3,000 a month, and I'm telling you this because in the letter you refer to 2,000. I'm not absolutely certain about this, but I believe I heard Aramburu say it quite some time ago.

Regarding my letter to Urrutia,[110] the following is true: Zarrabeitia[111] knew before leaving the conditions you mentioned to us. I explained to him what must be attended to during my absence from Paris:

110. Secundino Urrutia, member of the Basque Government Delegation in Paris.
111. Luis Zarrabeitia, member of the Basque Government Delegation in Paris.

• The payments on our house on Bassano Street (to help each other, we have the *traditional* rule that each absent *partner* pays their corresponding share of general expenses as if they were present).

• Deliveries to some distant relatives in France, and also possibly to my family in Bilbao, who might be in need, as has happened recently, and they have asked me for some clothing.

Zarrabeitia told me that rather than taking care of these matters himself, he would entrust the management to a friend in the same Delegation and that, for greater clarity, I should write a letter indicating who I designated to handle the matter, with the power to freely dispose of the money. Since Basaldua might also be away from Paris, I wrote the letter to Urrutia.

Regarding financial management, and following your instructions, we keep detailed notes of all expenses, even the most insignificant ones. We figure it would be worse for us to collect the amount in dollars and separate personal and administrative expenses ourselves. Because, while it's easy in theory, it's sometimes complicated in practice. The way we do it, everything is much clearer and gives us much more peace of mind. We present the accounts with all the expenses without leaving out a single one; and then the Treasury separates them and deducts what it deems fair, following the rules you set or others you think are pertinent. We will provide all necessary clarifications if needed. By the way, Basaldua told me that due to Zarrabeitia's absence, we would be told who we should send the accounts to, and we haven't received the notification yet.

With that said, you tell us what you think is best so that we can adhere to everything.

From the newspaper I'm sending you today, you'll see that for the 22nd we've organized a real Basque Day in Boise, which has had an impact even among Americans. We'll see how it goes; we expect a lot of people.

Agur, receive a very warm greeting from your good friend,

Antonio de Irala

[Letter from Antonio de Irala to Jose Antonio Aguirre, December 25, 1938]

His Excellency, Mr. Jose Antonio de Aguirre
Paris

Dear Jose Antonio,

This morning, I sent you a cable with the results of the Basque festival on the 22nd. I delayed the cable and this letter while waiting for the final settlement of the proceeds.

Every year, a Basque dance is held, which grows in importance each year; this year, with our presence and the film *Guernika*, it has been a reason for many to gather together. We organized the screening of the film, as you may have seen in the newspapers sent, in a local movie theater, with a continuous screening and a presentation by us to cater to the American public. The Basques all saw it, it was very popular, and it served to stir the spirit. They gave us $86 from the ticket sales. We got 30% of the ticket proceeds. It should be noted that the rest of the program was paid for by the company.

The dance is a reason for the people who spend the year in the mountains to get together. After so much time in isolation, they take advantage of this day to eat, drink, and dance. It was good for us to get to know each other. This year, due to the good weather, the sheep are still in the mountains, which has prevented many shepherds from coming. However, attendance has been higher than ever, and some have come from as far as two hundred fifty miles away to see the film.

The financial results have been good. Between tickets, raffles, and a collection, it amounted to $1,030. The money, as I mentioned in the cable, will be received by Leizaola[112] through the Red Cross. This has been done for the following reasons: when charging admission, the State of Idaho has established a tax on tickets sold. This tax is not collected if the proceeds are for charitable purposes, but this must be guaranteed by an institution of that nature. It seemed to us It would be better to send it

112. Jesus Maria Leizaola, councillor for Culture and Justice of the Basque Government.

through the Boise Red Cross to save on taxes and give the impression that the money is not being kept directly by us, thus avoiding sensitivities, and thus having a solid foundation for the future. The collection I'm referring to wasn't actually a public collection, but rather a kind of donation box placed in the ballroom. The money was sent to Leizaola's name because he is the one most closely associated with the Red Cross, and also because last year he received a small amount from that institution through the remittances here, which was for the benefit of the Basques in both areas. Now everything, and in dollars, is for the Basque refugees in France, with the money to be delivered in his name (Leizaola). Thus, the deposit was made at the Boise Red Cross.

You'll notice that we haven't done two things like we did in New York: a public event or rally and a public subscription. Before giving you the reasons, I will briefly point out the situation in which the Basques find themselves. We will explain this in detail in the general report.

The Basque colony in Idaho is like a small Bizkaia empire. There are an estimated seven thousand Basques in the entire state. The best of Bizkaia has emigrated here, healthy people, pure-blooded Basques, most from Ea, Amoroto, Lekeitio, and the entire Basque-speaking heartland of Bizkaia surrounding Markina. The Basque language is maintained with unexpected strength, and Bizkaian is spoken: the Basques from continental Euzkadi who reside here speak the Bizkaian dialect, and the few Basques from the erdeldun[113] area of Bizkaia who exist have learned it. I only know of one exception, a man from Bilbao; but he understands and speaks it quite a bit. Basque is strongly maintained in the first generation, that is, among the children of those who came from Euzkadi. The rule: almost all of them speak it fluently and naturally, without any significant distortions. They don't know a word of Spanish. They learn English in school and speak it, naturally, like an American. Basque weakens greatly in the third generation, among grandchildren, because their parents speak English perfectly, and the general environment has a strong influence, along with the ease and simplicity of English. The "little ones" of this generation understand

113. Erdeldun: non-Basque speaker.

our language but speak it with difficulty. These are not very numerous, and our observations were made in urban centers.

Among the Basques, three groups can be identified: shepherds, who are the majority; those settled in urban centers, owners of sheep, hotels, and other establishments; and finally, the children of Basques, who almost always work in the cities. It can be said that, in general, there are no political problems or divisions for this reason. There are very few who claim to be Francoists, but more than anything, it is to contradict others in conversations, etc. There is no activity in support of Franco. In terms of Basque patriotism, however, there is much to be done; they are Basques by virtue of their race, as if by instinct, but they lack a national consciousness, because they know very little about their homeland. Among the young shepherds who have come from the Basque Country, there are quite a few nationalists. Those who have settled in the cities are people fully dedicated to business and less spiritual than the shepherds. The children of Basques, except for the wealthiest who have been to the Basque Country or Spain, speak Basque, but their patriotic mentality is American, also a consequence of ignorance. What idea of the Basque Country would the children of a Nabarniz farmer who left his village at the age of twenty have? This is a common case.

Notwithstanding what has been said, the spirit of Gamboínos and Oñacinos is manifested here not politically but economically. This will facilitate our work if we proceed carefully. These Basques, like the good farmers that they are, have truly childish qualities along with other cunning qualities. The shepherd doesn't have a home; he depends financially on the sheep owner and, for everything else, on the hotel where he stays when he comes to town. And here comes the trouble between the hotel and bar owners and the sheep owners over financial matters and emotional rivalries, real jealousy over minor matters, mixed in with everything that is most important. The shepherd, being indifferent to such disputes, finds himself entangled in them.

There are four mutual aid societies in Boise: two for men and two for women. It would be logical to establish one with a view to efficiency, but no human force can achieve it. (We have not gotten involved in these messes.) Each society revolves around a hotel owner, and each of these dreams of maintaining their power.

Faced with this reality, our efforts have been directed toward doing something beyond these petty matters, gaining the friendship of the hotel and sheep owners. I believe we have succeeded. If it hadn't been for that, we would never have been able to do anything because there is no way to reach the shepherds against the will of those gentlemen. The shepherds live many miles from town, in the mountains, almost all year round.

During these days, we won't be doing the fundraising; it's not in our best interest; jealousy gets in the way. We must start at the top so that things go well, and it's necessary to prepare it, even with your involvement, and we'll have to direct it, but not from here. All this to avoid the suspicions that exist, and we've noticed them. Previously, one was done, and it turns out that influential people led it, and then the shepherds, to teach a lesson, signed up with higher amounts. I don't need to tell you how the others felt about it; they did everything they could to squelch it so as not to look bad. (This was two years ago.)

I'm giving you all of these details, so you know the inside scoop. This is the most unpleasant part of life here, a very small thing, admittedly, but important. You know how hard it is to get the baserritarras,[114] to do any order of things; the same thing happens here, and success often depends on the smallest detail.

As I told you in my previous letter and at the beginning of this one, we haven't held a proper meeting. Firstly, because people know enough about what we're trying to do now, the difficulty lies in channeling the action, and also because it's impossible to bring them together, especially this year. Most of them came to the dance hours before heading off to the mountains. We've followed the tactic of private conversations at family gatherings and in the press and radio. At the cinema, some discussion was held during the sessions.

The important thing we have here is the newspaper. The person in charge of the page has been dismissed because he can't write. This last thing I'm sending you is coming out without him. The title of the page has been changed; it's called "Basque Section." We will meet with the

114. *Baserritarra*: Basque farmer.

director tomorrow to see if we can arrange for us to do almost all of it ourselves, in the manner I indicated in the previous letter. It would be a great thing if we could do it.

We've taken advantage of our stay here, which may seem a bit long to you, to visit other towns and find some people in each one to support us. All of this takes a lot of time, and since the distances are enormous, time passes unnoticed. Whatever is done here has repercussions throughout the West, so we wanted to study the situation carefully and not leave anything up in the air.

I have a few other things to tell you, but since I'm running out of paper, I'm sending you this letter and will write again tomorrow or the day after.

Another dance will be held on the 30th to benefit refugees. On New Year's Day, we're leaving for Nevada.

Warm regards from your good friend and servant.

Antonio de Irala

Dance In Boise Yields $1013.75

Net proceeds of the ninth annual Basque Sheepherders' dance Thursday night at Riverside pavilion were $1013.75, Zenon Isaguire, general chairman, said Friday.

The money will be sent to the International Red Cross for the relief of Basque refugees in the Spanish civil war.

Auction of a lamb brought $160. Auction of a turkey brought $100. Several hundred dancers attended.

Idaho Daily Statesman, December 24, 1938, p. 2.

[Letter from Antonio de Irala to Pedro Basaldua, December 27, 1938]

Mr. Pedro Basaldua
Paris

Dear Perico,

I received your letters of the 1st, 2nd, 7th, and 9th of this month. The photos you mentioned have not reached me, but I assume they are in New York.

In the letter I am sending to the Lehendakari[115] you will see a paragraph referring to *Euzko Deya*[116] about the publication of something about the Basques of Idaho. Tomorrow, I will send you information about various things that might be useful for the newspaper; you can keep the rest for the archives.

Needless to say, I will take into consideration what you tell me about how to manage the photos you send me.

Regarding things here, I won't tell you anything specific about things in this letter because you will find out about them in the press, "our weekly newspaper." It's quite funny that, so many miles away, we can have a free "Basque section" in an English-language newspaper, *gratis et amore*, don't you think? Besides, so far, we've managed to destroy Cervantes and his wonderful language with another of our own invention... We'll see if we improve in the future.

I forgot to tell you about *Euzko Deya*. Whatever the Lehendakari thinks, you and Urkola[117] can work together to shape the matter quickly.

And that's all, Perico, I wish you all the best for the Bassano *Republics*.[118] One day I'll write a special letter to the Republic, with a photo that I hope will hang on the wall in memoriam. Don't forget to say hello to Don Alberto.

Agur, with hugs from your good friend,

Anton

115. *Lehendakari*: President of the Basque Country.
116. *Euzko Deya*: The Voice of the Basques, a newspaper published in Latin America as the official organ of the Basque Government in exile.
117. Felipe Urkola, editor of *Euzko Deya*. He was editor of the newspaper *El Pueblo Vasco* until its demise at the outbreak of the Civil War.
118. It refers to the apartment on Bassano Street where most of the Basque delegates in Paris lived.

Copia.

Boise Idaho. 6-39.

Sres. Sota e Irala.

Estimados Amigos

El dia 5 recibi su telegrama y esta mananala carta.
Le decia en mi anterior que me parecia que la gente estaba enfriandose debido a los triunfos de Franco pero veo es causado por una propaganda perniciosa hecha por algunos Fascistas contra este trabajo caritativo, y cuanto mas al Este penetramos mayor incremento tomaba la propaganda y determinamos dar fin a nuestra suscripcion.
Hace dos dias llegamos a esta y como mis companeros querian salir a trabajar a la mayor brevedad y yo queria que ellos estuvieran presentes al enviar lo recaudado fue el motivo para que le telegrafiase.
Nosotros estuvimos en Vale y Jordan Valley. En Vale vimos a Gandarias siendo este uno de los que se interesan por esta causa pero como Vds. bien saben ahi hay en esta muchisimos que aunque son Vascos trabajan con mucho celo contra la causa Santa de nuestra Patria y muchos de estos no reparan que esta clase de argumentos usan para desprestigiar la causa Nuestra.
Aqui no me parece que sea suceso el que se forme una junta permanente debido a lo que les he expuesto anteriormente y si viese que esto era conveniente seria el primero en proponerles se hiciera.
A los pocos dias de salir Vds. de esta tuve el gusto de hablar con Nick Mejias de Elko, Nevada el cual me pintoa a todos o a la mayoria de los Vascos de alli con sentimientos y propositos de ayudar a nuestros hermanos de raza y me parece que Elko se presta mejor para el objeto de poner un centro permanente.
Manana vamos a enviar a la direccion que Vd. nos indica dollars 1893 no me parece que es bastante para el fin a que se destina.
Pero estamos seguros que hemos hecho todos los posibles; tambien envio una lista con los nombres, direcciones y cantidades recibidos de cada persona y le ruego que bien por carta o personalmente haga que envian recibo personal a cada donante, que es lo que nosotro s les hemos prometido.
En breves dias espero salir a trabajar pero mi correspondencia me sera remitida de esta.

Deseandole buen viaje y con recuerdos de Matias y Landaluze Manden como gusten de su amigo M

Marciano Uriarte

Letter from Marciano Uriarte to Manu de la Sota and Antonio de Irala, announcing the sending of $1893 for Basque refugees, but lamenting the negative propaganda spread by some fascists. However, support is strong in Elko, and he proposes that a permanent sub-delegation of the Basque Government should be opened in this Nevada town rather than in Boise.

[Letter from Marciano Uriarte[119] to Antonio de Irala and Manu de la Sota, January 28, 1939]

Marciano Uriarte
1501 Hays StreetBoise, Idaho
January 28, 1939

Mr. Irala and Mr. Sota
Elysée Hotel NY

Dear Sirs:

I just learned your address from Nick Mejias of Elko, Nevada, and therefore I would like to take this opportunity to let you know how we are continuing with the fundraising we began when you left here.

When we began gathering contributions, we toured Boise, after which we went out to the surrounding area where we worked for two days, but we had to leave because the people working with sheep were very scattered, and we thought that by waiting a few days the sheep herds would be concentrated for the lambing, and this way it would be easier and more profitable for us.

We started again a week ago, and to date we have collected approximately 1,500 pesos. I expect it will take us another six or seven days to complete the entire route. It seems that with Franco's advance in recent days, there has been a slight slowdown in donations, but we will continue working with the same zeal with which we began. Since I lost the address in France that you gave me, please send me those details as soon as possible.

With regards to my colleagues, send whatever you wish, from your faithful servant,

Marciano Uriarte

119. Marciano Uriarte, head of the Basque Refugee Committee in Boise.

Emmett, Ida 29-I-39

Sr. Dn. Antonio de Irala.

New York, N.Y.

Querido amigo Antonio:

He recibido tu muy estimada por la cual veo habeis dado fin a vuestra patriotica jira, sin llegar a las bellas tierras californianas, en las cuales, debido al gran numero de españoles y mexicanos, entre los nuestros predomina y creo pertenecen a S. H. C. la ayuda al gobierno español.

En vuestras futuras actuaciones la fuente de ayuda a nuestros refugiados està, como diria el ''historiador de Aragon,'' en Idaho, Oregon y Nevada. Hace unos dias estuve, por muy poco tiempo, hablando con el '' Capitan''. Me manifesto, sin indicarme cantidad, como en Boise los trabajos han sido provechosos, pero no asi en lugares cercanos tales como Mountain Home y Nampa. En mi opinion, espero, aparte de lo que hayan recogido entre la llamada'' gente del pueblo,'' obtengan varios millares de Dollars, donados en los campos de ovejas, por nuestros horados y laboriosos pastores.

Tanto de tu simpatica persona como asi mismo de la de Manu, todos hablan muy bien. No hay ''vieja'' en este pueblo y fuera de el, que no sueñe con Manu, ni joven, mas o menos bella, que no suspire por Irala. Como ves el ambiente no puede ser, a lo menos en el presente, mejor.

Tomas y ANton ya marcharon al trabajo les he escrito una carta dandoles los recuerdos vuestros. Al lagun Anton le recomiendo el encargo de las pieles.

Esta semana no hemos tenido hoja vasca. Si en la proxima el periodico vuelve a publicar nustra seccion, cumpliendo tus deseos, le mandare a Basaldua semanalmente el periodico. A vosotros tambien os enviare uno, o cuantos numeros deseeis, en el supuesto que la hoja vasca vuelva a reaparecer.

Si tienes literatura vasca de actualidad enviame, yo te abonare el importe de ella.

Amigo Antonio, no ignores que ahora y siempre, tanto en lo

(vuelta)

First page of the letter from Jose Villanueva Amezketa to Antonio de Irala.

[Letter from Jose Villanueva to Antonio de Irala, January 29, 1939]

Emmett, Ida 29-I-39

Mr. Antonio de Irala
New York, N.Y.

Dear friend Antonio:

I have received your much appreciated letter, by which I see that you have ended your patriotic tour without reaching the beautiful lands of California, where, due to the large number of Spaniards and Mexicans, support for the Spanish government predominates among us, since I believe they belong to SHC.[120]

In your future endeavors, the source of aid to our refugees is, as the "historian of Aragon"[121] would say, in Idaho, Oregon, and Nevada. A few days ago, I spoke briefly with the "Captain."[122] He told me, without specifying the amount, how the work in Boise has been beneficial, but not so in nearby places such as Mountain Home and Nampa. In my opinion, I hope, apart from what they've collected from the so-called "townspeople," they'll get several thousand dollars donated in the sheep fields by our honest and hardworking shepherds.

Everyone speaks highly of both your friendly personality and Manu's. There's not an "old woman" in this town or outside it who doesn't dream of Manu, nor a young woman, more or less beautiful, who doesn't yearn for Irala. As you can see, the atmosphere couldn't be better, at least at present.

Tomas and Anton[123] have already left for work; I've written them a letter giving them your regards. I recommend the fur order to our friend Anton. We haven't had any Basque section this week. If the newspaper

120. SHC: Confederated Hispanic Societies.
121. He's referring to Damian Telleria.
122. Marciano Uriarte.
123. Tomas Arambalza and Tony Laradogoitia.

publishes our section again next week, fulfilling your wishes, I will send the newspaper to Basaldua every week. I will also send you one, or as many issues as you wish, assuming the Basque section reappears.

If you have any current Basque literature, send it to me; I will pay for it.

My friend Antonio, know that now and always, both in patriotic and personal matters, you can count on my humble person.

With affectionate regards from my wife to Manu and to you, your sincere friend says goodbye with a warm hug.

Jose V. de Amezketa

[Letter from Marciano Uriarte to Pedro Basaldua, February 7, 1939]

Marciano Uriarte
Boise, February 7, 1939

Mr. Pedro Basaldua
Paris, France

Dear Sir,

When Antonio de Irala and Manuel de la Sota were here, the Basques here proposed to raise money to attempt to, in some way, alleviate the situation of our brothers in France. Mr. Antonio de Irala instructed us to send the proceeds for this purpose to your address, and I am enclosing a money order for 1,893 dollars (one thousand eight hundred ninety-three dollars), along with the names, addresses, and amounts collected. As Mr. Irala told us at the beginning of the fundraising process, that when sending the donations, you would send a personal letter to each donor; we told them that while collecting funds, and so I ask you to write those letters.

Marciano Uriarte

Boise Febrero 7 - 59

Sr Pedro Basaldua

Paris - Francia

Muy Sr mio

Cuando los Señores Antonio de Irala y Manuel de la Sota estuvieron en esta, los Vascos de aqui se propusieron hacer una suscrición con el objeto de aliviar en algo la situación de nuestros hermanos en Francia. D. Antonio de Irala nos indicó que enviasemos lo recaudado para ese fin, a su direción, y adjunto le envio un giro por valor $1893.00 Mil ochocientos noventa y tres. Juntamente con los nombres direción y cantidades recogidas, como el Sr Irala nos dijo al empezar la suscrición que al enviar los donativos Uds mandarian de esa una carta personal á cada donante, nosotros al andár recaudando les hemos hecho ese ofrecimiento y por lo tanto les ruego escriban esas cartas.

Letter from Marciano Uriarte to Pedro Basaldua, Secretary to the President of the Basque Government in Paris.

[Letter from Jose Antonio Aguirre to Marciano Uriarte, February 22, 1939]

Paris, February 22, 1939

Mr. Marciano Uriarte
1501 Hays Street
Boise, Idaho (USA)

Dear Compatriot:

My Secretary, Mr. Basaldua, informs me of the contents of the letter you wrote to him dated the 7th of this month, as well as the enclosed check for $1,893, the amount of the fundraising you organized there.

Through the Basque Government Delegation in the United States, I learned of the work you were doing to help our brothers in distress. I wanted to write to you personally to express my gratitude, on behalf of all Basques, for your patriotic and exemplary conduct. I also ask that you forward it to Messrs. Landaluce and Bengoa,[124] my colleagues on the Committee, as well as to all the Basques who have come to the aid of our brothers.

Within a few days, I will arrange for all donors to begin receiving a token of appreciation and acknowledgment of receipt for the amounts they have donated. This money will be donated in its entirety for exclusively humanitarian purposes.

Very affectionate greetings.

J. A. de Aguirre

124. George Landaluce and Matias Bengoa, responsibles, together with Marciano Uriarte, for the Committee for Basque Refugees in Idaho.

Thank you cards from the Basque Government to donors supporting Basque refugees. "Good actions are never forgotten. By donating dollars, you will forever remain in the hearts of young Basques".

[Letter from Antonio de Irala to Jose Villanueva, February 23, 1939]

Paris, February 23, 1939

Mr. Jose V. Amezketa
Boise, Idaho (USA)

Dear friend Jose:

I don't know if in one of the last letters I wrote to you I mentioned my upcoming departure for Europe. In any case, I am now here in Paris, after an uneventful trip. I received your letter dated the 29th of last month (January) and I'm pleased with the good impression we were able to make there. The period for contributions organized by Marciano has now been closed. It amounts to about $2,000. The money has arrived in Paris, as have the proceeds from the "Sheepherder's Ball." Marciano tells me, in a letter he wrote to me in New York, that he has found that some people have taken issue with these contributions, and I replied that he should tell me their names because, if it is true, we will undoubtedly have to work on it. Do you have any information on this matter? Whatever you know in this regard, be sure to let me know, both now and in the future.

As for the rest, I can tell you little about the situation after the latest events, as you will be well informed by the press. Undoubtedly, the cause of the Republic is now entering a decisive period. At this moment, naturally, we have a serious problem with refugees; but, thanks to the organization of our leaders and the spirit of our people, it has been met with a dignity and effectiveness that is earning admiration, not only among individuals loyal to the Republic, but also among all French authorities, from the Government to the lowest of its agents. Today, the Basque Government shines brighter than ever and is appreciated and esteemed by all, so that it is definitively established, for it is in difficult situations that men and nations are best known. Do not think that these are mere words, but rather a sober impression gleaned from reality. This, combined with other very interesting factors, not only here but also in Spain and America itself, means that despite the bleak outlook, we can look to the future with peace of mind and confident that we will succeed in every way before long. I'll write to you again on this matter later. For now, I have no idea if or when I'll be back. In any case, we must work harder today than ever. I imagine you are as enthusiastic as ever.

Don't forget to say hello to Tomas and Antonio.[125] You can forward this letter to them so they can get the impression I'm conveying to you, which, as I said before, is not exaggerated in the slightest.

My best regards to your wife, and you know that your good friend hasn't forgotten you.

Antonio de Irala

125. Tomas Arambalza y Antonio "Tony" Laradogoitia.

[Basques in the Western United States][126]

Basque emigration to the United States has been concentrated primarily in the states of Oregon, Idaho, Utah, Nevada, and California. This emigration peaked from the beginning of this century until the beginning of the Great European War. It then gradually declined, and in recent years has been completely nonexistent due to restrictions imposed by American legislation.

Within the group of states mentioned above, there has also been a movement of the Basque population. The emigration trend was initially concentrated around the state of Idaho, but later, due to the progress of the cattle ranching business, they gradually flocked toward the state of California, a wealthier and more extensive area that offered them greater horizons for economic prosperity.

The total number of Basques residing throughout the West is estimated at around forty thousand. Their greatest number is in the state of California. Between Idaho, Oregon, Nevada, and Utah, there are an estimated fifteen thousand Basques, of whom approximately eight thousand are in Idaho. The remainder, approximately twenty five thousand, are in California.

The typical phenomenon of the preservation of Basque identity occurs in the state of Idaho, where there is no Spanish emigration at all. It gradually decreases in intensity in the states of Utah, Nevada, and Oregon, and then reaches California, where, although most Basques speak Basque, they speak Spanish fluently, due to the large Spanish-speaking population residing in that state.

The Delegation has specifically studied the situation of the Basques in Idaho, which is roughly the same as that of the states of Oregon, Nevada, and Utah.

Geographical Location of Idaho

The State of Idaho has a land area of 83,383 square miles, with a population of 445,032 (1930), giving a density of 0.4. The capital, Boise, has twenty six thousand inhabitants.

126. Report of the New York Delegation, March 2, 1939.

The climate is dry and stimulating. The altitude is generally high and varies between 723 and 12,655 feet. Economic activity is largely related to livestock and mining. It has two universities.

Basque Population

Almost all the Basques residing in the State of Idaho are Biscayan and Basque speaking. There are some who have come from the Spanish speaking areas of Biscay and have learned our language due to contact with the Basques living there. We only know of one case of someone who, while understanding and speaking some Basque, doesn't do so with the proficiency required for a serious conversation. The children of Basques are also Basque speakers. There is a phenomenon—with rare exceptions, due to having studied in the Basque Country or Spain—that they don't speak Spanish. It can be estimated that 45% of Basques do not speak Spanish, as many who arrived from the Basque Country with only a rudimentary knowledge have forgotten it.

Economic Situation

Among the Basques, the American-style rich are not common, due to the alternatives available to the livestock business, the basis of their activities. During the European war, prosperity reached its peak. A simple shepherd could earn $120 a month, with room and board. Today, wages have fallen to a minimum of $60 and a maximum of $85. The lower wage predominates.

On the other hand, sheep and cattle owners are not economically free, as many of them maintain ownership of their livestock with bank loans. Furthermore, the market for the sale of livestock products is controlled by large buyers in Chicago, Denver, etc., who set the prices.

Livestock, especially sheep, suffered a tremendous decline after the war. This decline coincided with the economic crisis in the United States and the bankruptcy of many banking establishments with which the Basques worked. When these closed and livestock depreciated in value, banks seized them to secure the loans they had made to their owners. This phenomenon had a major impact on the shepherds themselves. In general, the entire life of the Basques is animated by a traditional Basque spirit and based on good faith, as in the ancient times of our people. The shepherd who had a monthly salary, and who had gone to America to work for a few years, with the aim of building up a capital and returning to Euzkadi, never received his monthly or annual salary. He left the amounts on deposit with the owner, in order to help him by reducing his credit with the banks, and therefore, the interest. However, when the banks took over the Basques' businesses, many shepherds found themselves unable to collect from the owners the salaries corresponding to several years of work that had been earned. For this reason, many of our compatriots have had to stay much longer than they had anticipated when they left the Basque Country for America.

Currently, as we noted, they do not have large sums of money, but there is no Basque who lacks work and does not have enough dollars to live a comfortable life and be well positioned for old age.

Patriotic Situation

Given the era in which Basque emigration took place, our compatriots left without possessing not only a basic civic education, but also without having experienced the Basque Renaissance movement in the Basque Country. Therefore, most Basques, and their children, lack patriotic education. The most recent arrivals, especially the young people who experienced the national struggle in the Basque Country, retain all these concerns and maintain them with full vigor. They are limited in number and constitute a minority. In the rest, Basque sentiment has been awakened in a way they had not felt before, due to the war in the Basque Country, seeing the effects it had on their families, their friends, and their towns. Very few of them appear to be Franco sympathizers. The opposite is what predominates.

On the other hand, Basque sentiment is very much alive in them, as is only natural among people who have preserved their language as perfectly as the Basques of Idaho have done, using it frequently in all aspects of life.

Due to their spirit of honesty, hard work, seriousness, and respect for the law and for citizens, they have earned the sympathy of the entire American population, who know them as Basques, appreciate them as such, and distinguish them clearly from the Spanish. This has made them feel praised within the community where they live, for the mere fact of being Basque, and this feeling of legitimate pride has spread to their children, who, moreover, know very little about what the Basque Country represents in the world today.

In addition to their language, the Basques have retained other characteristics of Basque life, which are a consequence of our personality and organization in the Basque Country. Basque family life is far superior to American family life, without reaching the perfection of family life in the Basque Country. Americans themselves recognize and appreciate this.

In terms of popular sports, *pelota* is still practiced. In Boise, there are three quite good fronton courts. The specialty of *pala* is the most popular form of the game. However, it has declined recently because there are fewer young people than in the past, and those who previously played are no longer able to do so due to their advanced age. In almost every town where there is a Basque colony, there is a fronton court, of varying quality.

They preserve a repertoire of songs, which has not been cultivated, but which corresponded to those that existed a few years ago in the small villages of Bizkaia. The *Gernika'ko Arbola*[127] and the earliest patriotic songs are known. Some also sing in Spanish, to the sound of the guitar. This is not the most common practice.

Basque festivals are organized in which, along with the usual American dance, great preference is given to the Basque free-style dance, to the sound of the txistu and accordion, which arouses admiration among the Americans. The aurresku, pioneered by women, is also danced in the Lekeitio style.

Fraternity among the Basques is absolute. In Boise, there are two Mutual Aid Societies which function perfectly. It is common among them the maxim that "no Basque dies of hunger" there. In the face of misfortune of any kind, and in the face of the death of any of our compatriots, everyone comes together in mutual aid or in a public outpouring of grief. Basque funerals are considered the most well-attended in Idaho.

There is no such thing in Idaho as what we might call a political problem. It is easy to channel them into a national movement, to which they are naturally inclined due to the set of circumstances we have outlined. Naturally, there is no anti-Basque sentiment. Spanish sentiment is

127. *Gernika'ko Arbola*: The Tree of Gernika.

unknown. Differences or rivalries arise for personal reasons, over business matters. The basis of the rivalries revolves around the innkeepers, which is where the shepherds end up when they come down from the mountains, since they have no domicile, and the rivalries are ultimately nothing more than simple business competition.

Religious Situation

The Basques in this area are not religious. The men, not at all. The women, very few. And the youth, that is, the children of Basques born in America, follow the American way of life, which is cold in this area. There is no sectarianism.

The lack of religious practice has been caused by a combination of circumstances common to all emigration, plus some special circumstances. First, the environment, and then the regime of great isolation in which the vast majority live, outside the city, in the mountains, where they remain almost all year, circumstances that accustom them to feeling no concern for religious practice.

Currently in Idaho, and especially in Boise, the capital, there is an atmosphere of discontent toward the bishop, and they harbor unpleasant memories of a Basque priest who arrived in that area during the final years of the Monarchy, summoned by the previous bishop. This priest, named Don Bernardo Arregui, from Tolosa, once he arrived in Boise, took up a collection to found a church and a house in which he would reside. The Basques, being generous, spontaneously contributed to the collection, the necessary funds were raised, and the house and church were built in a central location in the town. Father Arregui seems to have shown excessive interest in financial matters and coupled with the fact that he was appointed by the Vice Consul in Idaho, mixing spiritual matters with temporal ones, he caused people to view him with distrust and suspicion, with the resulting separation of what he stood for and spiritual life.

When the current Bishop, Monsignor Kelly, arrived, he removed the Basque priest and forced him to leave his diocese. He personally went to live in the house the Basques had built for their priest, and used the chapel, which, by the way, is pleasant and well-appointed, as his private oratory.

Subsequently, a Flemish priest who resided in the diocese, in order to minister exclusively to the Basques, moved to Lekeitio, where he lived long enough to learn Basque quite perfectly. Upon arriving in Boise, the bishop assigned him to an area where no Basques resided.

This set of events, which undoubtedly reflects a lack of concern on the part of the ecclesiastical authorities regarding the spiritual situation of the Basques, has led to great animosity toward the bishop. The bishop devotes himself solely to making a few courtesy visits to wealthiest families, primarily intended—according to these families—to maintain relationships for financial gain. "When men foresee the event, they make themselves invisible and leave it to the women to settle the engagement more quickly and economically."

Some women have told us how difficult it is for them to practice their religion with the bishop. Last year, they asked for the priest we mentioned earlier, who knows Basque, to come so they could go to confession and celebrate Easter. They were promised this. The date arrived, and instead of the priest in question, an American priest who knew nothing of the Basque language occupied the confessional. Among the women, there are some who, despite their good intentions, have not confessed for a long time, due to the material impossibility of doing so. In general, the women know very little English, and the men do not know it well enough to make a confession of conscience.

Our Efforts

The members of the Basque Delegation who came to this area, Mr. Manuel de la Sota and Mr. Antonio de Irala, from the outset followed the tactic of gaining the people's sympathy through personal contacts, avoiding any cause for division, in order to first study the situation and then channel patriotic action. Success crowned their efforts. All those people welcomed them and treated them with the utmost affection and hospitality, even some who were considered Franco sympathizers.

Two dance festivals were organized during the Basque Delegation's stay in those lands to benefit refugees in France. A committee was later organized and held public fundraising, resulting in a sum of $1,838.

Coinciding with the annual Sheepherders Ball, a screening of the film *Guernika* was held around Christmas, the time when most of the shepherds descend on the capital. Prior to and after this screening, radio was used as a means of disseminating the concerns currently facing the

Basque Country. The event was a success, and all these activities were unanimously well received. The weekly Basque section of the local newspaper, *Boise Capital News*, was also used to maintain patriotic contact.

The report that will be submitted to the President[128] regarding possibilities for action in North America, will highlight those that, in the opinion of the Delegation, exist among the Basques of the West.

128. President, referred to the President of the Basque Country, Jose Antonio Aguirre.

Index of names

B

C

D

E

F

G

H

I/Y

M

N

O

P

Q

R

S

T

U

INDEX

Trip to Idaho

Speeches, letters and report

www.ingramcontent.com/pod-product-compliance
Lightning Source LLC
LaVergne TN
LVHW010546110826
845149LV00003B/574

* 9 7 8 1 9 6 7 1 7 9 0 8 4 *